# THE BRIGHT SIDE OF ADVERSITY

# THE BRIGHT SIDE OF ADVERSITY

*An Autobiography*

PARITOSH M. CHAKRABARTI

Om Books International

First published in 2025 by

**Om Books International**

**Corporate & Editorial Office**
A-12, Sector 64, Noida 201 301
Uttar Pradesh, India
Phone: +91 120 477 4100
Email: editorial@ombooks.com
Website: www.ombooksinternational.com

**Sales Office**
107, Ansari Road, Darya Ganj,
New Delhi 110 002, India
Phone: +91 11 4000 9000
Email: sales@ombooks.com
Website: www.ombooks.com



ISBN: 978-93-6395-732-9

Printed in India

10 9 8 7 6 5 4 3 2 1

To

My Grandson Deven

# Contents

# Epigraph

Out grandson Deven (our first grandchild) brought us so much joy that every other accomplishment in life paled in comparison. This poem my wife wrote when Deven was just two years old captures the spirit of that joy.

Don't promise me a Taj Mahal

Or a golden chariot fit for a queen

Don't shower me with precious jewel

Red, yellow, purple, and green

I do not cherish them anymore

I have Deven, a two-year boy

My Dadubhai who brings so much joy

And I wonder if this is not heaven, what is?

With his sparkling eyes and honey-sweet smile

He says, "Hi Did" and my heart melts a while

"Deven, Dida is leaving," I say

He says, "No Did you play?"

I say, "Dadubhai, I love you"

He replies "I uv you tu"

And I wonder if this is not heaven

Then what is?

A trip to Dadu's house is fun

As we hear him make his plan

"Dadu sit, I sit, blanket on and show"

Covering him and Dadu's lap with a throw

Deven rocks his head with Popeye tune

Noman Rockwell, you missed this view

In my mind I will hold these two

And wonder if this is not heaven

Then what is?

# Preface

In December 1999, I was honoured with a bronze plaque for Excellence in Entrepreneurship at the Global Bengali Conference held in Kolkata, India, by Chief Minister Jyoti Basu. The famous Bengali writer Sankar, who wrote a story about financially successful Bengalis abroad, highlighted my life's history in a commemorative book, *Smarak Grantha*[1]. During the conference, Sankar approached me with a proposal to write my biography to inspire young Bengalis with the life example of someone to whom they could relate.

At about the same time, the pro-vice chancellor of Calcutta University, Dr Surabhi Banerjee, whom I first met in connection with my endowment of a chair in chemistry at the University, also approached me about writing my biography. Dr Banerjee was also a well-known writer, and she had previously written the biography of Jyoti Basu.

I declined both requests. I did not think that I was such an example-setting character that someone would want to read my biography. If one considered my financial, academic, and

1. Edited by Sunil Gangopadhaya (a legendary literary figure in Bengal) and published by Saraswati Press, 1999

business successes worth writing about, I thought one could find much better examples. So, writing a simple biography did not interest me much. It would have been an act of self-propaganda, to which I have always been averse. What I thought could be worth writing about, however, were some deep-seated experiences that I had during the course of my long life. These might trigger new research to advance matters of societal interest. Such thoughts and experiences, of course, were intertwined intimately with my life, so they would not have the same impact if they were detached from my life history. Lessons of broad human interest can come alive only when we derive them from the real-life experience of the person who describes them. I thought if I had to write about myself, it had to be greater than myself. Hence the thought arose of writing a memoir rather than a simple autobiography.

Initially, I thought of writing my memoir as one book with several chapters. As the writing progressed, however, I came to realize that the material would not fit neatly in one book. The memoir has four themes: 1) An Autobiography; 2) The Making of a Corporation with a Soul; 3) A New Framework for Economics; and 4) A Treatise on Religion, Truth, Morality, and Purpose of Life.

These topics were so diverse that a single reader might not be interested in all of them. So, at the suggestion of a few friends, I decided to write a memoir series of four books with each book covering one of the four themes.

The first chapter of the first book starts with me as a boy who did not have a childhood. It describes my life until I was twelve years old. I was born in 1940 in Moulmein, Myanmar. Two years later, my family moved to our ancestral home in East Bengal (now Bangladesh). During my first ten years, so many events and so many changes occurred that, as I look back now, it seems like those years lasted an eon. During this time, my family was uprooted from the comforts of its elaborate ancestral village residence. Our home was dismantled and our future tossed into whirlwinds of chaos and uncertainty. I saw traditions vanish, communities dissolve, villages torched, a country transformed, and people killing people. I saw my family move from location to location, one home to another, each progressively worse, until the ten members of my family were hurtled into a two-room apartment in Calcutta.

Partly due to the disruptions caused by the sheer horror that was visited upon my native home, partly due to the tumultuous moves from one place to another, and partly because I was the fifth child in a family that prioritized educating its older children, I was never given the chance to attend primary and high schools. Nevertheless, I learned on my own, graduated from high school as a "private" student, and entered college at the age of thirteen.

During those horrendous years, my family stuck together. Adversity was the glue that held us together. We learned to share, respect our elders, and sacrifice our personal interests and comfort for the family's well-being. We developed into a tight-knit family. But bad times do not last forever, thank goodness. My family's problems disappeared as quickly as they unfolded. Each of my siblings soon became as successful as they could be, and we became affluent again. As close as we were, the family I was born into will also disintegrate one day as the whirlwind of time throws us around to various parts of the world, and the collective interest of our once-nuclear family will yield to the personal interests of each member.

The books end with a chapter on the purpose of life. I conclude that life has a higher purpose than one's own life. In this concluding chapter, I drew upon all my experiences and dissertations—as a student, a scientist, a teacher, an executive, an entrepreneur building a global company, formulating my thoughts about economics, and pondering on the nature of religion, truth, and morality. Those considerations, along with others, drove me to conclude that the higher purpose of life is not just living. It is to help humanity to reach its apex. This involves not only becoming the best we individually can be but also helping others to become the best they can be. We do this by bringing humanity together, and that requires understanding reality in both the physical and spiritual senses.

In presenting the narratives, particularly of books 1, 2, and 4, I had to dig deep into my memory. When I stretched my memory, what came forth were shards of experiences pertaining to the unusual events I encountered and the special people I met throughout my life. Those events both uplifted and depressed me; they were pleasant as well as sad and filled with hope and despair. Those events brought to me both ends of the emotional spectrum and everything in between—happiness and sorrow, pleasure and pain, sex and celibacy, peace and turmoil, health and sickness, faith and scepticism, morality and sin, right and wrong, good and evil, science and superstition, commitment and evasion; universality and narrowness, honour and disgrace, pride and shame, wealth and poverty, and success and failure.

The negative experiences seemed, at the time they were occurring, to emphasize the hardships of life, but when viewed in the aggregate and along with the positive experiences I have enjoyed, they represented an arrow flying towards the better end of the spectrum. My belief in that arrow provided me with the motive force to move forward in life, even in the face of adversity. When we lose faith in that arrow, we fail. My faith in that arrow carried me from a disastrously poor beginning to become one of the fifty richest people living in New Jersey and a thoughtful philanthropist, to engage in such diverse endeavours as instilling a soul in a corporation, developing a new framework of economics, and establishing a theory of truth. It also gave me a philosophical view of life that is both retrospective and prospective, and it led me to present this view in a treatise on religion, truth, morality, and the purpose of life.

Before I introduce each of the four books, I have a few other general comments about the memoir series.

## Equality from the Perspectives of Science and Morality

I examine two principles of science—the second law of thermodynamics and Darwinism—which deal with equality and inequality. The first principle, one of the fundamental laws of physics that rule the infinitely vast inorganic universe, uses inequality as the source of work as it strives to achieve equality figuratively at the graveyard of entropy. The second tries to maximize inequality in "survival of the fittest", with the law of the living world that represents the tiniest corner of the tiniest part of the universe.

I show how politicians, egalitarian philosophers, and economists, heedless of those laws, all fell into error while designing rules for human society. I show that both those principles of science can help us to design a process for reaching the ultimate truth about the goal of humanity. The laws of science, however, cannot reveal that goal—the "products" or the "ends" as philosophers call it—of the process. Those products reside in a unique set of rules, the rules of morality, that make us human. I discuss some of the debates that, for decades if not centuries, the egalitarian philosophers had on matters of equality. I believe their followers will get a new perspective on their thoughts in view of my discussion. Discussion of these principles of humanity, enshrined in the process and the products, runs through all four books at various levels of intensity but features most prominently in books 3 and 4.

## Biases

The books present several provocative thoughts and theories. These thoughts and theories are the products of my personal experiences and detailed inquiries regarding nature, human society, and Homo sapiens in general. Whenever we present thoughts and theories based on our own experiences and inquiries, our personal biases influence our discussions and presentations. These biases concern our tendency to emphasize the facts and other evidence that support our propositions and to minimize those that oppose our positions.

Biases also influence where one might draw the line between right and wrong, truth and untruth, morality and immorality. These lines are not always sharp like the difference between black and white. They often are more like transition zones from one way of thinking to another, each representing various shades of grey. Even so, we often see things clearly as black or white, and our biases are responsible for our taking such clear-cut positions. Though I endeavoured to found my ideas on reasoned arguments, I must confess that in each case I started with my personal beliefs and convictions rather than with a clean slate of mind.

For instance, I have never personally acted purely out of self-interest. So, it was natural that I did not quite agree with

Adam Smith's thesis that self-interest is the exclusive, if not the primary, source of collective interest. Similarly, I did not believe that science or scientific methods should be the gold standard for determining what is true or false. I have argued that the factor that differentiates humanity from the rest of the physical world is morality. The physical world and science, which represents the rules that the physical world follows, have no morals. Accordingly, I have argued that those who would have science dictate our lives are greatly in error. So, it should then not come as a surprise if I defined truth in two dimensions—scientific truth and moral (or spiritual) truth. I place moral or spiritual truth above scientific truth and have made the point that science, to be helpful to humanity, must always follow the guide of morality. I have argued with many examples, including that of the generation of nuclear energy, that science must follow the guidance of morality, or it will bring an end to humanity.

## Plain Language

In these books, I hope to reach intellectuals and educated men and women who have a keen sense of judgement and can make up their own minds about the substance of a topic under discussion. Only such people can be agents of change. We cannot ask the clerics, nuns, and bishops to reform religions; we cannot ask a modern economist to tell us in plain language what she/he wants to communicate. As Deirdre McCloskey put it "most journals of economics nowadays look like journals of applied mathematics or theoretical statistics … technical economics are no longer even superficially accessible to lay people," and yet to have any impact on decision makers, this is the worst language to communicate one's thoughts. I have tried to explain everything as simply as possible, even complex thoughts concerning economics, science, technology, and religion.

## Overview of the Four Books

### *BOOK 1—The Bright Side of Adversity: An Autobiography*

This captivating autobiography tells the story of a multifaceted first-generation immigrant from India who rose from a tumultuous childhood to achieve prominence in diverse fields as a scientist, inventor, educator, executive, entrepreneur, and philanthropist. He established one of the fastest-growing chemical and pharmaceutical companies in the world and chronicled it in *The Makings of PMC Group: A Corporation with a Soul*. After declaring capitalism morally bankrupt and socialism financially impotent, he developed a new economic framework called *Wealth of People*.

He made a convincing case why science and spirituality can peacefully coexist in the same mind, developed his own epistemology to decipher truth from falsities in religions, and argued that human life has a special purpose to serve in this universe. An eternal optimist, he shows in *The Highest Reality: A Treatise on Religion, Truth, Morality, and the Purpose of Life* that our ability to discover new things is as vast as the secrets of the universe and that there are no problems that human ingenuity cannot solve.

The primary focus of this biography, however, is not the life of the author or his accomplishments. The message is that life unfolds in the midst of adversity, and when we embrace adversity as a strength, it becomes a stepping stone to success. Similarly, when we face uncertainty with courage, a journey becomes an adventure full of excitement, awe, beauty, and fulfilment. The autobiography serves as a medium to bring these messages to life.

This fifteen-chapter book covers the length of the author's life from birth to age eighty-three, the year he finished writing the manuscript. However, he covers only the first fifty-four years of his life in detail and the next twenty-nine years in summary. This latter period is chronicled in detail in three separate books that belong to a four-book memoir series. Chapters 1–12 follow a chronological sequence. The remaining four chapters cover topics that do not belong to chronological classification; they are based on my experiences throughout my life.

## *BOOK 2—The Makings of PMC Group: A Corporation with a Soul*

The year 1994 presented a dilemma to me. At the time I was the Chief Technical Officer of PPG industries reporting directly to the Chairman of the Board. The dilemma was whether to launch a campaign for the chairman's job, which was becoming vacant at PPG and for which I had been shortlisted or form my own company. I opted for the latter and started PMC Group. My main reason for forming PMC Group was a firm belief that a corporation must have a soul, which corporate America was in danger of losing. Once I made up my mind and decided to form PMC Group, I resigned from PPG and bought one of its subsidiaries, the Polymer Products Company, which at the time boasted a revenue of only $16 million. From such a modest base, I built PMC Group at an accelerated rate.

As I concentrated on building PMC Group companies, it became one of the fastest-growing chemical and pharmaceutical companies in the world. Between 1995 and 2022, the annual revenue of PMC Group grew ninetyfold, from $16 million to more than $1 billion. We achieved leading positions in many industry sectors and established manufacturing facilities in the United States, Europe, South Korea, and India. Currently, we employ more than 1,500 people.

Before I started PMC Group, I wrote down the mission of the corporation that I envisioned. "PMC Group's vision," I wrote, "would be to build a success-model for twenty-first-century corporations that can grow rapidly, create jobs, promote social responsibilities, and generate the profits necessary to perform these functions well." In our model of a corporation with a soul, top- and bottom-line corporate growth would work in tandem with each other and with the creation of jobs and the discharge of social responsibilities. The purpose of PMC Group would be to embody and carry forward the dreams and aspirations outlined in its vision.

In 1997, I presented my vision of PMC Group to the US Commercial Development Association's annual banquet as their keynote speaker. Most of the corporate leaders in attendance praised my vision, but no one adopted the values that underpinned my company. By 2019, however, a similar group at the Business Round-table meeting that August debated the purpose of a corporation, and 181 of 188 attending CEOs adopted values that nearly matched those of PMC Group. So, I think the time has finally come for my memoir. I believe that all the success and satisfaction I've enjoyed have come from my enduring passion for discerning scientific truth and the ethics of human behaviour. By sharing this passion and the knowledge it brought to me with as many people as possible, I hope to spread the success and satisfaction I have known. I know of no better way to strengthen the foundation of an abundant, fair, and sustainable life for all.

I founded PMC Group on principles that we rarely see in corporations, such as loyalty to the communities in which we operate. Our products enhance the quality of life of people everywhere, and our business units invest generously in their communities. This is especially true of education, for it ensures moral and prosperous people.

## *BOOK 3—Wealth of People: A New Framework for Economics*

The idea behind this book began to germinate in my mind in the early 1990s when I was still working at PPG Industries. Then, while building PMC Group, I began to question whether a single success story, despite the business round table's deliberation, would change the behaviors of our corporations. The problem, I reasoned, was deeply rooted in our economic frameworks. Any efficient and morally bound economic system must have two important criteria: it must be able to generate wealth and distribute it to the people in a fair and equitable manner. Capitalism generates wealth but has failed to distribute it fairly. Socialism and communism strive to achieve fairness in distribution but have been impotent in creating wealth.

In 1997 I was invited to give a keynote lecture at a session on innovation at the National Conference of Agribusiness, hosted by Purdue University. It was during that lecture that I first expressed the idea that a fair and robust economic arrangement could be built using the laws of nature as templates. During my talk, which was well received, I condemned the way big corporations are run today and highlighted the strategy I was adopting in forming PMC

Group to remedy the pitfalls. After the conference, I joined several of its attendees, including the faculty members from Purdue's economics department, at an informal reception. The discussion turned to economic theories.

"Unless the basic economic theories are replaced by something better," I told the group, "a full-fledged assault on the issue of immorality won't be possible." When a faculty member insisted that I elaborate, I said, "The main frameworks of economic theories grew from certain ideas—like those of Adam Smith and Karl Marx—about human nature and at a certain juncture of socio-economic development in England and Europe, and as such, they carry with them the personal biases of the originators of those theories. For a framework to be unbiased and sustainable, it must have the rigour of a scientific process. Today's economic theories don't have that." Then I talked briefly about how such a new framework could be built using the laws of nature as templates.

The audience appeared quite interested in my thoughts, and one audience member suggested that I write a book articulating my ideas. Talking about a subject is one thing, I reasoned, but writing a book about it is quite another. However, the thought stayed with me. The details about such a book gelled over the next twenty-five years.

In *Wealth of People*, I examine two scientific principles—(1) the laws of thermodynamics, the second law in particular and (2) Darwinism—that explore both equality and inequality. The first principle, one of the fundamental laws of physics that rule the vast inorganic universe, is responsible for converting energy into work. It does so from unequal distribution of energy that strives to achieve equality.

The book opens with a primer on modern economic states by introducing essential economic terms. It then traces the origins of modern economic theories and the political and socio-economic climates in which they arose. Next, I introduce the most significant modern economic theories: the Smith-Ricardo-Mill-Malthus doctrine; the demand-side macroeconomic theory that Keynes introduced in the aftermath of the Great Depression; communism and socialism; and several morality-based theories. What follows is a critical analysis of the leading theories, emphasizing why socialism and communism are impotent as economic arrangements and why capitalism has become an immoral force.

In the final part of the book, I develop a new framework of economics that uses a process based on the irrefutable principles of the laws of thermodynamics. I begin by discussing several key concepts of thermodynamics. Then I draw a link between thermodynamics and economics, pointing out parallels between various economic and thermodynamic terms. The discussion of the thermodynamic principles and terms gets a little technical, but I've endeavoured to describe them simply and clearly.

Of course, the laws of nature are amoral; they adhere to no moral code. Any economic arrangement, on the other hand, must not only be consistent and reproducible but also morally acceptable. Science concerns natural phenomena, but morality belongs to humans—the only living species on Earth equipped with a fully developed conscience. Thus, as we seek guidance from nature for how to function, we must also seek guidance that serves our moral principles. I discuss morality in detail in Book 4 of my memoir, while in this book, I address it only briefly in connection with the proposed economic arrangement.

I was inspired to develop the alternative economic arrangement because of the absence of any better system. The current arrangements swing from capitalist instincts, which eventually lead to immoral excesses, to socialist instincts, which eventually bring forth misery because of socialism's inherent impotence, necessitating a return to capitalism. Socialism and communism were created in reaction to the capitalist excesses of monarchy and aristocracy, and the recent rise of socialist sentiment in capitalist countries is similarly a reaction to the surge of capitalist excesses. Wealth of People, fashioned after immutable scientific principles, creates wealth and achieves fair distribution—simultaneously.

I begin each of the first eight chapters (there are nine total) with a personal anecdote that relates the contents of the chapter to real-life experiences, thus turning potentially dry subjects into enjoyable reading. Many of these personal anecdotes are borrowed from Book 1 of my memoir series—my autobiography.

## *BOOK 4—The Highest Reality: A Treatise on Religion, Truth, Morality, and the Purpose of Life*

Life is a journey. It's also a learning experience. And it's not just a learning experience; it's about reflecting on what we learn. And it's not just about reflecting on what we learn; it's about discovering new things that go beyond how the physical world works. It also concerns non-physical things—the *spiritual* things. It's about discovering how the physical world interacts with our emotional world. It's about probing the nature of truth. It is about pondering about religions—the good and the bad in them. It's about understanding the importance of helping others and of philanthropic activities. It's also about pondering the purpose of life. This book, the last volume of my four-volume memoir series, is about all of the above. It brings everything together by relating each idea to my own inquiries and to the inquiries of those who have contemplated the same matters in the past.

I close the book with a chapter on the purpose of life, using examples from science, art, and philosophy to explore the concept that the grandest of all existences is nothingness and that nothingness is also the womb of all realities. All realities emerge as pairs of opposites from nothingness, and they end up again as nothingness upon their collapse. Our ability to create reality as pairs of opposites—our scientific, artistic, and philosophical advances and the fact that these realities can accumulate from generation to generation—gives humanity the power to one day fully understand the purpose that lies behind the existence of the universe. When humanity reaches that goal, we will have succeeded in fulfilling our purpose, which until then should be to do everything in our power to keep humanity alive and united at peace with itself.

# 1

# In the Beginning (Up to Age Thirteen)

## Earliest Memory

It was a grim evening dimly lit by a few gaslights on black iron posts. A gentle wind blew ocean waves against the moored ship—*chhallat, chhallat*—at regular intervals and sprayed a fine mist of water at every strike. The adults were talking in whispers. The eerie quiet broke only when we heard the thumping sounds of the soldiers' boots pacing back and forth on the dock. The atmosphere was thick with the anticipation of something ominous about to happen. We waited, ready to board the ship, a monstrous presence imbued with an air of steely apprehension. I clung to my mother, holding her sari tightly, a newborn baby on her lap.

Every time I scratch my head to retrieve my earliest memory, that scene appears vividly in my mind in an almost picture-perfect clarity. I also remember that as we settled into our cabin on the ship, Mother fed us *luchi* and *lady canning* (puffed bread fried in butter and golden-brown Indian sweets made from dried milk and cheese), my favourite foods. I cannot vouch that these are true memories or figments of my imagination, formed from the stories my mother told us.

The reason for my doubt is that if they are true, they would have taken place early in 1942, when the last civilian ship sailed from Myanmar to India before the Japanese invasion during World War II. I would have been two years old at the time, and the baby on my mother's lap would have been my sister Maya, who was about eighteen months younger than me. I do not remember anything else from my childhood until I was four years old. My memories of that age come in disjointed pictures: bushels of newly harvested rice heaped in the courtyard of our village home, ready to be half-boiled in large vats, dried, de-husked by dozens of women in large *dhekies* (manually operated hammering devices for de-husking rice), and stored in large silos on the compound where we lived. I also remember the rainy season when all the roads flooded, the water rose to the brim of our yard, and barges full of jute sticks arrived at our garden house. The next concrete memory is of being bitten by a snake when I was five years old. I will describe that experience later in more detail.

## Early Childhood

Though I describe myself as belonging to the Indian American ethnic class, my birthplace was in Burma. I was born in

Moulmein (now Mawlamyine), one of the most beautiful and romantic cities on earth. It was in this city on the pebble shores of the Andaman Sea where Rudyard Kipling was inspired to write a poem about a common British soldier recalling the beauty of a young woman he fell in love with there, half a world away from his home in rainy London. It was also the city from which another prominent writer, George Orwell, sent a powerful message against capital punishment while he was superintendent of police there. Orwell's message calling for the abolishment of capital punishment had a special significance coming from the city of love, beauty, and romance. It was in this romantic and picturesque port city that my mother conceived me, and I was born there on 1 April 1940. The time and place of my birth foretold that love for nature and humanity would come naturally to me, but many bad things happened to me before those portents became manifest.

The pristine beauty and tranquility of Moulmein with the blue ocean spread out before it, mountains in the background, and its many pagodas and monuments catering to its peace-loving Buddhist population, would soon be torn into pieces as World War II engulfed Burma and Japanese bombs poured like rain from the sky. Burma became a very troubled spot, as the early 1940s became a very troubled time for the world. Within four years of my birth, World War II spread like wildfire in the South-East Asian theatre. The war in Burma was far more brutal than many realize. The interests of four warring belligerents—the Axis forces led by Japan, the allied forces led by the British and including the Americans and Chinese, the Indian National Army led by the revolutionary Subhas Chandra Bose, and Burmese National Reactionary forces seeking the cessation of British rule—enveloped the region at the same time.

My father, after matriculation from high school, gained a civil service position in the Customs Department of British Burma, which paid a handsome salary. At twenty, he married his first wife and moved to Burma. Sixteen years later, after his wife died, leaving my father with two sons, aged fifteen and ten, my father married my mother, who is twenty years younger than he. During his work life, my father held various posts in major trade and port cities such as Akyab (now called Sittwe), Rangoon (now called Yangon), and Moulmein. My elder siblings were all born in Akyab or Rangoon. I was the only one who was born in Moulmein.

## A Brief History of Burma

Three Anglo-Burmese wars (in 1824, 1852, and 1865) consolidated Britain's total control over Burma. Until 1937, Britain ruled Burma as a province of British India. At that time, it gained a new colonial status, a new constitution, and a fully elected assembly with many powers going to the Burmese. Ba Maw became the first prime minister, but in 1939 U Saw forced him out. British authorities arrested U Saw in January 1942 for his cooperation with Japan, which launched a short-lived invasion of Burma soon after his arrest.

During Japan's 1942 invasion of Burma, the invaders drove the British out first from Rangoon, the largest city in Burma and capital of the Yangon region, and then proceeded to Moulmein, about 300 kilometres (about 190 miles) south-east of Rangoon. The Japanese occupation did not last long. It continued through 1943 into the early part of 1944. During the occupation, a (nominally) independent Burmese government under Prime Minister Ba Maw ruled the country. During this time, ethnic Indians fled from Burma in a massive exodus, as British officials no longer protected them, and the Burmese Nationalists persecuted them. They fled on foot principally to India, and mostly to Assam along barely passable tracks across mountainous terrain. Thousands perished along their way. To maintain a functioning government, Prime Minister Ba Maw did protect ethnic Indians in the civil service, keeping them safe from the Nationalists.

The year 1944 was the most eventful in Burma's wartime history. Bose's Indian National Army made a dashing entry into India during the early months of 1944 with the full support of the Japanese army, only to have adverse weather and the powerful British Indian Army repel them. In 1944, a British Indian Army counter-offensive began the liberation of Burma from Japanese occupation, and by 1945, the British gained back full control of Burma. Burma finally gained its independence on 4 January 1948.

During British rule, Burma became a prosperous country with a large colonial export economy. This was primarily due to its lush, dense forests that produced the most desirable teak lumber in the world, oil reserves, rubies, and plentiful production of premier-quality rice. Its resources attracted skilled and unskilled labour from neighboring India—mostly from Bengal and south India. They came as government civil service employees, doctors, lawyers, university professors, merchants, traders, engineers, moneylenders, dock workers, and migrant labourers. By some estimates, about two million Indians were in Burma in 1940—about 16 per cent of the country's population. They lived primarily around Rangoon. Indians went to Burma to make a fortune. My father was one such fortune seeker.

## My Mother and Our Ancestral Home

Although my mother did not receive much formal schooling, she was a very smart and resourceful woman. She managed our family prudently, and with the savings from my father's earnings, she expanded our ancestral home in the village of Silaur in the Brahmanbaria District of East Bengal (later East Pakistan and now Bangladesh) by acquiring lots of arable cropland. We rented these lands on a 50:50 basis, sharing the crops produced in a system known as *barga* (or the barga lease system). This arrangement generated a significant income for years and helped us maintain an affluent lifestyle for several years after my father's retirement. She also bought a lot of gold, both as ornaments for herself and as nuggets for economic security. She decorated our ancestral home with furniture made of choice Burmese *segun* teak.

She never neglected her children's education. Seeing the power that the Indian Civil Service (ICS, now the Indian Administrative Service) officers wielded in Burma and India, she always fancied that her children would one day become ICS officers. My elder siblings went to the English-medium schools in Burma. My family visited our ancestral home almost every year for two to four weeks. As the family left Burma permanently in 1942, the situation in Bengal became very perilous. Unrest and violent clashes between Indians and the occupying British personnel were occurring everywhere in India. Closer to home in the state of Bengal, a devastating famine struck in 1943, thanks to the misguided policies of Winston Churchill. This famine led to the starvation deaths of more than three million people (approximately 5 per cent of the state's population of sixty million).

## Building a Coherent Memory

There is no consensus among child psychologists concerning the exact age of children when their earliest memories occur. Estimates vary from two to seven years old. Aside from my memory (which may not be real) of the Moulmein dock when I was only two, I do not remember anything until I was four, and even that memory is quite fragmented. Clear and coherent memories began to build when I was five or six years old. I have no memory of anything that occurred before that age even though my imagination often tempts me to construct de novo what I have forgotten.

My first concrete memory is that of a snake bite when I was five years old. I was told that after our family settled down in our village home, my father took us for an excursion (some may call it a vacation) to Agartala, capital of the independent princely state of Tripura. Agartala was only about 14 miles (about 22 km) from our village. It had a good school system, and the king was completing the construction of a college there that would be accredited by Calcutta University. The idea, I suppose, was to have a second house in Agartala that might be convenient for the education of the children. During that vacation, my mother invited her mother and her family (my two uncles and an aunt) to join us since she had not seen them for quite a while. For this excursion, Father rented a mansion for a month.

One afternoon during that vacation, my immediate elder brother Gangesh and I went out to play in a large field next to the mansion. As we were playing, I stepped on a snake, which wrapped itself around my leg and bit me. Hearing Gangesh's scream that I had been bitten by a snake, everyone from the house came out. By then I had untangled the snake, and it slithered away. But while I was untangling the snake, it bit me again on my leg and hand. My aunt picked me up and laid me in her lap, and we all rushed to the hospital. The hospital treated me according to its standard procedures and released me with the warning that I should be watched carefully during the night. If my situation worsened, I should be brought back to the hospital immediately.

My parents also called an *ojha* (sorcerer) who uttered some hocus-pocus and advised that I should not touch the ground for twenty-four hours. So, for the next twenty-four hours, I became a fixture on the laps of my aunt, mother, grandmother, and uncles. My mother also promised to sacrifice a goat to the snake goddess Manasa if I survived, which of course I did. I will describe this experience in greater detail later in an episode in Book 4—*The Highest Reality: A Treatise on Religion, Truth, Morality, and Purpose of Life*—of this memoir series because it was a seed of my later exploration of truth and falsehoods in religion. During that stay in Agartala, my father bought a tract of land measuring about two-and-a-half acres in a prime location of the city in case he wanted to build a second house there.

## Memories of Silaur

When we moved from Burma to British India and our ancestral village of Silaur in East Bengal, the first order of business for my father was to enroll my brothers Suratha and Partha in one of the elite East Bengal high schools, the Iswar Pathsala, in the city of Comilla. Comilla was about 25 miles (40 km) from our village, accessible from our village at the time via 4 miles of village roads and 21 miles by train. At that time, a student's knowledge and comprehension of English were taken to a great degree as the measure of that student's education. This was so possibly because India had been under British rule for nearly 200 years at the time.

My brothers, having attended English-medium schools in Burma, received special treatment and gained admission to higher classes than they would normally have been. Suratha matriculated from high school in 1946 and entered Comilla Victoria Government College, from which he cleared his IA (Intermediate of Arts) examination in 1948. Partha created a sensation when he matriculated from high school with six letters (i.e., 80 per cent or more in six subjects), an exceptional scholarly performance. This marked him as a highly sought-after college recruit, and he received several offers with scholarships.

Since there was no girls' school in the vicinity of our village, and my parents did not want to send my eldest sister Charusheela (Sheela for short) to a faraway school in Comilla, she studied at home in tandem with Suratha, who is one year younger than she. She also matriculated from the high school system in 1946 and did her IA as a private student in 1948. She also pursued her higher degrees as a private student. Gangesh and I, on the other hand, did not receive much attention. We were home-schooled. There was some talk of enrolling us in the village school, but its quality was so poor that my father thought home-schooling would be the better option.

## *Our Village*

Our village was a caste-segregated community. The Brahmins, the affluent and landowning class, which included my family, lived in an area called the Brahmin-para, meaning the neighbourhood (para) where the Brahmin families lived. There were 18–20 families in the Brahmin-para. These families lived in two sections with a narrow road (a walking path, really) separating them. Each section was home to nine or ten families.

To the east of the Brahmin-para was a large pond or reservoir. Further to the east was the Sudra-para—an area where the Sudra (labour class) families lived. Still further east was marshy land, and further east was agricultural land. To the west of the Brahmin-para was a swamp, and beyond the swamp there was a large Muslim-para, and further west was agricultural land.

To the north of the Brahmin-para, separated by a narrow village road, was another Muslim-para. Further north was agricultural land. To the south of the Brahmin-para, there was another large pond, and further south still another Muslim-para. We called this pond the new pond (*natun pukur*), as my father told me that it was relatively new and man-made. On the western bank of the *natun pukur* was a *baag* (short for *bagan* or garden), but in our rural definition, it was an abandoned narrow strip of forest that belonged to no one.

Silaur did not have any shops or marketplaces. People would walk about 3 miles (5 km) to the south to another village called Sendah where a large group of the merchant class (Kayastha, originally Vaishya) lived. A few dozen Brahmin families also lived there; they represented an outflow from Silaur resulting from the village being too small to accommodate all the native Brahmin families anymore. Sendah was a big village. It had a marketplace that assembled every morning and lasted till noon or early afternoon. People from neighbouring villages would come to this market to buy fish, meat, vegetables, and other food items every morning.

About 3 miles to the north of Silaur, past the agricultural lands, a dead pond covered with water hyacinth, and a baag, was another village called Ablahucha. Its residents were also Brahmins, Sudras, Kayasthas, and Muslims. Ablahucha would host two markets a week in the afternoons; farmers, fishermen, and owners of stationery items would bring their produce and products for sale. Again, people from all the nearby villages would go there for shopping during the twice-a-week markets (called *haats*). I came to know those two villages, particularly their marketplaces, as I used to accompany my father when he went to the markets.

## *Our House in Silaur*

Our house was the largest in the Brahmin-para. The original compound from my grandfather's time had three parts—one for my father, and one each for his two elder brothers. My father expanded his section by acquiring two other properties. One was a garden property called the *chharabari*; it was attached to the south side of our main compound. The other was a separate house called the *natun bari* (new house); it was to the west just across the pathway that divided the eastern and the western segments of the Brahmin-para.

The main compound was rectangular with four large buildings made of corrugated tin with brick foundations and concrete floors. There were two yards—a private inside yard and an outside yard. This compound, with four buildings surrounding the inside yard, also had high metal-and-brick walls with two gates for security. The front gate was in the east wall, and the back gate was in the west wall. The gate in the west led, by a series of steps, to the narrow road that divided the eastern and western enclaves of the Brahmin-para.

Outside the front gate was a big outside yard with a brick building called the *dalan* in its southern part; it belonged to us, while two other large buildings belonged to my father's two elder brothers, both of whom were widowers. One of those uncles (my father's immediate elder brother) lived in the village with his daughter-in-law. The eldest brother lived with his son Kusum, who was a renowned medical doctor, in the city of Brahmanbaria. This brother came only occasionally to the village. The uncle who lived with his daughter-in-law in the village had a son, Chuni, who did not live in the village. Chuni worked as a wartime contractor. His job required him to travel from one city to another.

The natun bari consisted of two large buildings and a large yard. One of the two buildings was a godown (warehouse) to store paddy and rice during harvest seasons. The other was a guest house, sometimes used for local gatherings. We had a manual water pump in the yard of this property. The public had free access to this pump, villagers called it a tube well, and they used it to obtain water for drinking, cooking, and so on. My parents were happy that they could provide this facility for free to everyone.

The chharabari was essentially a large tract of land that acted as a big outdoor garden property. It had all kinds of fruit trees—mango, jackfruit, guava, banana, papaya, and what not! There was also a bamboo bush in it, and we could see white bamboo shoots coming out from the ground and growing to become green bamboo plants within a few months. Mother would often cook some delicious dishes from the young shoots. There was also an area in the chharabari with banana plants. Mother would also cook great dishes from banana flowers (the conical structures at the end of the banana bunch from where new bananas would come out—it has a layered structure like cabbage). There were all kinds of flowering plants in the chharabari. On the north-east side and behind some big trees was a small pond. This pond did not get much sun. Mother warned us not to get into that pond. Gangesh and I speculated that there must be a monster living underneath its dark water and so we kept away from it. During harvest season, the chharabari would double as a staging ground for jute and rice paddy.

## My Life in Our Village

The first thing that comes to mind when I try to remember my life in the village was that it was there that I first learned how to respect my elders; this was an integral part of our culture. Every morning when we got up from our bed, our first duty was to show this respect with *pranam* to our parents and elders, including the elder siblings. We did this by touching their feet with our right hand, then touching our forehead with it, and then our chest. This practice still exists, but not as a daily routine. It's now only for special days like the Vijayadasami (the final day of the five-day worship of Goddess Durga, which falls on the tenth day of the lunar calendar) and *nababarsha* (Bengali new year's day).

Unlike Western cultures, we never called our elders by their first names. Seniority was highly respected in our culture. We also had separate terms for male and female elder relatives. *Dada* for elder brothers, *Didi* for elder sisters; *Boudi* for elder brother's wife, *Jetha* for my father's elder brother, and *Kaka* for my father's younger brother. To show increased formality of respect, we would often add endings like *-masai* or *-babu* to the main terms like *Jethamasai* and *Kakababu*. In this book, I have not used this formalism. I used the first names of my elder brothers, though I never used those names to address them. I called my immediate elder brother Gangesh *Sejdada*, the next higher-up Partha *Chinidada*, and the eldest Suratha *Borodada*. I simply called our eldest sister Sheela *Didi,* since there was no other elder sister. If I had had another elder sister, I would have called the eldest *Borodidi*.

Every morning, Gangesh and I picked fresh flowers for puja (worship of the family deity), which my mother performed after she bathed. We would always pick the flowers from the chharabari, and many times we went to other houses to pick exotic flowers. My favourite flower was the *sephali*. Its small white flowers have an exceptionally pleasant fragrance when they fall to the ground from the trees at night. Before anyone could walk on them, Gangesh and I would fill our small flower baskets with them. Flower picking was a big event during the main *parvans*—formal religious festivities that involved offerings to various deities. Such festivities occurred almost once every month. As the saying goes, Bengali Hindus observe thirteen parvans in twelve months.

I remember the evenings of my village life with nostalgia. In our inside yard, there was a tulsi plant on a raised earthen platform, called the *bedi*. Every Hindu house had such bedi and tulsi plants. Many consider this plant sacred and an embodiment of Vishnu. Every evening as darkness descended on the village, my mother would put an open-flame mustard-oil lamp in front of the tulsi plant, bow down with the folded end of her sari around her neck, and make the *ulu* sound by moving her tongue rapidly inside her mouth. Though none of the other housewives planned any synchronization, they would do the same at around the same time, and the effect would be a grand chorus of ulus. Along with the open-flame lamp, my mother would also put some incense sticks under the tulsi plant along with a plate of sugar cakes, called *batasha*. The sound of all the ulus that broke through the quiet of the village evenings and the scent of the incense cast a spell of tranquility over me, making me feel the divine and be peaceful. My mother would then distribute the batasha to all the family members. We would eat them, and then it would be time for dinner. By that time, our domestic helpers had put kerosene safety lanterns in every room.

Every morning we would eat our breakfast, which was boiled eggs, homemade sweets, puffed rice, and milk. Then it was time for studies. As both Gangesh and I were home-schooled, our tutor was our eldest sister, Sheela, our Didi. Though I do not remember all the books I read, I remember my first English book and its opening sentence. It read, "Bengal had had many famous children, and Sir Ashutosh Mukherjee was one of them." Sir Ashutosh Mukherjee was a very famous Bengali, and in Bengal we learned about Ashutosh Mukherjee, Vidyasagar, and a few other famous Bengalis just like American children learn about Abraham Lincoln, Martin Luther King Jr, and other American luminaries.

The reason I remember the opening sentence of that book so vividly is not because I suddenly started to emulate the great characters. The main reason was that I was fascinated by the repeated use of the word "had". Though Gangesh was three years older, he and I studied at the same level and read the same books. For me, the most interesting things I learned at that age came not from those books but were what my father taught me during our trips to the markets. It was during those trips that I learned simple addition, subtraction, multiplication, and division—all without the aid of slate and chalk. I learned to do those operations in my mind. I suppose that is why I later excelled in arithmetic.

Gangesh and I spent most of our free time playing in the chharabari. When the village fell silent after the midday meal (it was the biggest meal of the day), Gangesh and I would sneak out with *khejur gur* (molasses made from date-tree sap) and *chira* (beaten rice) to the chharabari, sit on hay bales, and eat our treats. We had two milking cows that would also roam around in the chharabari. We had our most fun in the chharabari during summer in the mango season right after a storm. The cows seemed to have an extra sense to foresee when such a storm would be coming. When they sensed the coming of a storm, they would start crying *humbaa* and run to their sheds. When we saw the cows running, we followed them and took refuge inside a building.

We called these storms *kalbaishakki* (severe storms of the Bengali month of *Baishak,* April–May in the English calendar). They were a sudden gathering of dark clouds that would soon erupt with violent winds that would tear branches from trees and create havoc all around. These storms, however, were very short. They came, danced their monstrous dances, and disappeared as quickly as they came, as if opening the door in the sky for sunshine to come beaming back. Gangesh and I liked these storms because our fun times began after such storms. As soon as the storm was over, we ran to the mango trees and collected all the green mangoes that fell from the branches. Gangesh knew how to de-skin them, cut them into narrow slices, and season them with salt and sugar to make the most delicious pickle I ever ate.

In our village, the rainy season was a scene to behold. Water would submerge everything around the villages. Gangesh and I would sit at the edge of the chharabari and watch the water rise. In a few days, the entire Brahmin-para would become an island, and we relied on dinghies for all transportation to other villages or marketplaces. At the beginning of the rainy season, we moved a couple of our dinghies from the ponds next to the chharabari. My memories of the chharabari are among the most cherished of all.

There are other memories of my time with Gangesh in our village that also come before me but not in any conscious order. I remember how I used to cling to Gangesh all the time. I remember both of us venturing through the baag on the bank of the natun pukur, looking for exotic plants and creatures. We would discover certain tubular flowers that grew in the baag, and each had a drop of sweet nectar inside it. We would suck out the nectar from the stem side of the flower, and it tasted sweet like honey. Maybe we were competing with the bees for these nectars, but that didn't bother us then. I also remember another scary experience Gangesh and I had while exploring a neighbouring village. The following episode describes this experience.

### *Episode 1-1: Brahmadaishyu*

Gangesh and I decided to venture to Ablahucha on a day when there was no bazaar there. We wanted to explore the area where the bazaar assembled to see if we could find some interesting things that the stationary shopkeepers might have left behind. We started walking after the midday meal, when most people, except possibly a few farmers, took their afternoon naps.

It was a very hot summer day. Even the farmers were not on the croplands. We walked through the agricultural fields and approached a baag with huge trees on it and a pond below on the right thickly covered with water hyacinths. To go to Ablahucha, we had to walk along a narrow track in the baag. Gangesh told me that he heard that a *brahmadaishyu* haunted the baag, and people saw it when the place fell quiet in the evenings. Nobody, he said, would venture through the baag alone in the evening for fear of the brahmadaishyu, which Gangesh told me was a fearsome ghost with its head not on its shoulders but coming out of its belly.

Though it was daytime, both Gangesh and I were terrified to walk through the baag because no other people were around. I had always been afraid of ghosts. Mother told me that if I ever feared a ghost coming at me, I should utter "Rama", the name of the supreme Hindu God. Ghosts are afraid of God's name, and if I uttered "Rama", all ghosts would disappear. It was like the sign of the cross for Catholic Christians, the behaviour that drives evil away. Gangesh and I decided to chant "Rama" as we walked through the baag.

As we started to go through it, some birds startled us with shrill calls that sounded like someone crying for help. We began to chant "Rama" more rapidly, but when we did, the word sounded like *mara*, which means a dead body (in other words, the source of all ghosts). We thought that the brahmadaishyu had overtaken our speech and changed "Rama" to "mara". We became frozen with fear. Then we turned around and started to run. That was when we saw a farmer coming towards us, and we breathed sighs of relief. With our hearts still pounding, we walked back to our house, never to venture to Ablahucha on our own again.

I remember when our cousin Chuni came to the village for a few days. Gangesh and I admired him and clung to him like his shadow. We would feel obliged if he gave us any orders. He looked like a hero to me, something one would aspire to become. My father told Chuni that he could stay in the dalan. While barbers came daily to shave my father, Chuni used "7 O'clock" blades for shaving. I discovered the glossy cover of the blade that was lying near his bed and asked Chuni if I could have it. He said yes, and it became one of my most precious possessions. I kept it inside a beautiful metal box. Among my other precious possessions were horse and cow figurines that Partha had made from clay when he came home from school during holidays. Both Gangesh and I would go with Partha to the marshy lands at the end of the agricultural area to the north of our village to collect good clay soil. Partha was very artistic. He could make various types of figurines from clay. When sun-dried, they looked so real!

When Chuni came to the village home, his wife stayed with him in the dalan. We called her Chuni-boudi. Several months after Chuni left, Chuni-boudi gave birth to a beautiful baby boy. I remember my mother giving the baby a gold bangle as she blessed him with a long life. Mother did not like Chuni-boudi living with her father-in-law when Chuni was gone. She thought it did not look good for a young housewife to live with her widower father-in-law when her husband was away. So Mother asked Chuni-boudi to live with us, but it did not happen.

I heard of terrible Hindu–Muslim riots breaking out in various parts of the country, though our village remained relatively calm. When Gangesh and I went to the Muslim-para, the Muslims, many of whom were our *bargadars* (sharecroppers of our croplands), treated us very well. They all had dogs and puppies and allowed us to play with the puppies. Outside our village, however, inter-religious relations were becoming tense, Father told us. Fearing armed riots, my brother Suratha bought half-dozen swords in Comilla and brought them to our house. I fancied that, as I was small, if rioters came to our house, I would sit low with one of those swords and cut off their legs.

Though Gangesh studied at the same level as I did, he was much more physically active than I was—partly because he was several years older than I. He could climb trees that I could not. The village boys taught him how to catch birds. He would climb a tree, put glue on a piece of wood, and tie the wood to a branch. Then he would put a few earthworms or a butterfly on the glue. When a bird stood on the piece of wood to eat the butterfly or earthworm, it would get stuck to the glue. Gangesh would then bring down the piece of wood with the bird and put the bird in a cage.

Gangesh also could use a bow and arrow to hunt little animals. He looked like a warrior when he used his bow and arrow. I remember an episode involving Gangesh, with a bow and arrow made by one of our handyman helpers, that prompted me to ask the handyman to make a bow for me too. This resulted in my committing a guilty act—my first guilt—that will remain with me for life.

### *Episode 1-2: My First Guilt*

We had many helpers in our house, including several handymen who worked part-time outside the house. One day I found that one of them was making a bow and arrow for Gangesh. I asked him to make one for me also. He said that he would be glad to make one for me if I paid him as much as my brother was paying. I told the handyman that neither my brother nor I had any money, so how could we pay him? The handyman said that I should get money the same way my brother got it. I asked him how. He said that my brother got the money from my mother's cash box, and I should do the same. He warned me not to tell any of this to my mother. If I did, he would never make anything for me.

I knew where my mother's cash box was and where she kept the key. I opened the cash box when no one was around, took some money from the box, and gave it to the handyman. The handyman said that he would start making my bow and arrow, but it would take much more money because my brother gave him more. By putting Gangesh and me in competition, the handyman extorted a lot of money from us.

Initially, my mother did not suspect anything. Soon she appeared to be concerned that money was disappearing from her cash box. But she did not suspect either me or my brother. Her suspicion fell on one of our resident domestic servants. She told my father that the servant was somehow stealing money from her cash box. My mother and my father decided to terminate the "unfaithful" servant.

As soon as I knew their plan, I became restless. I did not want the servant to lose his job for no fault of his own. I went to my mother, broke into tears, and confessed the whole thing to her. My mother thanked me for my confession and punished Gangesh by confining him to his room for one full day. When she told my father what had happened, he called the *choukidar* (the village sentry) and told him how the handyman was extorting money from us. The choukidar handcuffed the handyman and sent him to the police station, which was about 5 miles (8 km) from our village. I do not know what happened to the handyman. I guess the police released him after they took a bribe because they never asked us to testify.

The whole episode shook me to the core, and it left an unforgettable feeling of guilt in the mind of this six-year-old. I promised myself that I would never again lie to my parents, a promise that I did not keep (in spirit) a few years later. I will describe that occasion later in another episode (Episode 1-5).

That episode and the one that I will describe later left a permanent mark on me. I would never again knowingly participate in any wrongdoing, no matter how compelling the cause could be at the time. But for now, I will get back to describing some of my village experiences.

One memorable event occurred when I was still six. It was the *upanayana* (sacred thread) ceremony. A boy born to a Brahmin family does not become a full Brahmin unless he wears a sacred thread around his shoulders because that is a sign that he performs certain routine religious rites every day. Like a bar mitzvah or a christening, the upanayana is an important religious ceremony that all boys born to Brahmin families must perform.

### *Episode 1-3: Our Upanayana Ceremony*

I remember my and my brothers' upanayana ceremony quite vividly. My parents wanted me and three of my brothers—Suratha (fifteen years old), Partha (twelve), and Gangesh (nine, I was six)—to receive the sacred thread at the same time. Since this was a big occasion, my parents combined all four ceremonies to reduce the cost and workload. The only problem with this ritual was that the participating boys must be between seven and fourteen years old; Suratha already passed that age, and I had not yet reached it. Among all the turmoil of settling down in our village after moving from Burma and getting the older boys, Suratha and Partha, admitted to school, Suratha's upanayana could not be done on time. There was also a problem with me. I was underage for this ceremony, but the system allowed all kinds of violations if we could pay the heavy rectification fee to the priest. For that fee, the priest performed special pujas (offerings to God) that allowed a waiver to Suratha and a religious sanction for me, which added the nine months I spent in my mother's womb to stretch my age to seven. Suratha and Partha came from Comilla for the ceremony.

I will describe the upanayana ceremony in detail in Book 4, in connection with my grandson Deven's upanayana. The difference here was that while I performed Deven's upanayana as a cultural thing, ours was a fully religious event with full adherence to the procedures laid out in the Hindu scriptures.

During the upanayana ceremony for my brothers and me, Father invited many of our relatives from near and far to stay with us for at least the duration of the ceremony, which lasted three days. At the end of the third day, Father invited all Brahmins from our village and the two nearest villages to a celebratory feast. I later learned that the Brahmins of all those villages were all related to our family. As our village could not accommodate all the descendants of our predecessors, they established new villages and took residence there.

During the three days of the ceremony, we were supposed to perform *brahmacharya*, which means extreme self-control. We already had our heads shaved to become *brahmacharis* (ones who practise brahmacharya). No female except our mother was allowed to visit us. According to custom, we ate only fruit, milk, and rice gruel. We were forbidden from eating any other cooked food.

In the early morning of the third day, we four brothers went to the natun pukur to bathe. We took three dips in the cold water and came out of the pond. It was deep winter, and I remember shivering the whole time. We then put on a new set of saffron clothes and went out for ceremonial alms-taking. We went to about twenty Brahmin houses nearby and asked them for alms. They put rice and pulse in our alms bags, and we came back darn tired. The priest then permitted us to eat normal food. Mother had already prepared the most delicious dishes that we devoured rapidly.

On the same day, a midday feast was scheduled, to which we invited all the Brahmin families from the three villages—Silaur, Sendah, and Ablahucha. To prepare for the feast, my father summoned all the fishermen from the nearby villages, asked them to bring their entire morning's catch to our house, and promised them handsome prices. They obliged. All the village people came to see the fresh and live fish that these fishermen brought to our yard. As with the fishermen, Father asked all the milkmen to bring all their milk and promised them a premium price as well. Father also did the same with the providers of goat meat and all kinds of vegetables. About a dozen cooks and helpers began cooking all the delicious dishes and dairy sweets in the wee hours of the morning. The feast was a grand success.

After the upanayana, we performed ritualistic prayers three times a day, reciting the Gayatri hymn. Gangesh and I did it for a few days, then reduced the frequency to once in the morning. Partha and Suratha gave up the practice as soon as the ceremony was over because they had to go back to their boarding schools.

The fun and festivity of our upanayana were soon followed by an experience, the danger and frightfulness of which one can scarcely imagine if they have not experienced such an assault. It was the experience of dacoity in our house, which I describe below.

### *Episode 1-4: Dacoity, the Armed Robbery that Terrified My Family*

*Dacoity* is a common term in India for armed robbery. The British coined the term by anglicizing the Bengali word *dakat* or the Hindi word *daaku*. The Merriam-Webster Dictionary defines it, using the Indian penal code, as "robbery by an armed gang of not less than five men". A more practical definition of dacoity in an Indian context is an armed attack on a rich person's home by a group of bandits who might arrive as a large gang. Often, the bandits begin by sending a threat; with this, they expect the homeowner to understand that if he removes any valuables from the house, he does so at the risk of his life. That is what happened in our case, although of course, our case was unique in its details.

Hardly a week had passed after our upanayana when my father received an anonymous letter. Suratha and Partha had already gone to their respective boarding schools in Comilla. The letter was from the dacoits. They knew Mother had brought all her and my sister's jewellery from our safe-deposit box at the bank to wear during the upanayana festivities. Father also had to withdraw a lot of cash to pay for all the things that were involved in the upanayana. We purchased new clothes and luxury items in Brahmanbaria.

The dacoits somehow knew all this and warned Father not to remove or hide anything. If he did, he and we would be killed, the letter warned. The letter also gave a specific date when the gang would raid our house. It warned my father not to inform the police and specified the dire consequences that would follow if he did. Anyway, informing the police would not have helped. The nearest police station was 5 miles away in Brahmanbaria, two hours by foot through croplands and muddy tracks. The letter was in the tradition of grand dacoities that were perpetrated against some legendary rich people in India, although we were nowhere as wealthy as they were. The dacoits, however, thought otherwise. They thought Father had brought great wealth from Burma, and that it was now all in our village compound.

Though Father did not inform the police, he hired a couple of dozen people who—armed with lathis, machetes, spears, and bows-and-arrows—guarded our house during the threatened time. Many of these guards were also our tenant farmers, and they had unfailing loyalty to our family. Our whole village and the villages around ours were also on the alert. We asked the choukidars of the nearby villages to warn us if they saw anything suspicious. The day that the dacoity was to occur passed with a lot of anxiety but no action. No dacoit showed up to challenge our guards. Another seven days then passed without any incident. Everybody, including the village elders, thought that the letter was a hoax. Father disbanded the guards' nightly vigils.

In the middle of the night about ten days after we expected the assault, the entire village lit up with flaming torches, and the residents woke up to the sound of gunfire. My parents knew the long-dreaded dacoits had arrived. All of us children came from our rooms to our parents' master bedroom. Soon we heard that the dacoits had broken open the main gate of the compound. The dacoits were at our main door. Father reached out for one of the swords that Suratha brought from Comilla and prepared to take a position on the side of the main door as if he would cut each bandit in half as they tried to enter our room. Realizing this would be a futile effort against a few dozen dacoits, and fearing that if they saw my father armed with a sword, the first thing they would do would be to kill him, Mother snatched the sword away from my father's hand and threw it under the bed. I forgot my fantasy of lying low and cutting the legs of the miscreants and was shivering in fear. Soon the bandits broke down our front door and swarmed inside our building.

Mother told the dacoits to take everything but not to hurt anyone physically. For one hour they ransacked all the rooms and took almost all the valuable items, which included all our clothes and even the sewing machine and our gramophone. (Clothes were considered valuable at that time because India was experiencing an acute scarcity of fabric, as freedom fighters had interrupted imports from England.) When they asked my mother where she kept her jewellery, she took out her necklace, bracelets, and earrings and threw these towards them. When they asked where she kept the rest of the jewellery, she pointed to the drawer of a mahogany chest and gave them the key that she had tied at the corner end of her sari. Anticipating that something like this could happen if the dacoits came as they had threatened, Mother filled a metal box with fake jewellery and kept it in the chest of drawers. She hid the real jewelry in a blind pocket underneath a study desk. None of the dacoits thought of checking underneath a desk drawer. For one thing, no woman would normally keep her most precious possessions in a simple place like behind a desk drawer. Mother outwitted the dacoits. They were happy to take the metal box with fake jewellery.

In the middle of all the commotion, my mother suddenly noticed that my sister Sheela, who was sixteen at the time, was missing. My parents became frantic. After the bandits left, our neighbors began to emerge from their homes and suddenly my parents found my sister in one of the neighbours' houses. When the bandits entered our compound, my sister sneaked out of her room and escaped through a hidden escape door in the north wall of the compound and reached the neighbour's house, where they hid her behind a closet.

The next morning, the village elders arrived. Father sent the choukidar to the police station in Brahmanbaria. Several policemen came to our village to investigate the dacoity. Father thought that he recognized some of the dacoits, but they were wearing camouflage so he could not be absolutely certain. The police interviewed quite a few people from the village and arrested a few on suspicion. Realizing that it was not safe to keep my sister in the village, my father sent her to Kusum's house in Brahmanbaria by a palki (palanquin) with an armed guard of about a dozen people.

After the dacoity, my parents decided that it was no longer safe to live in the village. India had just gained its freedom from British rule and our village was now part of the newly formed country of Pakistan, a Muslim nation. My parents decided to move the family to Agartala. Agartala, the capital of Tripura, was an independent princely state, and its king decided to join the new, secular, nation of India. Father asked the police chief of Brahmanbaria, a position still held by a British officer, to provide armed police protection for our family in the village as we prepared to move out. The police chief stationed two constables in our house, but my family had to bear their cost. Father gladly accepted the offer. The constables stayed in the dalan.

There was also a severe shortage of building materials at the time. In fact, there was next to none. So, Father decided to dismantle our village dwellings and move all the material to Agartala and reconstruct the dwellings the same way they were in our village on the property Father acquired just a year or so ago in Agartala. The plan was that Father would stay in Agartala to supervise the construction and Mother will stay with me and the other younger children in the village with police protection until we could all move to Agartala.

The process of dismantling the buildings then began in all earnest. Mother, Gangesh, my younger siblings and I moved to the smallest building in the compound. A large crew of labourers began dismantling the large buildings brick by brick, post by post, beam by beam, corrugated sheet by corrugated sheet, nail by nail, and screw by screw. We had these materials carried by foot to large barges docked about a mile away on a waterway that reached Agartala.

In Agartala, my father started to prepare the land for our new house. He had a big pond dug in front of the property and had the foundations excavated. He used the soil from the excavations to raise the elevation of the property, giving it a prosperous hilltop look. When the building materials arrived in Agartala, a large crew started to assemble them the same way they were in Silaur. The people of the neighbourhood were amazed to see such construction under way when no one could find any building materials. Our new neighbours in Agartala gave us the nickname *lakhpati*, meaning something like "millionaire" in English.

Back in the village, Gangesh and I loved to hang around with the two constables. They would show us their rifles and we looked with wonderment when they cleaned the barrels of their guns and loaded them with bullets. They became part of our family. They would address Mother as "mother" and behaved like her obedient children. Mother also treated them well and served them new and delicious dishes every day, which they appreciated. Mother, however, warned them not to get too friendly with Chuni-boudi, who we felt wanted to hang out with us when we hung out with the constables. Mother's watchful eye prevented that from happening.

At least once a week, the constables would explore the surrounding villages. Mother told us that they made some money during these trips by threatening poor villagers. During those nights, my mother was afraid that thieves could be stealing crops from the godown (warehouse) of the natun bari. She would wake me up several times at night, and I had to accompany her as she watched the natun bari with a powerful flashlight to make sure that there were no unusual movements there. Mother soon sold the contents of the godown, and we no longer had to watch the natun bari when the constables were out on their nightly adventures.

## Life in Agartala

Within six months of the dacoity, our new home in Agartala was complete, thanks to the gigantic number of workers Father hired to complete the construction in record time. The new house contained all three relocated buildings, a large stand-alone kitchen building, a cow shed, and a place for ducks. A six-foot high fence surrounded the entire compound of two-and-a-half acres for our security. We no longer needed the constables in Silaur, and our family moved to Agartala.

Sheela did not return to Silaur after she went to Brahmanbaria—from there she went directly to Agartala. We now had all our wooden furniture that came from Burma to Silaur moved to Agartala. We bought two milking cows and several ducks. The ducks swam in the pond and lay eggs at night. The cows gave plenty of milk, enough for the entire family. Partha entered the newly opened college in Agartala for his Intermediate of Arts (IA) studies. Suratha, who completed his IA from Victoria College in Comilla, joined the college in Agartala for his BA studies. Sheela would also continue her BA as a private student, but she could now borrow texts and reference books from the college library. Gangesh and I were not yet the focus of much attention. The idea was that we should pass the school final examination as private students and then join the college in Agartala. It was only after we had become safely ensconced in Agartala that Mother, for the first time, told us about how she outwitted the dacoits and saved most of her gold and jewels.

In Agartala, my parents, Sheela, and the children younger than me slept in the largest building. Suratha and Partha were in the medium building with their beds and study desks on either side of the room. Gangesh and I slept in the smallest building, which also served as guest quarters. When our uncle Sailesh came to visit, he would sleep in a guest bed in our room.

By the time we came to Agartala, Gangesh had told me everything about how children are born. He learned it from a Muslim boy while we were in Silaur. The boy told Gangesh that he saw how his parents did it. In poor households in the villages, many members of a family lived in a single room, and there was little scope for adult privacy. One night while in Agartala, I woke up in the middle of the night. When I looked outside, I saw Mother and Father on the verandah of their building, completely undressed. I immediately thought that we were going to have another brother or sister. But that did not happen.

Another day I found one of our cows lying down and a slimy secretion coming out of her vaginal orifice. She was also making loud *um-baaa*... sounds. Mother told me that she needed to see a bull. I immediately knew what she meant. Gangesh and I already knew of the place where people took their cows to mate with a bull for a fee. We took our cow there. We paid the guard two rupees. He opened the gate to a large fenced-in area where a powerful bull was running around. The bull looked ferocious. The guard tied our cow on a post inside the fence. The bull ran around a few times, came behind our cow, and jumped up on her rear with his two front legs around her body. Soon after that, the guard brought our cow out. Nine months later the cow gave birth to a beautiful calf. When you grow up in places like Silaur and Agartala, you learn about adult things quite early in life, as I did.

The birth of the calf was a great experience for me. I witnessed the entire process, from the mating, the way her pregnancy progressed, the way I could feel the calf kicking inside her when I put my hand on her belly, and how her vaginal orifice started to grow bigger as the delivery time approached and rather rapidly during the last hour or so before the delivery. I saw how the front hooves of the calf came out first and how a neighbour helped to bring the calf out by pulling the hoofs that started to come out. I saw with amazement how such a large baby could come out through the normally small vaginal orifice. I saw how the helping neighbour cut the umbilical cord and tied it and how, within a couple of hours, the cow delivered a large placenta. I saw how the cow licked the calf clean of slime as it came out and how within a couple of hours, the calf first tumbled while trying to stand up but in a few hours was running around. I saw the beauty and perfection of nature in procreation. I saw sex between the cow and the bull and found nothing shameful or indecent about it. I developed a new perspective on life and its continuation—in animals as in humans. I also felt sad that the bull never saw what a beautiful calf it fathered or if he at all cared to know about it. I thought about my father caring about me and how humans differ from other animals.

While we lived in Agartala, my father would visit our village house to collect the proceeds from the sale of our share of crops from the barga croplands. He appointed one Abdul Karim to oversee crop production on our agricultural land to the west of our village and one Manjur Ali to do the same with the agricultural land to the north. They received a small percentage of the income, which I believe was somewhere between 2 and 5 per cent. Manjur Ali was very loyal to my parents, he was very trustworthy. His two boys, Hiru and Mukul, were contemporaries of my brothers in school and college in Bengal. These two boys were the only two Muslim boys from our village who got a college education.

In Agartala, Gangesh and I were in charge of all shopping except for big-ticket items. Gangesh was quite tall, he could ride a bicycle. I would sit on the rear seat, and we would explore all parts of Agartala by bicycle. For daily grocery shopping, we would normally go to the local market, and sometimes we would venture as far as Vishalgarh, a suburban city on a hill about 5 miles from Agartala, to buy special items. Not going to school helped in this regard. In our spare time, Gangesh and I would plant various types of flowers and fruit plants to give our house in Agartala some of the character of the chharabari that we missed so much.

In 1949, an episode occurred that would shake my conscience to the core. This is the episode that I hinted at before after describing the episode about my first guilt. This episode would become my second guilt. Here it is.

## *Episode 1-5: My Second Guilt, Stealing Mother's Gold Nugget*

I talked about my first guilt before. In that episode, which took place when I was six, I stole money from my mother's cash box to pay a crooked handyman who promised to make me a bow and arrow. When I confessed that mischief to my mother, she pardoned me but made me promise that never again in my life I would lie to her. I broke that promise—a commitment that I made to my mother and myself—with worse mischief within four years.

When we moved from Silaur to Agartala, my mother allowed Gangesh and me to do the daily shopping for fish, meat, and vegetables from the local market. But she would not allow us to make the big purchases, particularly our once-a-month purchase of 100 pounds of rice. That task was for Suratha, though I normally accompanied him when he made such purchases. This episode occurred on such an occasion. Suratha and I went to the main market about 3 miles from our house to buy rice. Mother gave Suratha 40 rupees for the purchase; this represented the cost of the rice plus the rickshaw rental to bring the rice home from the market.

On this occasion, a big fair was in progress at the main market. There were all kinds of temporary stores selling various novelties. As Suratha and I were going around and looking at these novelties, we stumbled in front of a gambling shop. It had all kinds of novelties, from spring-operated toy cars and Swiss army knives to big items like fancy flower vases, nice kitchen equipment, bathroom mirrors, and many other eye-pleasing items. These were not for sale but could be the stakes for gambling, and people succumbed to the lure of a one- or two-rupee bet possibly fetching items worth 200 rupees or more. Suratha, as much as he was a wise college student, thought he could win and started placing bets. Every time he lost, he thought about recouping the earlier loss and making an additional profit by placing an even larger bet.

Of course, this continued until he lost all the money, and he did not know how to face our mother with this news. He concocted a story, saying that for some reason, the ideal rice was not available, and the rice merchant promised to have it the next day. He told me not to tell the truth to Mother. He also said that I would have to steal a small gold nugget from her hidden drawer in the black mahogany almirah in her bedroom. Mother would never suspect me of any wrongdoing if I were loitering in her bedroom. I used to do that all the time. But Suratha normally did not do that. So, he said, it would be easier for me to steal the nugget. He said that there were so many small nuggets that our mother would never notice if one was missing. He planned to sell the nugget the next day at a jewellery store and buy rice with the proceeds. Mother bought those pure gold nuggets when we were in Burma and was saving them to make jewellery for our sisters' weddings.

I dared not disobey Suratha's orders. None of my siblings dared disobey him. We knew the consequences—a severe beating. Suratha was also our hero. He could do so many amazing things. He inspired awe among the younger siblings with what he could do. He knew how to cast a fisherman's net in our pond and catch fish, he could milk a cow, and could perform many magic tricks. To disobey him would mean that I would no longer be his companion. I convinced myself that if I listened to him this time, he would teach me the Lilliput magic. By this magic, he could make a big boy into a little boy. He showed this magic many times before, drawing admiration from his audience. So I agreed to his plan, although unwillingly. That evening when our mother was busy preparing dinner for the family, I entered her bedroom as Suratha stood guard near the door to give me a signal if he found someone else entering the room. I successfully stole a decent-sized gold nugget from the hidden drawer and gave it to Suratha.

The next day, Suratha and I left for the market somewhat early. The first thing Suratha did was to stop at a jewellery store. The store owner guessed that it was a stolen piece and threatened to call the police unless we sold it to him at a very low price. That low price, 60 rupees, was more than enough to cover Suratha's losses, so he sold the piece for 60 rupees. We then went to a sweet shop and ate a lot of delicacies. Suratha bought the choice quality rice, and we came back in a rickshaw. Mother was happy to see the rice and she appreciated the quality of it. Suratha kept the surplus money to himself to spend as his pocket money.

Everyone was happy, but I was suffering inside and not just for stealing the gold nugget from my mother. I was now also bearing the burden of keeping a mischievous act secret. Suratha had sworn me to such an extent that I could not disclose it even to my constant companion Gangesh. So, I made another vow that no matter how much beating I would have to endure or how much hardship it might cause, I will never do such a thing and lie to anyone. White lies, as I will describe later in Book 4, became an exception in later days.

I kept the secret from my mother and everybody else until Suratha became a high-ranking Indian Police Service (IPS) officer. At that time, I revealed the secret to her in the presence of Suratha and others, and she laughed it away. She said that it only showed how resourceful it was for Suratha to come up with such a clever idea at the time! Resourceful? Clever idea? I thought that such reasoning was hypocritical when the definition of a virtuous or vicious act depends on the power of the actor. Suratha was now an important officer, so his mischievous act of several years earlier became a source of amusement. Anyway, my guilt was gone, and life moved forward for me without further suffering from the act that happened in the past.

I now return to how our life evolved in Agartala. Within a few months of our coming to Agartala, my father caught typhoid fever and remained bedridden for three months. Since there were no telephones either in our house or at the doctor's office, Gangesh and I had to go to the doctor's office almost daily to describe our father's condition and bring the medicines that the doctor prescribed. Our not going to school helped in this situation as well.

At about this time, communal riots broke out in East Bengal, where Muslims were slaughtering Hindus. The independence of India that accompanied its partition into secular India and Muslim Pakistan bought the worst miseries to the residents of the states of Bengal and Punjab. Eastern Bengal and western Punjab were Muslim-majority regions, and they became the new nation of Pakistan. After the first riots broke out in Pakistan, and Muslims began killing Hindus, India experienced a wave of retaliatory riots in which Hindu mobs killed Muslims, and the secular Government of India was unable to control the bloodbath.

The Indian subcontinent, particularly its eastern and western parts, became the scene of some of the worst bloodshed that anyone in India had ever seen. Trains full of Hindu bodies, people who had been passengers trying to escape from Pakistan to India but who were killed en masse, shook the conscience of the region to its core. The mass exodus of Hindu refugees from East Bengal migrating to the west and Tripura created a nightmare for social workers. The sight of endless columns of Hindu Punjabis walking across the border to India while an opposing column of Muslim Punjabis was crossing the border to Pakistan would live in infamy.

Fortunately, our village remained relatively calm. Though my father was not able to travel to our village because of his illness and even after that for fear of being killed by the rioters, our loyal caretakers Abdul Karim and Manjur Ali walked to Agartala, bringing our share of the barga income to us. They would not take the train or travel by normal routes for fear of being caught by Pakistan's Muslim radicals and being accused of being Hindu spies. Our family was lucky to have such faithful and loyal friends.

Partha made another sensation in the final IA examination in 1949 when he stood third among all the students within the accredited colleges under Calcutta University. Every year, the top ten students are said to "stand", and colleges recruit them eagerly to enroll at their institutions. For the Agartala college, it was a particularly prestigious event because Partha was in the first graduating class of that college. It would also remain a historic event for the next fifty years, as no one else from Agartala would earn a "stand" position during that time. Overnight our family became the talk of the town. Everyone now knew who Partha was, and if I told someone that Partha was my brother, I received special respect.

Partha received invitations from most of the colleges in Calcutta for admission to their BA programmes, and these colleges offered him all kinds of scholarships and free boarding to entice him. He finally decided on Surendranth College in Calcutta. He received loads of financial incentives in the form of generous scholarships and free room and board at their hostels. He started his BA programmes there with a major in mathematics. While in Calcutta, Partha witnessed more ugly Hindu–Muslim riots there. During those riots, the authorities locked the hostels where students lived so that they could not participate in the riots. That may have saved his life.

Other than the disturbing news from all around, things were going well for us in Agartala until a calamity hit. My youngest sister, Ratna, who was just a toddler at the time, came down with measles, and one night she developed a breathing problem. Gangesh and I went to the doctor's house in the middle of the night. When we told him the symptoms, he said he would return with us. After examining Ratna, he decided to give her an injection of penicillin, the World War II miracle drug that had just become available for public use. Perhaps the doctor used the wrong dose or Ratna was allergic to penicillin, but in either case, she became restless after receiving the injection and died within a few minutes. Her death was devastating to my family. I will describe this in Book 4, along with an incident in which a tantric (a mendicant who worships gruesome-looking images of Goddess Kali of the cremation grounds) took advantage of the tragedy and swindled my mother.

Soon after this tragedy, Suratha received his BA degree with distinction from Agartala College in 1950. Sheela also passed the BA examination as a private student in the same year and immediately got a job as a teacher at the local high school. Suratha knew that Agartala would not offer the proper opportunities for his future. Mother also thought that there weren't enough eligible bachelors in Agartala from whom to choose a groom for Sheela. In other words, a plan for another migration of our family was taking shape. Our family now planned to move to Calcutta—its third move in less than six years. Partha was already in college in Calcutta. To prepare for the move, we sold our cows, gave our ducks to our neighbours, and rented out the house in Agartala. With only essential belongings, the family ventured to Calcutta. Sheela and Suratha went first. They rented an apartment before the rest of us could go.

## Early Years in Calcutta: Ages 11–13

The advance party of Sheela and Suratha rented a four-bedroom house in Behala, a Calcutta suburb, and then wrote to us to say that we could now come. So our journey from Agartala to Calcutta began. The first 5 miles were on foot to the rail station in Akhaura, with a hand-cart driver carrying all the belongings in his cart. We boarded the train and started to spread our blankets on the seats to chalk out our areas. Gangesh and I put all the luggage up on the bunkers. Mother kept the tiffin carriers in which she bought prepared food near her. As the train started, I found myself caught between sadness and excitement—sadness because we were leaving behind everything I cared for, and excitement because we were going to a new dream city called Calcutta that we had all heard so much about but that only Partha, Suratha, and Sheela had yet seen. As it would turn out, we were in for many surprises—good, bad, ugly, and supreme.

After about twelve hours, the train pulled into Sealdah station in Calcutta. We were expecting Suratha and Sheela to be waiting for us, but they were not there. In those days there were no cellphones, so we could not check where they were. After waiting for an hour, my father hired a horse-drawn coach. The coach driver put all our luggage on the top of the coach and tied them firmly. We all crammed inside the coach. Thus began the three-hour horse-coach ride to Behala.

We arrived at Behala but were not sure where the apartment was. We saw a group of boys sitting on a raised concrete platform in front of a big house on the roadside. I poked my head out of the coach and asked the boys if they knew where the apartment was. They said *agey* (Bengali for "before"), and so I took the meaning that we had gone too far. I told the coach driver, but just then one of the boys said "here comes another *Bangal* family that does not know what 'agey'" means. That was when I realized that the boys were making fun of us. They thought people from East Bengal, whom they derogatorily called Bangal, were uncultured and could not speak good Bengali.

I figured out the cultural difference that made the same term mean different things to the people of West Bengal and East Bengal. It turns out that, in addition to meaning "before", agey can also mean "forward" as in "going forward". The first meaning refers to time the second to space. When used alone, the word connoted a time perspective. When used with some other words, it indicates movement along a path; here it had the perspective of space. I felt a need for cultural exchange if we were going to eliminate the demeaning of one group by another. Anyway, we finally arrived at our destination.

When Suratha and Sheela arrived, they were surprised to see us. They had gone to the station with the wrong information about the arrival time of our train, and when they could not find us at the station, they thought that we must have missed the train. Anyway, everything worked out fine. The apartment was nice. It was a single-storey, masonry bungalow with four bedrooms, a nice kitchen, and a bathroom with a water tank and an electric pump to bring water from a reservoir. There were several other similar apartments in the compound, and Hindu families occupied them all. They were victims of communal riots, displaced from their homes in East Bengal or East Pakistan (now Bangladesh).

When my family decided to move to Calcutta, we did not fully understand the financial stress we would face. For one thing, my father's pension, which was 50 per cent of his salary when he retired, did not amount to much in Calcutta even though it was a handsome amount for living in Silaur or even in Agartala. Second, we could no longer access the income from our barga land in Silaur. Abdul Karim and Manjur Ali could travel to Agartala, but they could not travel to Calcutta. The pressure of the situation fell particularly on Suratha and Sheela, who now needed to earn a livelihood for the family. Suratha took up private tutoring, and Sheela accepted a job as a schoolteacher. Those jobs, however, were in central Calcutta, and commuting there from Behala became very strenuous. To reach their jobs, Suratha and Sheela first had to walk to the tram depot and then transfer to other public transportation lines a couple of more times. They would start at about six in the morning and would not return home until 10 or 11 at night. This was not going to work. We had to find a place to live in central Calcutta.

The huge migration of Hindus from East Bengal led to an acute housing shortage in central Calcutta because of the huge city's economic opportunities. Sheela found a rental place in the centre of the city, in Bowbazar. We moved from our decent-size apartment in Behala to a one-room apartment in Bowbazar. We had the room partitioned with corrugated iron sheets to create separate sleeping quarters for the males and females. There was a small separate kitchen for us, but only a windowless common bathroom for all tenants of the floor. The bathroom always radiated the pungent smell of urine because there was no structured urinal to catch urine and flush it out. People urinated on the floor far from the floor drain (in my dreams I still see this nauseating scene). The attractiveness of this apartment was that it was in the centre of the city and close to all activities. The university that Partha attended, the students Suratha taught as a private tutor, and the school where Sheela taught were all within walking distance. This saved travel time and money.

While the elder siblings were busy at their jobs, the daily burden of buying vegetables and groceries fell to me. Neither my father nor Gangesh could do these jobs as efficiently as I could. They were easy marks for the cheating traders of Calcutta. I learned quite early how to avoid such treachery.

At about the same time, Gangesh and I were both thinking about appearing for the School Final examination as private students so that we could enter college. To appear for the

School Final examination, any private student had to first take a qualifying examination, otherwise, the number of students sitting for the final examination would have been unworkable. Every senior high school student from displaced families was hoping to sit for certification as a private student. This was due to the disruption of their studies that resulted from being driven away from their ancestral homes.

The year was 1952. I was twelve and Gangesh fifteen. Both Gangesh and I thought of taking the qualifying test that year so that we could sit for the final examination in 1953. We both submitted our photos to the authorities, and they gave us documents with our photos that permitted us to sit for the qualifying examinations. The bar for passing this examination was significantly lower than what we would face at the final examination. I passed the qualifying examination, but Gangesh failed. So I started to prepare for the school final examination in 1953. For the first time, Gangesh and I were separated in our studies.

As I was preparing for the final examination, I had an accident that did not look too bad initially but soon took an ominous turn. To get a few books from one side of the partitioned room to the other I jumped from one bed to another through the opening in the corrugated iron sheet that divided the room. During this jump, my left knee hit the sharp end of the divider and a big chunk of flesh came out as a result. I had the open wound stitched at the hospital, but it soon became septic. I received a penicillin injection despite my mother's reservations—her memory of our youngest sister dying from such an injection was still vivid in her mind.

As 1953 arrived, I sat for the School Final examination with a messed-up wound in my knee. I passed the examination—not with flying colours but high in the second division. I felt disgraced by this, as I came from a family in which my elders had high scholarly records. Fortunately, the wound dried up and healed, although slowly. As a reminder of that accident, I still carry a prominent scar on my left knee.

I was now thirteen and excited to enter college. The obvious choice was Surendranath College, which was where Partha studied. He was just finishing his master's course at the university campus. Our one-room apartment in Bowbazar was on the fourth floor. Talking to other tenants on our floor, my mother learned that a few single girls lived on the ground floor (in the United States, we call it the first floor) and that their profession was prostitution. Mother became very concerned because Sheela was of marriageable age. If any prospective groom's family found out that we were living in a building also occupied by prostitutes, the prospect of her getting married would disappear. So, we soon moved to another apartment in a more respectable area, about a mile to the north in a place called Hedua.

This apartment was more spacious and had two bedrooms. But it was on the ground floor, and it was damp and dark. We all fell sick there. So after a lot of searching, Sheela found a two-bedroom apartment through one of her friends in a decent area that was known as the Mullick Para, off Mirzapur Road near College Square and close to the university. The rooms were very big, about 400 square feet each. The apartment did not have a kitchen, but it had a verandah that was about 8 feet wide and 40 feet long, and it was fenced off to create a kitchen, a dining area, and servants' quarters. Though the bedrooms were on the second floor, we had a small private yard and a private bathroom on the ground floor. Though still small for a large family like ours, it was a vast improvement over the previous dungeons. Our fortunes started to turn while living in this apartment.

## Conclusion

After leaving Burma, we barely spent three years in our ancestral village even though we came with the intent of making it a permanent home. The same thing happened when my father built a new house in Agartala; we all expected that we would finally live in peace for the rest of our lives and be happy. That dream also failed to last more than three years. Then we moved to the uncertainty of rented apartments, moving from one apartment to another. At our lowest point, we had nine people crammed into one partitioned room with access only to a common latrine redolent of the acrid stench of urine. It would take another two years in Calcutta before we could see the light at the end of the tunnel, or at least start thinking about what that would look like.

As I look back at those seven or eight years, I find that they contain an extraordinary compilation of memories. I am often amazed at how my brain could etch so many impressions into itself in so little time. What is even more amazing is that among those memories were some of the fondest ones—of the times I spent with Gangesh in our village house. Those memories also include the most dreadful experience of being victimized by armed bandits, losing my youngest sister to measles, and living at the bottom of Calcutta's congested centre. But the terrible experiences were also the ones that would make the future feel so much better when it arrived.

# 2

# College and University Life in Calcutta

## *A Turning of My Family's Fortunes*

## (Ages 13–19)

As I noted, I passed the School Final examination in the second division. Different people had different opinions about it. Most thought that it was a miracle that I passed under such adverse conditions and at the tender age of thirteen, while Gangesh, who was three years older and of the target age for the examination, failed. My mother thought that it was a miracle, but she did not believe I was any better at my studies than Gangesh. Mother believed that I could present things much better than my knowledge justified, and that was the reason I passed.

I thought differently. By one measure I felt disgraced. My brothers Suratha and Partha had not only passed this examination in the first division but also with letters of excellence in many subjects. Partha particularly was a student of stellar reputation.

And here I was, the black sheep of the family, who, excuses notwithstanding, disgraced the family by passing the School Final examination in the second division. By another measure, I blamed my results on my poor performance in Bengali and Sanskrit. The Bengali alphabet has three letters that represent variations of the *s* sound, two letters to represent variations of the *j* sound, and many other letters and diacritical marks that represent slight variations in pronunciation. Ordinary people, particularly Bangals, used only one pronunciation for all the variations. So everyone tried to remember what version to use in different words. Having never attended any school, I did not receive proper training in Bengali phonetics. The slightly differing sounds of some Bengali and Sanskrit letters totally confused me.

My way of learning was logical consistency. In Bengali, I memorized the various uses of similar-sounding letters in various words, but before that, I messed up the spellings in my writing. This was the primary reason for my poor grade in Bengali. The same way applied to my Sanskrit. My Bengali spelling might also have influenced my scores in other subjects such as history and geography, which we studied in Bengali. Had it not been for Bengali and Sanskrit, my record showed that I would have easily passed in the first division. So, when it came to deciding whether to study arts or science in college, I had already made up my mind. I said goodbye to the arts subjects except for English (English was compulsory at intermediate colleges) and embraced science; although all my elder siblings studied arts, and no one in our family studied science before.

Though I eliminated Bengali and other literary subjects from my college curriculum, I did not completely abandon them. The sting of poor performance bore heavily on me. I decided to master those subjects—particularly Bengali and English literature and other arts subjects such as history and geography as extracurricular studies. Later, in 1966 and 1967, two of my articles would appear in the annual issues of the prestigious Bengali literary magazine, *Betar Jagat*, published by All India Radio. In addition, in the examination of my DSc thesis, Professor R.D. Haworth, FR. of the University of Manchester, wrote that my "literary style [in English] is excellent".

## 1953–55: The ISc Years

I began my studies at Surendranath College for the Intermediate of Science course. My subjects were English, physics, chemistry, mathematics, and biology. Biology was my "fourth" subject, which means that it was optional. A student could study ISc without taking a fourth subject. Everyone had to take three science subjects from a list of physics, chemistry, mathematics, and biology, and one could take a fourth if she / he wished to do so. Most students who took a fourth subject did so to improve their chances of passing with a higher rating. I would receive credit for any points over the passing grade in the fourth subject in my total points for the regular three subjects, allowing for the ranking of the three grading divisions—first, second, and third. In other words, the fourth subject was insurance in case the scores in the first three subjects fell short. On a more serious note, it gave the student exposure to an additional field of knowledge.

Another reason for my taking biology as a fourth subject was to show off. When I studied biology in the 1950s, I needed to bring a set of animal dissection tools in a black box to class.

If a kid carried such a dissection box, it showed that he was a college student. For me, a diminutive thirteen-year-old, it was important that people recognized me as a college student. Style triumphed over substance here.

On my first day at college, I had an embarrassing experience. I did not stand up while declaring my presence by saying "yes sir" during the opening roll-call, as convention required. Having never attended any school before, I was unaware of this custom. The professor thought it was very arrogant of me to answer him while seated. He also thought that wearing shorts at the college was inappropriate, and as I was wearing shorts, he assumed that I was making a deliberate attempt to disregard tradition. He sarcastically addressed me as a "child" and punished me by making me stand on the bench for fifteen minutes. As it happened, I did not have long pants; all I had were shorts, which all young children wore. When I returned home that afternoon, I told my mother that I would not go to college unless I had long pants (we called them "full pants" as against "half pants" for shorts). She gave me money to buy three ready-made long pants from a store on College Street.

I enjoyed my ISc college years very much. I enjoyed my studies and began to receive high praise from my professors for doing well. For the first time, I also had what people call classmates. I developed special friendships with several of my classmates. Many of them wanted me to help them with their studies. I felt good that my peers appreciated my knowledge and ability.

I remember a friend with whom I went out to catch frogs. Our practical biology class required us to dissect two types of animal: frogs and lobsters. For frogs, we were to find their circulatory system and for lobsters, their alimentary system. My friend and I thought that we could practise frog dissection outside our classroom. He lived in Beleghata, a near suburb of Calcutta where there were open fields and many swamps with plenty of frogs in them. On weekends, we would catch frogs in Beleghata, anesthetize them with chloroform, and dissect them. We became experts in frog dissection. During my final examination, I did very well in dissecting the frog. While most students could hardly expose the intact heart, I was able to expose the heart intact, full of blood and beating. Though I got good marks for dissection, the thought that the heart would soon beat no more made me sad. So I decided not to pursue biology beyond ISc.

Among the other subjects, mathematics came very easily to me. I was fascinated by physics and chemistry. As I came to learn those subjects, the thought that immutable laws of nature guided our physical world fascinated me. These were laws that existed from eons ago and that would continue as far into the future as anyone could imagine. I thought that being a part of the physical universe meant that some immutable laws that God imposed when he created us might also regulate our future. I was intent on learning the laws of human evolution. But before that, I had to learn the laws of the inanimate physical world of chemistry and physics. My interest in those subjects deepened as I also started to become increasingly interested in religion. I hoped that one day I would be able to understand how we might mould our future to meet any higher grand patterns that might bind science and religion together. These thoughts inspired me to exert myself more in my studies and I continued to do well in my classes.

As I felt confident in my studies, I thought that if I tried, I could be good at whatever I did. I wanted also to be good in my daily routine of doing "bazaar", i.e., family shopping like buying fish, meat, vegetables, and other groceries. I learned how to determine if a *hilsa* (shad) fish had eggs in its belly (those with eggs do not taste good). Initially, I would ask the trader if the fish had eggs or not. But my mother once told me that the fish I bought had eggs in its belly, even though the fishmonger said it had none. When the next day I confronted the vendor who told me that the fish was egg-free, he retorted: "Tell your mother, how could I possibly know what a young female fish could be doing in the darkness under the water with her boyfriend?" Of course, I did not tell this joke to my mother, but I got a lot of big laughs when I told it to my friends. The most important takeaway from this was that rather than asking the fishmonger, I should learn how to determine the quality of a fish.

I learned how to determine whether a fish was still fresh or not by rolling my fingers along its back. The pressure of my fingers would not leave a mark on a fresh fish, but it would on a fish that was going bad. I also learned to determine the quality of other grocery items; to test if milk had been adulterated or diluted with water, I dipped my fingers into it and watched how the creamy white fluid ran down my finger. I could tell if a squash (gourd) was young or old by poking my fingernail on its skin and observing how easily the nail penetrated the skin. With okra, I could tell if it was good—that is, a baby okra—by breaking its tip; a clean break indicated youth. Older okra pods are fibrous and do not break well, so they are not good to eat. I could tell if an eggplant had seed or not by giving it a gentle squeeze in my palm and feeling how it rebounded. I could tell if eggs were fresh or rotten by making them spin on one another.

I learned these techniques by watching how the vendors tested their produce, and eventually I became as good as they. When my father went to buy these things, he would ask the trader whether the item was good or not. This is what he used to do while in the village, but in Calcutta, where the traders' self-interest was more robust than their honesty, *trust*—the ultimate currency of human interaction—had lost most of its value. Quite often, we had to throw away items that Father bought after Mother had used them in cooked dishes. Like a skilled doctor practising internal medicine, who knows how to diagnose disease by an external examination of a patient, I also learned how to test for the quality of produce by examining them from the outside.

I did not, however, lose trust in common people but learned where trust required the supplement of independent confirmation—an approach that decades later Ronald Regan would popularize with his famous line: "Trust but verify." I would vouch and dramatically illustrate the importance of not losing trust in people in an episode in Book 3—*Wealth of People: A New Framework for Economics*. That episode happened about a couple of dozen years later, in 1977 in the same type of bazaar in Calcutta.

I also bought coal for cooking. I learned how to separate the porous pieces that burnt well from the heavy rocks. I would hire a rickshaw to carry the sack full of cooking coal. Of course, along with the coal I also bought cow-dung cakes that served as starter fuel for the coal. These skills made me the natural choice for doing the family's daily shopping.

In those days of scarcity of everything, Indian mothers learned not to waste anything. My mother would not throw away the skins of a gourd or its seeds. She would make tasty preparations from this would-have-been refuse. Bengali mothers would not throw away even the head of a big fish like carp. They would cook the most delicious *moori-ghanto* (fishhead preparations with beaten rice) from them. They would also cook mouth-watering dishes from unripe jackfruits, cooking them like goat meat when there was no goat meat to be had. They called the unripe jackfruits vegetable goat.

Lacking refrigeration, people preserved fish by drying them under the sun while they were still fresh, particularly in East Bengal. The product, called *shootki* (dry fish), was a protein source during the season when people generally could not get fresh fish. In East Bengal, shootki was a key ingredient in many delicious preparations. When you do not have much, you learn to make extraordinary things from the ordinary. Our mothers knew how to do this and do it well.

At the time I was in college in the ISc course, things started to turn for the better for our family. Suratha passed the IPS examination and went to Mount Abu for training. This was great news not just for our family but also for the entire neighbourhood. People we never knew came over and congratulated us. More great news: Sheela married a Class-I government officer! Her husband was the sub-editor of *Betar Jagat*, the print journal of All India Radio. He lived in a posh government apartment in the prestigious Ballygunje area. Sheela moved out of our family home and into her husband's quarters.

The riots in Bengal subsided, and people could now travel back and forth between the two halves of Bengal. My parents visited our ancestral village to collect our barga income during the summer. Those trips were during my summer vacation, so I would accompany them. In that way, I became better acquainted with the people and culture we left behind. Partha completed his MA in statistics around this time and accepted a well-paying job at the Life Insurance Corporation of India. Things were turning out better for our family.

There was an episode, a funny anecdote, that occurred at this time that I cannot resist telling. It is about a household servant we hired at the time.

## *Episode 2-1: Trust Rewarded, a Guru*

At the time I was studying for my ISc, we lived in an apartment in Mullick Para. As I mentioned before, that was where we created a kitchen, a dining area, and servant's quarters by fencing in a verandah. As our fortunes started to turn, we hired a male servant, Montu, to help my mother with her daily chores. He had the servant's quarters as his bedroom. Montu was a refugee from East Bengal. He would tell me stories of how he had several servants attending to him when he was the son of a wealthy zaminder (landowner) there. All refugees had one or more such stories—whether completely true or embellished—and those tales helped them face the dire conditions they faced to earn a livelihood.

In those days, masters were generally rude to their servants—I was an exception. I paid attention to what Montu had to say. He called me his guru (although not in the literal sense of a spiritual guide). One of Montu's jobs was to cook rice in the evening while radio dramas captured the attention of my family. My mother would cook all the dishes during the day and all Montu had to do for dinner was to cook rice. One day as we finished listening to the drama, my mother called Montu to start serving rice for dinner. But he was nowhere to be found. Along with his absence, everybody's shoes were also missing, except mine. He had run away and stolen a few more items besides the shoes. Mother was furious. She wanted my father to report to the police station. Of course, my mother knew as well as my father that making a police report would not lead to the recovery of the stolen goods. The police had more important things to do with their time than chasing fleeing servants, an occurrence that happened every other day. I wondered why Montu did not steal my shoes.

Then I discovered a letter on my study desk. He wrote that he was going to the Himalayas to become an ascetic. Life as a servant was unrewarding, he wrote. He had to steal a few things so that he could sell them to get some money to help him travel to the Himalayas. He asked me to understand him. He was not a habitual thief, he wrote. If he could become a successful ascetic and could reach God, he would come back and let me know. He said that I was his best friend, his guru—and that is why he did not steal my shoes. He wanted me to wish him good luck. I thought that good deeds do not go unrewarded in this world. Montu rewarded my trust in him by not stealing my shoes. I wished Montu good luck in my mind. I hoped he could get what he was looking for. I did not tell anyone of that letter until a long time after.

In 1955, I passed the ISc final examination, not only in the first division but also securing very high marks in every subject. My professors congratulated me, including the professor who made me stand on the bench on the first day of my class. When he heard that I had no bad intentions on that day and that, not having attended school I did not know the protocols, he felt sorry that he had punished me.

## 1955–57: The BSc Years

After seeing my ISc examination results, the principal called me to his office. He congratulated me on a job well done and expressed the hope that I could repeat Partha's results in BSc. He was referring to when Partha earned his BA, ranking first in first class with the university gold medal. He majored in mathematics. The principal told me that my results entitled me to major in any subject, but he recommended mathematics. If I majored in mathematics and had Partha's guidance, I would be able to repeat his stellar performance. My mother's opinion of me, however, seemed to have remained the same. I suspected that she still believed that my results came more from my ability to present things in a certain way than from my real knowledge. She was sad that Gangesh again failed the School Final examination and thought it was because the university had a messed-up evaluation system. The only person on whose scholarship Mother had an unfailing trust, and justifiably so I must add, was Partha. For his part, Partha also maintained the highest reverence for my mother and held her next to God in importance.

As advised by the principal, I enrolled for the BSc class with honours in mathematics at Surendranath College. I had physics and chemistry as minors. All my friends who had passed ISc with me said that I made a good decision in taking mathematics as my major. With someone like Partha in the family guiding me, they said, I was sure to get a first-class in mathematics honours. I did not feel good about those remarks. I felt that Partha would be standing like a shadow to take all credits if I did well in mathematics. I was even more concerned about what my mother would say if I got a first class in mathematics honours. She would undoubtedly continue singing Partha's praises for my success, so I decided to change my major. It would be either physics or chemistry—the one that all my friends would think would be the toughest.

All my friends opined that if I wanted the challenge of taking the toughest major, it should be chemistry—not because it is harder than physics but because of the head of the department of chemistry at Calcutta University at the time. Department heads then decided how many first-class candidates there would be in a subject from all the accredited colleges under Calcutta University. At the time, Dr Pulin Behari Sarkar, DSc was the head of the chemistry department at Calcutta University (also called the University College of Science, or simply, Science College). He chose the questions for the final examination and he had a reputation for selecting questions that even the professors would have difficulty answering. I found my challenge.

I changed my major to chemistry. But was it a good decision? With the benefit of what unfolded in my career, the answer is certainly yes. But was it the most rational decision at the time? The answer is no. The most rational decision would have been mathematics, the one that I initially took. We humans, and especially the younger among us, are poor at seeing the future and even poorer in making what we call "reasoned decisions". That is why, once a decision is made, it is futile to look back and ponder much about "what could have been better". It is better to concentrate on the challenge at hand and do your best at it, so that is what I decided to do.

The problem, however, was the principal. When he heard that I changed my major, he called me to his office again. He told me that I was making the biggest mistake of my life by neglecting certainty and throwing myself into uncertainty. He asked me, saying that it was for my own good, to change back to a mathematics major. I told him that I liked the challenge that a chemistry major presented. He threatened to call my father and tell him that I was making a big mistake. I told the principal that I had made up my mind, and that if he called my father, I would change my enrolment to another college. He shook his head at my arrogance but gave up his harangue.

One person who was very happy with my decision was Professor Priyanath Kundu, who was the head of the chemistry department at Surendranath College at the time. Professor Kundu congratulated me on my decision. He told me that if everyone went for certainty and avoided taking any risk, it would be a very boring world. But this same Professor Kundu would one day scold me and threaten to call my father.

The scene was the fish market across from Surendranath College. Both Professor Kundu and I were there in the morning to buy fish. He asked me what I was doing in a fish market when I should be home, studying. I told him that my responsibilities to my family included the daily shopping for fish and other produce. He said that that must change, that my parents needed to find someone else to do it if they did not want to ruin my future. I told him that there was no one else who could do it in our household. I assured Professor Kundu that I would not neglect my studies. I then touched his feet in reverence and asked him for his blessings. At this, his anger melted away and he told me not to hesitate to ask him if I needed any help with my studies.

The two years of the BSc programme went by with very few surprises. I passed at the top of my class with a silver medal, making all my professors happy. I was now ready to enroll at the Science College for my master's degree.

## 1957–59: The MSc Years

I enrolled at the University College of Science for my master's degree in chemistry. I was excited to be in the Science College, about which I had heard so much. During the first year (which was called the fifth year—counting from the first year in college) we studied the three branches of chemistry—physical, inorganic, and organic. In the second year, we had to choose which of those branches we wanted to major in, the other two would then become minors.

On the first day and for the first time I met the legendary Professor Pulin Behari Sarkar, DSc. His hair was all white, and he was wearing a white *dhuti* and a white *punjabi*—the typical Bengali outfit. He also was a chain smoker; he smoked a Charminar (a low-cost brand) cigarette as he talked. He was very easy to talk to. I instantly developed a liking for him. He also seemed to have liked me. We talked for more than an hour at our first meeting. He told me that I could interact with him as much as I wanted. He said that his mission was to build character and prepare the chemists of the future. He talked about other college professors and said that they did not take their subjects very seriously. They remained stuck in the past and did not grow with their fields. He wanted to prepare chemists who would want to remain students forever.

Science, Dr Sarkar said, was knowledge in progress. Once you stop keeping up with progress in your field, you stop being a scientist. Every year during BSc honours and MSc examinations, he tested not only the students but also challenged the professors to show how much they were keeping up with the progress in their field. His bad reputation as a tough professor, he said, was because he wanted the examinations to reveal how the faculty and students were keeping up with advances in science. I was fascinated during our first meeting. I felt good that during my BSc studies I frequently visited the library at the British Council, which had some of the most recent journals in chemistry, and I enjoyed glancing through them.

Though Dr Sarkar was the head of the chemistry department, the department also had divisional heads. The head of organic chemistry was Professor J.C. Bardhan, DSc, and that of physical chemistry was Professor B.N. Ghosh, DSc. Note that to be a full professor at the Science College at that time, you had to have a DSc degree—not the other (lower) doctoral degree of PhD or DPhil. Indian universities adopted this dual doctoral system from England. In the United States, we do not have such a dual system. There is only one doctorate degree in the States—the PhD. In the United States, people judge the quality of a PhD degree by the reputation of the university from which you receive your degree and the reputation of the professor whom you work with for your dissertation.

As an inorganic chemist, Professor Sarkar was also the divisional head of inorganic chemistry. Each of these divisional heads was among the luminaries in their fields. There was not a single organic chemistry professor in the world who would not have recognized the name Bardhan, known for the Bardhan–Sengupta synthesis. Similarly, there was not a single physical chemistry professor who would not have heard of the contributions that Dr B.N. Ghosh made in the field of colloid chemistry. He was also famous for formulating the theories and equations of ionic solutions, where his name would appear side by side with the pioneers of the field such as Debye-Hückel. We also had Dr Ashima Chatterjee, DSc, who would become a world-renowned natural-products chemist and even receive India's third highest civilian award, the Padma Bhushan. I was excited to attend the lectures of these luminaries; I was ready to soak up the knowledge they were to transmit. Later, however, I would discover that their brilliance sometimes masked their skills in dirty power politics, which led to my dwindling respect for some of them.

Many decades later, in January 2018, I was asked to deliver the Ashima Chatterjee Centennial Lecture.

During that first year, the professor I interacted the most with was Dr P.B. Sarkar. His passion was in designing micro-tests—he called them drop tests—for the qualitative analysis of inorganic chemicals. He would provide the students with glazed white ceramic plates with rows of fingertip-sized depressions that served as reaction chambers. He would then add a single drop of the analyte into each depression. In the next step, he would add drops of various organic reagents (ligands) to each depression and observe whatever colour change or precipitation occurred. From the combined observations, he could then roughly identify the analyte. The key was the unique reaction that a specific inorganic cation would undergo with each organic reagent, producing a change that you can easily visualize against the white background of the depression.

He challenged us to read about developments in organic chemistry and come up with new reagents. The drop test, he said, saved time and chemicals. They were also much safer than conventional macro-tests. He said that we should reserve macro-tests for confirmatory analysis after we established an initial rough identity for the chemical by drop tests. I was also fascinated by his thought process. I discovered an analogy with the techniques I used to test the quality of fish or other produce when I did my daily shopping at the bazaar. This also reinforced my belief in the broad parallelism of processes and methods that occur in one field with those of another.

I became a fan and frequent companion of Professor Sarkar. He found me a willing listener. At the end of the day, when it was time to go home, he and I would often walk together to the bus stand. On our way, he would stop at the corner cigarette store to buy a pack of Charminar. During our walk, he described the various experiences he had working with chemists at home and overseas. This reminded me of my childhood experience of learning to perform simple mathematical operations while going to market with my father.

When it came to choosing a major during the second year, Professor Sarkar was convinced that I would choose inorganic chemistry. But my mind was fixed on learning about drug molecules and how those structures interacted in the human body to create miraculous results; so I chose organic chemistry. Professor Sarkar was disappointed, but he understood. After all, he was scheduled to retire in 1960. Many years later, my wife and I came to know Dr Sarkar's son, Bijan Sarkar, when we were living in New Jersey. Bijan would tell me about conversations at his home during which his father would talk about me. His wife Chaitali would also tell us that she heard about me from her father-in-law. I was surprised that such a famous and absent-minded scientist would remember and mention the name of one of his students during conversations with his family members.

At the time I was in my second year, conformational analysis was a relatively new field in organic chemistry. Conformations denote the various configurations or shapes that organic molecules, including very complex ones, could assume by free rotation around single carbon–carbon bonds. In the spirit of my discussions with Professor Sarkar about keeping up with progress in a field, I began to research the advances the field of conformational analysis made in the wake of the pioneering work of Professor Melvin Newman, who in 1952 proposed the use of projection structures to study conformations (Newman 1963, p. 5).

My research led to me delivering a seminar in the lecture hall of the chemistry department; all the faculty and students of chemistry were invited. Since we did not have molecular models in the department (a disgrace) I made several clay-and-stick models and used them to illustrate my talk. The faculty and students alike all received my lecture very well. One faculty member, Dr Dhananjay Nashipuri, who was a reader at the time, later asked me to see him in his office. After I entered, he closed the door of his office and told me that what I had done was a disservice to the other students. By moving far ahead of our curriculum, I made the other students appear backward. I was surprised to hear such comments coming from a university faculty. It was probably this kind of faculty that Professor Sarkar was talking about during the first day of our meeting. I was disappointed by Dr Nashipuri's comments, but they did not discourage me.

As our final examination approached, I did not want to leave anything to chance. I decided to be prepared for any type of question. I knew that in the final examination, your ability to answer a question counted for only so much. You also had to answer them quickly so that you would finish with enough time remaining to review your answers; that is what made the difference between being the best or the second best. We had to deduce chemical equations, conceptually reconstruct complex structures, logically determine possible isomeric structures of complex molecules, know most of the named reactions, and remember the structures of various dye molecules (azo, triphenylamine, and heterocyclic), sulfa drugs, general and local anesthetics, various types of antibiotics, and various steroids, terpenoids, chlorophyll, haemoglobin, and other complex molecules. We had to remember various natural products and their physiological activities, identify how and where to apply what analytical approaches, remember the half-lives of most heavy-metal isotopes for the determination of geological ages and ages of other materials, remember the values of various physical constants, remember various synthetic designs, and many, many more theories and equations, including thermodynamic equations, how to deduce those equations and recognize various other physico-chemical phenomena.

I spent every waking hour during summer vacation preparing for the final. Since I found it difficult to remember all those facts and theories, I made a dozen three-inch by four-inch notebooks in which I could write in miniature letters all the relevant information. I carried them with me in my pocket wherever I went—even when I was in my bed. As I walked or lay down, I would try to remember all this information, and if I could not, or got stuck with any, I would immediately consult those little notebooks. In essence, those notebooks contained most of the information that the hefty textbooks of organic chemistry, physical chemistry, and inorganic chemistry contained. I wanted to be ready for the final examination anytime, anywhere, and under any circumstances. I would soon put this strategy to the test, as I was about to sit for my final MSc examination.

I found the value and importance of having full command over the type of information mentioned above when my brother Suratha was married in Dhanbad (a few hours by train from Calcutta). The *boubhat* (a reception given by the groom's side) took place during my MSc examination. We all had to go to the wedding (I took most of my notes with me), and when we returned, all members of my family moved to a big house temporarily rented for the boubhat. I stayed at our Mullick Para apartment alone.

As luck would have it, I caught a cold in Dhanbad, and it developed into bronchitis while I was staying alone at the apartment. As I developed a breathing problem the night before my final examination was to begin, I rushed to the hospital and begged the doctors to give me whatever was necessary so that I could be alert and breathe freely the next day. The alternative, I told them, would be that I would have to wait another year before taking my MSc examination. The doctors gave me a few medicines and a penicillin injection. The next morning, I was fit and ready to take the examination.

When the results came out (a list of the successful candidates hung on a wall of the university's Senate Hall), I saw my name at the top of the list. I remember running non-stop and as fast as I could from the Senate Hall to my house, which was about a mile and a half away, to tell my family. I then went to Science College to see the professors. They all congratulated me. I also hung out for a while with some of my closest friends, among them Dulal Mukherjee and Prabhat Bhattacharya. I then went to Professor Kundu's house to give him the good news. He was happy beyond imagination. As I tried to bend down and touch his feet, he lifted me up, held me against his chest, and told me that this was where my place was. That was a very emotional moment for me.

The day my MSc results came out was perhaps the happiest day of my life. When the mark sheets were available several days later, I found out that I did not just top the list but also set new records in every subject. The preparation paid off not only at the time but for years to come as I faced the challenges of difficult chemical problems. Even today, more than sixty years later, I still have some of those three-inch by four-inch notebooks.

This chapter of my life, my life as a student, started with a dark mark after the School Final examination and ended with a golden light—a gold medal in MSc. I had entered Science College as an aspiring student and emerged as an accomplished chemist. With the end of formal student life, I would now face the challenges of what to do next.

# 3

# Sharing My Family's Financial Burden

## *Obtaining DSc Degree, College Professorship, Supplemental Income*

## (Ages 20–24)

When I brought home the news of my first-class-first in MSc, my mother's first comment was that I had the luxury of studying for a master's degree because Partha was bearing the financial burden of the family. After Suratha and Sheela left home—Suratha became an IPS officer and held various posts in various parts of the country, and Sheela moved in with her husband—their income no longer came to the family. So it fell on Partha to pick up the slack; without his income, it would not have been possible to maintain the rest of the family together.

Mother had a valid point, but her comment hurt me. I just wanted her to recognize that I was as good as her other sons, and particularly Partha in educational achievement. Partha also did not seem to have been very happy with the news of my results. This was also understandable. The brilliant Partha ended up with a less-than-stellar performance in his MA in statistics. Anyway, I told my mother that I would now be able to share the family's financial burden. By now, Partha had passed several sections of the London School of Actuary examination and was on the way to becoming a fellow of the institute—a very coveted qualification that made him highly valuable to the insurance industry. His salary of Rs 500 per month in a quasi-government job was a handsome one at a time when highly regarded IAS and Indian Police Service (IPS) officers' starting salary was only Rs 350 per month.

When the major newspapers reported on my MSc result, I became a highly sought-after candidate for college teaching positions. The head of the chemistry department of Bethune College, an all-girls college, Dr Devi Chakravarty also reached out to me on behalf of the parents of chemistry honours students at her college, asking whether I was interested in private tutoring. She had connections with many of the famous and wealthy people in Calcutta. She said that I could ask for a high rate, Rs 100 per month for three one-hour sessions of private tutoring per week.

Within a week of my results being out, I visited the principal of the morning section of City College on Amherst Street in Calcutta, which was within walking distance from my home. The City College had two sections—a morning section from 6 a.m. to 11 a.m. for girls and a day section from 11 a.m. to 4 p.m. for boys. I was interested in teaching the morning section because it would keep the rest of my day free to do research if I chose to do so. When I visited the principal of the morning section, he immediately offered me a position as a full-time lecturer (we were called professors) and asked me if I could start the next day. The salary from the college would be Rs 125 per month, and the University Grants Commission (UGC) also provided a supplementary amount of Rs 125 per month, resulting in a total monthly salary of Rs 250. I accepted the position on the spot and started my job the next morning. I also accepted two private tutoring assignments, which generated an additional income of Rs 200 per month.

## Honorary Lecturer at the University College of Science

In August 1961, less than a year after I obtained my MSc degree, the secretary of the Councils of the University Colleges of Science and Technology, B.K. Mukherjee, recognized my record performance by informing the head of the Department of Pure Chemistry that the vice chancellor of the university had appointed me an honorary lecturer to deliver "lectures on the theoretical basis of organic chemistry" to the post-graduate classes. Though the appointment did not carry any financial remuneration, it was a great honour and a hint at a future appointment to the regular faculty of the university.

## Financial Sufficiency

The combined income that Partha and I brought in, Rs 950 per month, was a godly sum in those days. There was practically no inflation, and the value of the rupee on the international market was fixed at five per dollar. Our family income of 950 rupees per month put us in the top tier of the upper-middle class. Until now, we lived in the Mullick Para apartment. We now moved to a much bigger rooftop apartment in a building on Baithak-khana Road. This apartment had four bedrooms, two bathrooms with running water, a modern kitchen, a separate prayer room, and large sections of an open concrete roof with railings both in the front and back of the apartment.

These open areas looked like a rooftop garden, and we put various potted flower plants in these areas. We converted one of the bedrooms into a drawing room (living room in the US), though with a couch in one corner, like what in the US is called a daybed. From a cramped, one-bedroom partitioned apartment in Bowbazar to this airy and roomy modern apartment was a great improvement. Suratha was now posted in the prestigious position of Deputy Commissioner of Police in Calcutta. He lived with his family in a luxurious government quarter, and Sheela with her covenant officer husband also had an affluent lifestyle. To accomplish all this in less than nine years after moving to Calcutta was a massive and welcome change in our family's social standing. People started calling my mother *ratna-garbha* (jewel-wombed).

## In the Midst of Uncertainty

### *Failed Initial Attempts at Doctoral Research*

Though I had a good income, teaching at City College and private tutoring on the side was not the permanent future that I had envisioned. I had to think of a better, steady, and more sustainable future. If I wanted to become a permanent faculty of the university, I would need to have a doctorate degree. So, I decided to get a PhD degree; I had ample time after my teaching in the morning section of City College to do research.

For this, I had three options. I could join the laboratory of either Dr Bardhan, Dr Ashima Chatterjee, or Dr Nashipuri. I eliminated Nashipuri for two reasons: 1) my earlier encounter with him, in which I gained the impression that he was a narrow- and backward-minded individual, and 2) he was still a reader, an intermediate position between a lecturer and a full professor in the hierarchy of university teachers. I considered Dr Chatterjee's laboratory seriously because she had already made a good name as a leading scientist and had more research funds available for her research associates. She had three PhD candidates in her group at the time, more than in any other group. The third option was to join Dr Bardhan's group. At the time, he was the university's head of organic chemistry.

Dr Chatterjee was involved in phytochemistry research, and though it involved some synthetic work, it was mainly about the isolation, identification, and investigation of properties of novel plant-based chemicals. Dr Bardhan's work was almost entirely in synthetic chemistry, and he was well known in synthetic chemistry, having been the lead chemist of such well-recognized named reactions as the Bardhan–Sengupta synthesis. My interest in drug molecules and synthetic chemistry drove me towards Dr Bardhan's group.

The negative was that he did not have a good reputation among his research associates. One Dwijen Mukherjee, who just earned his PhD after working in Dr Bardhan's group for seven years, did not have any compliments for him. Dr Bardhan could not attract many brilliant students to join his group. A lifelong bachelor, he was rumoured to have a liking for women. At the time he had one Gita Mukherjee (no relation to Dwijen), his only research associate, working on her PhD in terpenoid synthesis. She was a beautiful woman of exceptionally fair complexion and had a very rich husband. She did not have a good academic background—she passed with a third class in MSc. Her only goal, it seemed, was to have a PhD title degree. She had no interest in pursuing a research career or a paid academic job. On the positive side, Dr Bardhan valued my academic accomplishments highly and heaped all kinds of praise upon me. I fell for the praise and decided to join Dr Bardhan's group.

Within a few months, my opinion regarding Professor Bardhan began to sour. For my first assignment, he asked me to help Gita Mukherjee with her research. Initially, I thought he wanted me to learn the various synthetic techniques by helping Gita. But later, through conversations with Dwijen Mukherjee, I learned that, by having a newcomer finish the work of an existing researcher, Dr Bardhan kept his PhD students from leaving his group. If a researcher spent several years doing work that another person would use for their thesis, the new researcher would have nothing to show for his achievement if he wanted to leave. Dr Bardhan would then tell another newcomer to work on a project for which the preceding colleague would write her/his thesis. I did not know how much truth was in those stories, but I was getting restless without a project of my own.

I also discovered that Dr Bardhan was the most ruthless political power broker that I had ever known. When it came to politics, he was either for you or against you. There was nothing in between for him in that game. His politics were blind to competence. He could be your best friend or your worst enemy. If he became your enemy, he would try to destroy you; if he befriended you, he would push you forward in everything. To be his friend, however, you had to declare unquestionable loyalty to him, and I was not willing to sacrifice my integrity to gain his favour.

The time I spent in Dr Bardhan's lab, however, was not wasted. I learned a few laboratory techniques from him that I could not have learned elsewhere. One special case comes to mind. It was how to make "molecular" sodium. In many organic syntheses, a researcher uses metallic sodium as a reagent. In these reactions, you get the best results if the sodium metal (a soft metal generally stored under kerosene) is in the form of little beads with a relatively large surface area. But breaking down the metal into tiny beads is not easy. Dr Bardhan showed me how he did it. He cut the soft metal into small cubes with a knife. Then he put the cubes in a long-neck round-bottom flask under xylene (a hydrocarbon solvent). He then heated the flask on a sand bath and watched the meniscus of the condensing xylene vapour move up the neck of the flask. When the meniscus approached the top of the neck, he took the flask out of the sand bath, wrapped it with a towel, closed the flask with a rubber stopper, and gave it a quick jerk with his hands. When he opened the flask, we saw that the entire mass of sodium had broken up into tiny silver-white beads under the xylene. We nicknamed the beads with enormous surface area "molecular" sodium. I tried the process myself several times, and every time it worked perfectly. I have used "molecular" sodium many times in my research projects.

## *Trying an Industrial Job*

I also had other options to consider, but continuing to teach at City College and earning more money through private tutoring was not one of them. One ostensible option was to go to the UK or the United States and do my PhD there. I was sure that I would have no problem securing a graduate fellowship in a reputable laboratory in either country. But this was not a real option because, as a graduate student in the UK or United States, I would not be able to help my family financially. Although my mother or Partha might have agreed if that is what I wanted to do, I was not willing to renege on my financial responsibilities to my family.

I thought of giving up my research ambitions and seeking a well-paying job in industry. I saw an ad in the English-language daily, the *Hindustan Standard*: a big textile company led by the noted industrialists Bharatram and Charatram was looking for two senior-level chemists' positions. The minimum requirement was a first-class master's degree in organic chemistry from a top-ranking university or a PhD. Knowledge of dye chemistry was preferred. I do not quite remember the name of the company; it could have been Bharat Mills or Bharat Textiles.

India was beginning to industrialize, so capable chemists and chemical engineers were in high demand. The textile and dye industries were growing very fast. Without thinking about it too much, I applied for such a position. The company invited me to interview with them in New Delhi, and they paid all my travel expenses, including travel by first-class train. I had never visited New Delhi before. The opportunity to visit Delhi and travel first-class was incentive enough to accept the invitation, though I was not at all sure if I would get the job.

When I arrived for the interview, I was surprised to see several dozen candidates, with more than half of them PhDs. I gave up any hope of landing the job. To narrow down the list, the company first gave us a written exam with many questions about cellulosic polymers and dye chemistry. I found the questions quite easy—my extensive preparation for my MSc examination came in handy. After the company evaluated the written examinations, they narrowed their list down to ten candidates, and I was one of them. Several senior officers interviewed us, after which they selected three, including me, to meet the chairman. They told us that out of the three of us, they would select two—a chief chemist trainee and a deputy chief chemist trainee. The chairman told me that I would hear from them soon.

Soon after I returned home, I received their offer letter. They selected me for the chief chemist's position—starting salary of Rs 600 during the training period with a raise to Rs 750 upon completion of the training. No one to whom I talked about it, including my IPS brother and my sister's husband, believed me. They wanted to see the offer letter. They were amazed at the salary offered. I went to see the principal of Surendranath College to seek his advice on whether to accept the offer or look for an opportunity to pursue PhD work. He said that such an opportunity comes only once in a lifetime. Even if I returned with two PhD degrees, I would not get such an offer. He had spent his whole life in the academy. My salary, he said, would be higher than his. I also went to see Professor Kundu, but he was ambivalent. He said that this was an unbelievably lucrative offer, but I would also be giving up the chance of being a great scientist.

After various considerations, I accepted the position. I would work in New Delhi for three months and then relocate to the central technical department in Gujarat. The deputy chief chemist's position went to a PhD. When I arrived in Gujarat, twelve junior chemists and the deputy chief chemist would be reporting to me. I later heard that the reason I got the top job was that I scored 100 per cent on the written examination. Things, they said, started to go in my favour from then on, with the chairman's final decision to offer me the top position and to make the offer so attractive that I could not refuse.

Having lived with my family all my life, I felt terribly lonely in New Delhi. I also was having second thoughts about my decision. Was I selling myself off to the highest bidder while ignoring other personal motivations and expectations of people such as Professor Kundu, who had invested quite a bit of emotional capital on me? I heard of Professor Seshadri, FRS, of Delhi University—a highly respected researcher with an international reputation. I went to see him, told him my dilemma, and sought his advice. I told him that I was torn between two extreme emotions—money on the one side in amounts that I might never earn otherwise, and achieving something of sustainable value with my life on the other.

He told me not to think too narrowly. Money, he said, was important in life but it was not everything. Furthermore, he said the company did not hire me as a personal favour. They hired me for my capabilities. If I could not prove my worth, they would not keep me for life. And if indeed I had the capabilities they hired me for, there will be other such opportunities. Considering my background, he suggested that my immediate goal should be to get a doctorate degree. This is something I would not be able to do if I did not work for it now. He hinted that if I wanted, he would be glad to accept me in his group.

I thought that if I had to move to Delhi for my research, I might as well go to England or the United States. Yet, there was another distant possibility for me to consider—a Sir P.C. Ray Fellowship at Calcutta University. It would give me a chance to have my own laboratory and conduct independent research, which I would like very much because it would also allow me to work directly for a DSc degree and skip the PhD. It was a distant possibility because the position historically went to people who already had a PhD and wanted an opportunity to continue their research interests further.

So, I left the industrial job and came back to Calcutta. To satisfy my family, I told my mother that until I decided on my next step, I should be able to match my income to Partha's with my salary at City College (which had assured me that I could have my job back anytime I wanted) and three private tuitions. After returning to Calcutta, I decided to take a bold step. I went to see the vice chancellor of the university and told him why I could not work for Dr Bardhan. He knew the political atmosphere at the Science College and sympathized with me. I told him that I could easily go to either the UK or the United States and I would only consider such an option if I did not get an opportunity to do independent research at the Science College. I told him that it would be possible only if he gave me the Sir Prafulla Chandra Ray Fellowship (popularly known as P.C. Ray Fellowship). I told him that if he placed his confidence in me, I would do everything in my ability not to disappoint him. He told me to see him again in seven days.

## *The Break Finally Comes*

When I returned to see the vice chancellor after a week, he gave me the good news. He said that he talked to the fellowship committee and the members unanimously agreed to offer me the fellowship. The stipend was Rs 250 per month plus a generous grant for buying chemicals and other research supplies. He told me that I could start immediately. To add to the good news, he also told me that I did not have to worry about Dr Bardhan.

Dr Bardhan would be leaving the university soon to take a top-level job at the Industrial Research Institute in New Delhi. With the two jobs—teaching at the City College's morning section and the P.C. Ray Fellowship—I would be making almost as much money as I would have at the industrial position.

In the meantime, at the request of Dr Devi Chakravarty, I also agreed to tutor two first-year chemistry honours students at Bethune College. One of them was the daughter of a powerful cabinet minister from West Bengal (who will remain anonymous) and the other a daughter of the wealthy Paramanik family of north Calcutta. With the tutoring income added to my two salaries, my total income soared to an astronomical Rs 700 per month. My mother was happy. As an aside, I may mention here that decades later, on 28 December 2011, I would be giving the prestigious Surendra Paul Lecture at the Ramakrishna Mission Institute of Culture—an annual invited lecture that had been delivered by people such as the president of India in other years—to commemorate the 150th anniversary of Sir Prafulla Chandra Ray.

## The Research Years in Science College: Sir P.C. Ray Fellow

I started my fellowship in 1961. It came with a full office-cum-laboratory module like the ones that lecturers, readers, and professors had. Full professors had two modules each. The lecturers and readers had only single modules, the same as mine. It was customary for each faculty member to put his/her name and degree on a shiny brass plate and attach it to the entrance door of their office. For instance, the nameplate in front of Dr Bardhan's office read "Professor J.C. Bardhan, D.Sc." I did the same. Mine read "Paritosh M. Chakrabarti, M.Sc. (Gold Medalist)." It was like back in my college days when I carried a black biology dissection box around to advertise that I was a college student when I was in the ISc programme. Self-advertisement in India was and still is a common practice. I was also sucked into it.

On a more substantive note, I immersed myself in my work. I would arrange my lectures at the morning section of City College so that I could be free by 9:30 or 10 a.m. I would then go home, eat a full meal, and go to my fellowship laboratory at Science College to work on my research project. These places—City College and the University College of Science—were both within walking distance from my home. I would generally reach Science College between 10:30 and 11 a.m. I would conduct my experiments until 6 p.m. and then go for tutoring. The tutoring required brief bus trips. I would finish my tutoring and be free by 9 p.m. If I had experiments running in my lab, I would go back to Science College to finish the experiments or go home. During weekends, I would spend most of my time at Science College.

I had a great time teaching and doing my research. The very nature of experimental research is that, once you start your reactions, it often takes several hours of running before completion and work-up. In between, you have ample free time. This was when I would hang out with my friends in my lab. Two of these friendships were especially dear to me. Dulal Mukherjee, who was doing research in physical chemistry at the time, would later become a professor at Science College. The other was Prabhat Dutta, who took a teaching position at an engineering college after his MSc degree and wanted very much to do research under my guidance.

## *Mixing Teaching and Research with Romance*

During my time at Science College, my female students from chemistry honours classes at City College would often come to see me. Some of these visits would take romantic turns. I enjoyed those encounters and cherished them dearly. To look macho, I became a chain smoker. In picking up smoking I might also have been trying to imitate my hero, Professor Pulin Sarkar. (I would later give up this bad habit in 1967 after a bout of asthma attacks.)

I very much enjoyed the romantic aspect of my life during my time in India between 1961 and 1964. My laboratory gave me the rare privacy to have romantic conversations with the girls who came to visit me. In India, unlike in Western countries, young women preferred scholars to athletes. Being a first-class first in MSc and doing independent research, I was very much in demand by girls of marriageable age and their parents. In addition to my female students, I also enjoyed romantic advances from the students I tutored. But our culture did not allow our romantic adventures to progress very far. I would go out on dates with some of my romantic fans, but my advances would mostly stop at embraces, sometimes passionate embraces. Restaurants had booths with curtains to provide privacy for romantic couples. In India, boys and girls did not kiss in the mouth—at least not when I was in India. Mouth-to-mouth kissing was considered unhygienic and as such was out of style. I kissed the girls I liked on their cheeks to show affection and on their eyes to show loving emotion.

There was something else I did during my breaks from research. Though devoid of musical talent, I loved to fantasize that I could be a good musician. So I bought a guitar and kept it in my lab. When I was free and no none was with me, I would try to strum the guitar into a melody, but it never came close to any music, let alone a melody.

## *Partha's Marriage*

As our household income soared, and we were now also living in a spacious apartment, my mother wanted Partha to get married. In those days in India, most marriages were arranged, though Suratha did not abide by that practice. Suratha chose his own bride. But Partha was different. He was my mother's favourite child, and she wanted to decide what was best for him. At my mother's request, my father summoned a marriage broker. The broker brought proposals from the parents of many eligible brides. My parents chose the daughter of a wealthy tea plantation owner as Partha's prospective bride. Her name was Gayatry. She was one year older than me—five years younger than Partha. She was twenty-three and Partha twenty-eight when they became engaged in 1962.

Partha was not eager to get married. He was having a secret love affair with his secretary—a middle-aged Anglo-Indian woman. We discovered this when one evening Partha did not come home on time. When it was 10 p.m. and Partha was not yet home, we all became worried. Mother called Sheela, as she knew many of Partha's colleagues. After calling these colleagues, Sheela told our mother that Partha's colleagues saw him going out with his secretary. Sheela also knew where the secretary lived. So, in the middle of the night, my mother and I went to his secretary's house. An elder gentleman came out and told us that she was not home. He told my mother not to worry too much. Partha was fine. We returned home, but my mother could not sleep. The next morning Partha came home, and he had a hangover. He must have drunk a lot the night before, he was embarrassed. He did not go to work that day. My mother urgently wanted to arrange Partha's marriage, as his engagement with Gayatry was settled. Partha did not have much say in it. He could not disagree with his mother's decision.

The formal engagement ceremony took place at the bride's house. In our society, we called it the blessing ceremony. The father of the groom gives a gold necklace (or any other gold ornament) to the bride and declares that the arrangement is final. On Partha's blessing day, I went to the bride's house with my father. Partha did not have any role in it. The formal ceremony consisted simply of my father blessing Gayatry, putting the gold necklace, which my mother had a jeweller make from her gold reserve for this occasion, around her neck in the presence of the bride's many relatives. The bride touched my father's feet while accepting the necklace. At that moment, the bride's father gave my father a thick envelope and my father gave it to me to carry in my pocket. After the bride's family provided refreshments, the ceremony was over. Gayatry then signalled me to come to another room. She said that she heard a lot about me, and she hoped that we would be good friends when she came to our house. I liked the way she talked, and we became friends from that day.

When my father and I returned home, I found out that the envelope contained Rs 5,000 in cash—a huge sum in those days. I also learned that after the marriage, Gayatry's father agreed to give Partha a brand-new Ambassador car. Most middle-income families did not own cars in those days. Having a car was a status symbol. I did not think about the envelope or the car anymore at that time.

The wedding took place with pomp and splendour in the mansion of Gayatry's father. Hundreds of guests attended. Everyone talked about how lucky Gayatry's father was to get such an illustrious groom for his daughter. After the marriage, it was our turn to arrange for a boubhat. This is a formal reception of the bride coming into our house. The responsibility for arranging for this occasion fell on me. I arranged for a big tent to be erected in front of our apartment. As I mentioned before, the building had a 40-foot by 80-foot concrete roof extending from its facade. The tent was erected in that area. I hired decorators to adorn the house with flowers and lights. I hired several chefs to cook for the 150 guests that we expected. Of course, even all these arrangements were no comparison to what the wedding that Gayatry's father had provided. Yet I was pleased and thought Gayatry would appreciate my efforts. The reception went well, and Gayatry told me that she liked the arrangement very much.

Partha and Gayatry moved into the most spacious corner room in the apartment. The newly-weds usually rose late in the morning and kept the door of their room closed most of the time when they were inside. My mother did not like that. She wanted Gayatry to get up early, look after the household chores, and stay with her to help prepare meals for the family. Though we had a full-time household helper, we did not have private chefs to prepare our meals. Gayatry told me that she was trying to help my mother as much as she could, but she was not accustomed to much work. Partha, she said, would not listen to any complaint about my mother.

I told my mother to take it easy with Gayatry and allow her time to learn about our system. Mother told me not to poke my nose into these matters. I could see that cracks were beginning to appear in Partha's marriage, which did eventually fail despite my efforts to make it work for them. I shared some guilt for not protesting the dowry-taking and for not being able to return part of the dowry that I carried in my pocket. Gayatry, however, remained my friend. She would confide with me most of her secrets—her souring relations with my mother and Partha's coldness in dealing with their relations. There was no problem, she said, with their sexual competency. But Partha did not seem to love her. They made love when they were together, but there was no love in their lovemaking.

Later, when Gayatry needed my emotional support the most, I could not respond to her for a variety of complex reasons. At that difficult moment, I forced myself to forget about her. The guilt, however, never disappeared. A few decades later, it came roaring back when it was too late to do anything about it. It is an emotional story that unfolded over an extended period of my life. I describe it in an episode (Gatu: A Debt Never Paid) in Book 2.

## *A Fight with Our Landlord Dr Haldar*

During the 1950s and '60s, Calcutta experienced a severe housing shortage because of the continued influx of refugees from East Pakistan (now Bangladesh). Consequently, landlords could extract extra money in the form of "salami" (initiation fees) or huge advance payments on rents. The government's efforts to control rental costs by imposing rent-control laws backfired. The owners of good apartment buildings found ways to overcome rent-control laws through short-term lease agreements and asking for hefty advances on rents. The rates for good apartments under the short lease arrangements were also very high. A major share of people's earnings went towards paying rent.

The monthly rent of the four-bedroom apartment we leased on Baithak-khana Road was more than the salary of a college professor. We also had to pay twelve months' rent in advance. Our understanding was that our monthly rent would come from the deposit, and after twelve months we would pay a new deposit to renew the lease. But after we entered the apartment, the landlord demanded that we pay monthly rent. The advance, he said, would stay with him until we left, when he would return it. The landlord, Dr Haldar, was a notorious and powerful man. He owned many nursing homes and rental buildings in Calcutta. We heard bad stories about him. In many cases, he did not return the deposits when the renters left. If they protested, he threatened them with violence by his goondas.

After the two episodes, "My First Guilt" and "My Second Guilt", I vowed never to lie again. Now, inspired by Tagore's line "[Lord] may Thy wrath fall equally on those who do injustice and who tolerate them," I expanded my vow to include never participating in or tolerating injustice. I approached our landlord and after praising the beauty of the apartment, I said that we proposed that he deduct our monthly rent from the deposit we paid. When eleven months' rentals had been deducted, we would renew the lease with another twelve months' deposit. He declined. He was using those deposits to invest in new buildings, which I saw as an abject injustice. I told my parents and Partha that we should stop paying monthly rent, otherwise we would never get our deposit back. They agreed with me. I told Dr Harder what we intended to do. He warned me that I did not know with whom I was dealing. He would have me beaten up badly if I tried to go against him. To this, I replied that he also did not know with whom he was dealing. If he proceeded to implement his threat, it would be the end of his elaborate scam.

After that occasion, I filed a report with the local police detailing my conversation with Dr Haldar and mentioning the threat he posed. I also told my neighbours about the incident. I did not tell any of these things to my parents.

True to his threat, a few days later as I was coming back from routine grocery shopping with our household help carrying the purchases, Dr Haldar's guard blocked our entrance to the building. I dared the guard to stop us, and I proceeded to push my way forward. During the tussle that ensued, all the groceries that our helper was carrying fell to the ground. I had reached the end of my patience. I went to the police station and asked the inspector to arrest the guard and his boss. The inspector knew how connected Dr Haldar was to the political apparatus and advised me that my best bet would be to file a complaint at the criminal court. The court could issue a restraining order on Dr Haldar and ask the police to investigate the matter. This would empower the police to do what they had to do. Though my brother Suratha was a powerful police officer, I did not want to get him involved.

Later that day, I went to the criminal court with a lawyer. I told my entire story to the magistrate. The magistrate was in his late twenties or early thirties. When he heard who I was—a college professor and a researcher with a brilliant academic background—he sympathized with my cause. He immediately issued a restraining order on Dr Haldar, his guard, and his other associates. He also asked the police to conduct a thorough investigation and report to his court within a week. The upshot of the police investigation was a criminal case filed against Dr Haldar and his guard.

The case proceeded rapidly. Both Dr Haldar and his guard appeared before the court and avoided incarceration by posting bail. Dr Haldar was surprised by the speed at which the criminal case against him proceeded. The guard who tried to block our entry now would give me a military-style salute when I entered our building. Dr Haldar engaged some of the best criminal lawyers but to no avail. Both Haldar and his guard were convicted on my testimony.

The news of Haldar's criminal conviction was front-page news in the Calcutta dailies. Many of Haldar's other tenants congratulated me. It was a moral victory. Dr Haldar would not bother us anymore. When the year was over, we sent our rental check by registered mail to him. When he refused to accept the mail, we began to deposit our rent to the rent-control office. I could not do all these things alone. Partha was with me every step of the way.

Haldar appealed the conviction and the case eventually went up to the Supreme Court. I was not in India during most of those appeals. But every appellate court upheld the conviction order of the lower court.

## *Encounter with a Sanyasi in a Railway Station*

There was another incident—an encounter with a fake sanyasi in a railway station during my research years at the Science College—that would permanently change my outlook towards religion. It triggered a cascade of events in my life that would eventually help me to come up with my own theory about religious truth and religious falsehoods. This is why I have left it for Book 4, *The Highest Reality: A Treatise on Religion, Truth, Morality, and Purpose of Life,* where it fits better.

## *Starting an Education Chain*

The meeting with the so-called sanyasi in the railway station was a disappointment, but the spirit of making personal sacrifices for the benefit of others, which led me to search for a guide in a sanyasi in the first place, did not die with it. I diverted my attention to finding worthy causes for sacrifice. I knew that India faced a massive problem in educating its vast population. This was not because people were unwilling to learn but rather because of a shortage of teachers. A strong and ardent believer in the power of volunteerism, I thought of a scheme that I believed could help solve the problem. I called it an "education chain". I did not just think about this scheme, but as soon as I thought that it could be a reasonable solution, I started a pilot experiment.

One major problem with educating the masses in India was that most poor children did not have anyone to guide them. The masses of slum dwellers want their children to escape the rot into which they were born, but they do not know how to do this. I tried to address this problem with my education scheme.

I knew the financial worth of my private tutoring skills—it was Rs 100 per month for two hours a week. Only a few students, and the most well-to-do among them, could afford to pay such a fee. For my pilot, I selected ten students from the chemistry honours classes and began giving them two one-hour lessons per week for free. It was a group lesson, but the lessons were not free in the literal sense. Although I asked for no money from these students, I did require each of them to promise to give similarly "free" lessons to ten deserving high school students. That is, in return for receiving "free lessons" from my students, the high school students were to extract similar promises from their students.

My goal was to reach the children of the slums. The driving force was the spirit of volunteerism. When volunteerism starts at the top and helps one directly, the beneficiary is often inspired to contribute as a volunteer as well. The project started and began to progress well, but before it could take a solid hold, it was time for me to leave the country for postdoctoral work in the United States.

When I later returned to visit India, on 8 December 1966, I wrote to Bijoy Singh Nahar, minister-in-charge, Labour Department, West Bengal, to see if we could institutionalize the scheme. But as it always happens, politicians are never of much help unless an idea dovetails with their immediate interests. The project died, but it eventually came back on a much stronger and more formal footing when I started the Chakrabarti Foundation scholarship. Making a promise to spread the benefit of the scholarship is an implicit requirement for being qualified to receive it. The concept also helped me design and/or lead many philanthropic projects in the future. I describe these in detail in the chapter "Beyond Self-Interest" in Book 4.

## The Youngest DSc

After I got the Sir P.C. Ray Fellowship, my immediate concern was to choose a worthy research project, something that would not be too close to the type of research that was being conducted elsewhere on the campus at the time but also lofty enough to be worthy of a DSc dissertation. At that time, the total synthesis of complex natural products caught the fancy of chemists around the world. Robert Robinson and Robert Burn Woodward each became celebrity chemists by independently publishing the total synthesis of cholesterol in 1951 and 1952, respectively. Two years later, Woodward's group would publish a total synthesis of strychnine, for which he received the 1965 Nobel Prize in chemistry. Dr Carl Djerassi, who joined Stanford University in 1959, also made a sensation by synthesizing certain antibiotics and the hormone cortisone.

I wondered if I could identify some interesting natural products, the total synthesis of which would enrich our current knowledge of organic syntheses. The molecules I selected for synthesis were brazilin and haematoxylin—two compounds that eluded attempts for total synthesis for more than a hundred years. I immersed myself in the task. When I undertook the project, I did not realize the extent of the difficulties I would encounter. In quick succession, I was able to synthesize several new classes of compounds. Among them, indeno-(2',3':3,4)-coumarins and dihydro-anhydro-trimethy-brazilin. That work would have been enough for a PhD but probably not a DSc dissertation. I was obsessed with completing the total synthesis of brazilin and haematoxylin. A lucky break came early in 1964, and I submitted my 314-page DSc dissertation in April of that year. Three of the most renowned chemists of that time examined my dissertation, and they were highly complimentary. I quote part of their reports below.

> The thesis of Mr. Chakrabarti is a very good and diligent work which proves that the author has much experience in the syntheses of organic chemistry. His synthesis of indeno-(2',3':3,4)-coumarins and dihydro-anhydro-trimethy-brazilin, dihydro-anhydro-tetramethylhaematoxylin, and related compounds are an enrichment of our knowledge of this class of heterocyclic substance.
>
> —Professor Paul Karrer,
> Nobel Laureate,
> Technische Hochschule, Zurich, Switzerland

> The thesis relates to a topic that had interested chemists for very many years partly because of the complexity of the problems and partly because of the interesting structural rearrangements encountered in this field of study.
>
> The work in the thesis is extensive and important. Ingenious and elegant synthetic methods of general application have been devised in the synthesis of derivatives of brazilin and hematoxylin series. The experimental work has been carried out with utmost care and skill and considerable novelty and originality have been shown both in devising new theoretical routes and in their experimental exploration.
>
> The presentation of the thesis is quite first-class, the literary style is excellent.
>
> —Professor R.D. Haworth,
> FRS, University of Manchester, UK

> I am happy to state that I regard his synthetic work as outstanding. The work was very well conceived and beautifully executed. Chakrabarti is particularly to be complimented on his perseverance in the face of discouraging results. His successful work has opened up new lines of synthesis that may be further applied in the synthesis of natural products in the indenocoumarin series.
>
> —Professor Melvin S. Newman,
> Regent Professor of Chemistry, the Ohio State University,
> Member of the American Academy of Science

Based on such lavish praise, Calcutta University awarded me the DSc degree in 1965. I had submitted the thesis in April 1964, when I was just twenty-four years old.

Reporting on this achievement, the Sunday *Hindustan Standard* of 7 March 1965, had this to say:

The degree of Doctor of Science has been conferred on Sri [a Bengali honorific] Paritosh Mohan Chakrabarti by the University of Calcutta for his outstanding contributions to Synthetic Chemistry. Aged only 24 years, Dr. Chakrabarti is the youngest recipient of this top honour of D.Sc. from the University.

Dr. Chakrabarti's thesis entitled "Synthesis of Brazilin and Haematoxylin Series" relates to a complicated field of research, which has interested chemists over the world for a century. His work has been widely acclaimed by eminent scientists from U.K., U.S.A., and other countries as "outstanding," and "an enrichment of our knowledge of this class of heterocyclic substances." According to them, the results achieved by Dr. Chakrabarti have "opened up new lines of synthesis" in this complex field of chemistry. The novelty and originality shown by Dr. Chakrabarti have been highly praised. The presentation and literary style of Dr. Chakrabarti's thesis was ranked as excellent.

In 1959, Dr. Chakrabarti stood first in class I in the M.Sc. in chemistry at Calcutta University. He was Sir P.C. Ray Fellow of Calcutta University and a popular professor in Chemistry, Rammohan College, Calcutta. Dr. Chakrabarti is currently carrying on advanced research in the field of Cancer in the U.S.A. as Visiting Post-Doctoral Research Fellow.

(Note: The newspaper made a mistake. I was a professor in City College, not Rammohan College.)

What gratified me the most was that I was able to keep my promise to the vice chancellor of Calcutta University that he would not be sorry that he granted me the Sir P.C. Ray Fellowship.

# 4

# The Transition Years, 1964–69

(Ages 24–29)

## In the United States: Visiting Postdoctoral Fellow at the Ohio State University

Conventional wisdom had it that becoming established as a professor-cum-researcher, which was my primary intention at the time, involved getting some postdoctoral research experience. Such an experience provides the opportunity to expand one's research horizons and learn how other professors look at problems, but more importantly, it exposes one to new laboratory techniques, experimental design, and analytical equipment. Accordingly, as soon as I submitted my thesis for DSc in April 1964, I started to write letters to a few renowned professors in the United States.

Within just a few weeks, I received several positive responses, including one from Professor Melvin S. Newman of Ohio State University. I was particularly happy with Dr Newman's invitation because of my interest in stereochemistry and conformational analysis. Professor Newman was known for his pioneering work in those areas. Recall that when I was an MSc student at Calcutta University, I gave a seminar on conformational analysis and illustrated the concepts with home-made ball-and-stick models because we did not have commercial molecular models at the university. In that seminar, I mentioned Newman's work in this area. Now I had an opportunity to work with the same famous chemist. I was excited at the prospect and decided to accept his offer. (As fate would have it, after I became the director of research at PPG Industries, the same Professor Newman came to work for me as a consultant.)

The research project I undertook with Professor Newman concerned a mechanism of chemical carcinogenesis. For a long time, it was known that polycyclic aromatic compounds present in coal tar were potent carcinogens. The prevailing mechanism attributed the carcinogenic properties of these materials to their rigid polycyclic aromatic molecular architecture. Our goal was to determine if the prevailing mechanism was correct or not.

We synthesized a highly potent carcinogenic polycyclic aromatic compound, 20-methylcholanthrene. The name indicates a methyl group (–$CH_3$) at the twentieth position of the cholanthrene molecule. This molecule exists in two mirror-image configurations known as optical isomers (in the way that one's right hand is a mirror image of one's left hand), in which the only difference was the spatial arrangement of the methyl group. In coal tar, the compound occurs in equal quantities of each isomer. Laboratory synthesis also produced equal mixtures of the two isomers. These isomers were similar in all respects, including the number and juxtapositions of all the single and double bonds that bind the atoms together in the molecule. The only difference between them was the spatial arrangement of the methyl group; this made one arrangement a mirror image of the other.

No one had ever separated a mixture of these two mirror-image isomers of hydrocarbons into two pure samples until we undertook the project. To do so, we used a designed complexing agent with a carboxylic acid group that could exist in two optically isomeric forms, and we were successful. The only way to know which isomer was which was to transmit polarized light through the pure solutions of the isomers—one rotated the polarized light to the right and the other to the left. The preferred isomer of the complexing agent formed a distinct complex with each of the two optical isomers of 20-methylcholanthrene, and each of the complexed isomers had a distinct solubility in organic solvents. Taking advantage of this differential solubility, we separated the two isomers and then de-complexed them by washing the separated isomers with an aqueous solution of sodium bicarbonate.

We tested the two isomers of 20-methylcholantrene for carcinogenic potential and found, to our delight, that only one isomer was carcinogenic, not the other. We argued that, as nature made the molecules of life in one type of spatial arrangement exclusively, only one of the isomers of 20-methylcholantrene could interact with those molecules of life and the other could not. This work debunked an earlier theory of carcinogenesis of polycyclic aromatic compounds. Had there been another planet in our vast universe where the molecules of life had the opposite spatial arrangement—a perfectly logical possibility—the isomer that was non-carcinogenic in our world would have been carcinogenic in the other and the one that was carcinogenic in our world would have been non-carcinogenic in the other.

Our work had significant implications for drug design. Some drug molecules have two or more spatial arrangements of their atoms; that is, they are isomers. So, it was logical to assume that not all the isomers would be physiologically active, and indeed, this is the case. Being able to separate the various isomers of a drug molecule would allow the manufacture of more potent drugs that would be effective at lower doses and thus have fewer and/or less severe side effects. Later work on stereospecific synthesis and/or resolution of the isomeric mixtures helped to realize that potential, but cheap resolution methods were unavailable then, and they still are.

While at the Ohio State University, my next endeavour was to design simple and economically attractive methods of resolving optically isomeric compounds, but before I could make much progress, I received very disturbing news that made me abandon everything and return to Calcutta. Later on, other pressing issues and different priorities prevented me from revisiting the project. Maybe I will leave the thought with my grandchildren in case they want to work in the area.

As I mentioned at the beginning of this chapter, postdoctoral experience is not only about making discoveries. It is more about learning things that you cannot learn from books. It is about seeing how other people handle their tasks. It is about learning new skills and techniques. Here are a few examples of what I learned during my brief year and a half as a postdoctoral fellow at Ohio State University. Each had a lifelong impact on me.

## *Runaway Reactions*

I completed the main goal of my research project in less than a year, which is something that usually takes between two to three years. Professor Newman was very pleased to see that I accomplished the tasks in such a short time. But this did not come without risk.

In my synthesis scheme, a large stock of a critical intermediate was key to shortening the time to reach the end product. I decided to run a large-scale reaction to make this critical intermediate. It involved heating certain chemicals (supposed to be carcinogenic) in benzene (also carcinogenic) in a three-neck flask fitted with a long condenser and adding a funnel to deliver another reactant dissolved in glacial (anhydrous) acetic acid to the flask.

The entire system was closed except for the top of the condenser; it had a drying tube on the top with open communication with the environment. To carry out the reaction, the contents of the flask had to be kept at reflux temperature. The reaction was exothermic (it released heat as the reaction occurred). Because of this, I had to add the reactants through the funnel at a slow yet steady rate. That way, the contents of the flask remained at a controlled reflux temperature.

It so happened that the onset of the reaction was slower than I anticipated, and I had added more than the optimum amount of the reactant through the funnel before the reaction started. As the reaction was exothermic, the excess reactants caused a runaway condition once the reaction finally started.

The cooling capacity of the condenser was not sufficient to remove the heat of the reaction. The liquid from the flask started to come out with a gust, blowing off the drying tube and spraying the hot liquid containing benzene, acetic acid, and other chemicals all over the wall and me. I cooled down the reaction with ice and cleaned up the mess on the laboratory bench, then I went home, removed my clothes, and showered for about an hour with repeated shampooing of my hair.

I was afraid that the benzene and other chemicals that sprayed on my head could one day cause brain cancer. That was the reason for the long shower and repeated shampooing. Fortunately, I have never had cancer or any impairment of my brain function. In fact, an active brain has been my biggest asset as I progressed through life.

There is a widely held belief in biomedical sciences that the definition of a chemical as a drug or a poison depends on its dosage. Chemicals that are poisons in large doses are often drugs at low doses. This is a maxim that many environmentalists ignore at a significant cost to our economy and our health. Maybe that is what happened in my case. The repeated shampooing might have reduced the concentration of the spilled chemicals to a beneficial level.

I learned a hard lesson that day. Never take exothermic reactions lightly. One should always design experiments so that no excess reactant ever accumulates, and one should always provide a sufficient outlet for the heat (i.e., cooling) in real time. These lessons also have analogues in society and business. If any uneasy situation (such as anger) is allowed to accumulate for too long without finding an outlet in real time, the anger will find its outlet through violent revolution or devastating labour strikes.

## *Patience Pays in Resolving Bottlenecks*

Professor Newman invited all the researchers working in his group—graduate students and postdoctoral associates—after dinner every Friday evening to his home for an informal discussion of issues faced by the researchers. The idea was for everyone to learn from the experience of others. The get-togethers often involved fun as well. Some of the researchers played billiards as they discussed their problems. Each week, one of the researchers would give a talk on any aspect of chemistry he or she chose.

Within a month of joining the group, Professor Newman asked me to present my thesis work at one of these evening meetings. I talked about all the complicated reactions, but just about when I was about to finish my talk, I stopped for a second and changed course. I said that it was not the complicated reactions that made my total synthesis of brazilin and hematoxylin successful. No, the success came about because of how I solved a bottleneck that outwardly looked so simple! It was about how to conduct a bromination reaction that we do so routinely. In my case, however, it defied all logical approaches. I tried all possible conditions that I could think of, and every attempt failed. I was determined, however, not to give up. In my mind, I knew there must be a trick, and I had to find it. Eventually, I succeeded by carrying out the reaction in dry ether mixed with a chlorinated solvent at a subzero temperature. The brominated product came out as crystals that looked more beautiful to me than anything I ever saw. I had resolved the bottleneck, and the rest was history. With this I stopped. People listened to my presentation with occasional questions and interruptions, but there was pin-drop silence as I narrated the last part.

After I had finished, Professor Newman thanked me for an excellent presentation and then said, drawing the attention of everyone, that the most important takeaway from my presentation was the patience that was required to resolve the bottleneck. Every major project in life presents a few bottlenecks. The difference between those who are successful and those who are not is the patience necessary to solve those problems in the face of repeated failures. That night I came home with Newman's comments ringing in my ears as a friend drove me to my apartment.

## *Better Faster than Slower: Flash Distillation*

One day I was carrying out a messy distillation of a semi-thick reaction product at ultra-low pressure and heating the distillation flask in a hot oil bath. I kept the oil bath at 20 °C, higher than the boiling point of the colourless liquid that I was trying to recover from that dark-brown viscous material (a standard practice). At that point, Professor Newman entered my lab. Seeing me toiling at recovering my desired product, he took the flask out of the oil bath. Then, with an open flame of the Bunsen burner, he heated the flask directly, and within a few minutes recovered a thin, light-brown liquid in the reception container. He then told me to do what I was doing with the oil bath, meaning the finishing step.

What he did was a flash distillation to first recover a semi-pure product. The yield of the final pure product that I recovered by using this two-step process was much higher than what I would have obtained by my original technique. Exposing the material to the moderate temperature of the oil bath for a long time was more detrimental to the stability of the product than exposing it to a much higher temperature over a shorter time. I learned that there are times when fast, draconian approaches are better than cautious slow approaches. Later, when I joined GAF corporation as a group leader, during my first week I solved a long-standing problem using the same principle. That first success put me in the good graces of the company's management.

### *Teaching Techniques and Communication Skills*

While at Ohio State University, I often attended undergraduate lectures by prominent professors. The purpose was not about learning the subjects that I already knew well. The purpose was to learn the professors' communication and presentation techniques. I learned why some of the best researchers were lousy teachers while others, who might not be stellar in their research, were excellent teachers. Professor Newman was one of the best teachers I met. His presentations were lucid, full of fun, and he connected them to our everyday experiences. It was this last quality that made the subjects so memorable. He also told us that every phenomenon follows certain patterns that are common to all occurrences—in science, in nature, and in life. Later I would use those techniques in my lectures and writings with great success.

## Life in Columbus, Ohio

My first experience in Columbus—the capital of the state of Ohio and the seat of the Ohio State University's main campus—was a jaw-dropping surprise. Professor Newman came in person to the airport to receive me as I arrived in the United States from India. Not only did he pick me up, but he also took my suitcase from my hand, saying that I must be very tired from the long journey. Coming from India, where the less important person treats the more important one with reverence, being treated like this by Professor Newman was startling. I saw how reputation and high social standing can become a virtue. The formula is simple: Add humility.

Humility means treating all people with respect, extending the same courtesies to all people regardless of their standing in society, and behaving with others with the same courtesy that you would expect from them. Humility is then courageous, not servile, behaviour. It requires being comfortable with yourself and not letting your accomplishments go to your head. It is a moral value. On that day, I saw the beauty of humility and vowed to adopt it as a personal value from then on.

Professor Newman took me to a hotel and told me to take it easy for the rest of the day and that he would see me at the department the next day. Upon my arrival at the department the next morning, Professor Newman introduced me to his secretary, who gave me my monthly salary in advance and in cash. He then took me around to introduce me to the other members of his group and showed me my lab and desk.

I looked around the other chemistry labs on campus looking for Indian faces. I saw a few but was already feeling homesick. One great benefit of homesickness is that you make quick friends with anyone who looks familiar. In India, we talked about Bengalis, Punjabis, and Gujaratis, but here I talked about Indians. The parochialism returned to a limited extent, however, when I met several Bengali students and postdoctoral fellows. Most of the students were single and had already adjusted to the local way of life, including some having American girlfriends. The Bengali postdoctoral fellows, particularly the ones I met, were mostly married people, but they did not have their spouses with them. I became an instant friend with another post-doc, Shyam Sundar Bhattacharya. He was from Dhaka, East Pakistan (now Bangladesh). Shyam helped me find a lodging just a few blocks from the department. I moved from the hotel to my rented room.

## *Social Life*

My social life in Columbus, Ohio, was mostly confined to the Indian community. There were a few established Indian families in and around Columbus. They would invite me along with other Indian students and post-docs to their homes for dinner on weekends. I enjoyed those visits. I particularly remember a couple in Marysville—the Raychaudhuris. The husband worked for Nestlé and his wife was very lonely since she did not have any friends. They had a little boy. Whenever I visited them with some of my other friends, she was very happy. She would show pictures of her younger sister and express her wish that one of us would marry her and bring her to the United States.

Though most of the students and post-docs lived in lodging houses (these featured single bedrooms with a common kitchen), I soon moved out from mine to an attic apartment. It had a bedroom, a living room, a kitchen, and a large bathroom. I had the entire suite to myself and that gave me full privacy. The apartment came furnished—the only thing I had to do was to buy a TV with a rabbit-ears antenna. This apartment became a gathering place for my friends during the weekends. I learned to cook a few dishes, and whatever I cooked my friends enjoyed. To express my appreciation for the way I had been welcomed earlier, I occasionally invited the Indian families, including the Raychaudhuris of Marysville, to visit me in my apartment. They admired my modest arrangements.

## *Magazines, Nightlife, and Movies*

In my early twenties, I taught at a girls' college, and in my classroom I tried to maintain an air of gravity and act like a father figure to my students. When I was with my parents, I would not look at attractive girls or talk about my interests in girls. Doing so would have been impolite. In India, magazines did not publish pictures of naked women. The only nude pictures I saw, if one could call them nude, were those of the scantily clad "Agfa girl" (Agfa was a brand of colour film that used suggestive photos of women in their ads). I remember one of a young European woman with her legs exposed up to her hips. We would never look at such pictures when we were with our elders.

In Columbus, those restrictions were gone, and without any fear of being caught by my elders or my students, my friends and I would buy copies of *Playboy* magazine and keep them in our rooms. We would also go to X-rated movies, which most cultured Americans avoided. Having no other outlet for our suppressed sexual urges, we took advantage of these opportunities.

One day, a friend of mine, Dr Chatterjee, whom we called Chatterjee-da, bought a used car. Before coming to the United States, he had spent several years in Germany and so was familiar with German nightlife. Chatterjee-da used to take us to nightclubs around Columbus in his car. We would each buy a glass of beer for 50 cents and watch the naked young women slide up and down slippery poles on a stage. I had never seen the naked body of a woman before except for my mother, and that was only for a moment when she was frolicking with another naked body, that of my father, on the verandah of their room in Agartala in the light of the full moon.

I found the obscenity laws of America amusing. These laws required women to keep their nipples and vaginas covered. Everything else could be exposed. Taking advantage of the laws, or rather to make a mockery of them, the strippers would highlight their nipples by pasting little decorative stars on them and cover their genitals with strips of the narrowest possible pieces of cloth, often with arrows drawn pointing toward their vital parts.

## *Lavern Love*

Though I had an enjoyable time in the lab and lovely experiences interacting with fellow researchers, my social life was limited to just a few friends. The university was aware of this problem with foreign scholars, so they had a programme in which local families would host the university's foreign personnel during the holidays. One day, the department secretary told me that a local family had invited me to spend Christmas with them. I was excited by this and eagerly accepted the invitation.

When I arrived at the home on Christmas Eve, I found that my host was not a family but rather a single woman. Her name was Lavern Love. She was attractive and about twenty-five years old, and she lived with her eight-year-old daughter. She graciously welcomed me into her home, telling me to feel at home and asking her daughter to show me around the house. During the evening, several other people dropped by, and some of them brought gifts. Lavern cooked a turkey for dinner and prepared several side dishes. Her twenty-something cousin also came with her boyfriend to join us for dinner, which we all enjoyed.

Lavern served both white and red wine during dinner. Her cousin and her boyfriend drank red and white wine alternately. Lavern drank a few glasses of red wine. I just kept sipping my first glass of red wine. At around midnight, we had a round of coffee, and Lavern's cousin and her boyfriend left. Lavern kissed her daughter goodnight and took her to her bedroom. I went to bed in the guest room.

Something unexpected happened as I was about to fall asleep. Lavern came to my room in her nightgown. She laid down next to me, put her hand around me, and asked me if I was having a good social life in America. I knew I was being seduced, but I did not need to be seduced. The warmth of her body made my adrenaline flow. I did not, however, want to have a bodily interaction with a woman I did not know. I was also afraid that the invitation might have been a ploy to trap me. I was torn between my blind urge on the one side and rationality on the other. I went to the bathroom and returned after relieving myself of my erotism. Realizing what I did, Lavern told me not to do such a thing again in my life when I was with a woman; it was an insult. After that, she went back to her room. In the morning, things looked normal. Lavern served breakfast, and after finishing, I said goodbye to Lavern and her daughter and left. Lavern said she hoped to see me again.

In the ensuing weeks, Lavern called me several times at my department. When people answering the common phone told me that Lavern was on the line, I would tell them to tell her that I was busy at the time and that I would call her back later. Of course, I never meant to call her back. I did not want to get involved with a woman whom I did not know much about. After trying several times, Lavern ultimately gave up.

## *Falling in Love*

There were only a few single Indian women on campus at this time. Those who were there were brilliant students but not physically attractive. Yet based on the supply-and-demand equation, they were very much in demand by single Indian male students. For their part, the young women were generally more serious about their studies than their male counterparts. A few of them would often come to me for help in their chemistry courses. I would help with no romantic interests from either side.

For quite a while, even before I came to Ohio State University, I saw in my dreams a vivid picture of a young woman—slim with a long neck, sharp features, and intelligence beaming from her face; she was dressed in an all-white outfit—long and sleek trousers reaching to her ankles, and a thin turtle-neck sweater with sleeves reaching to her wrists and fitting gracefully on her body and highlighting its contours. She was very pleasant and smart. I fell in love with this girl of my dreams and thought of meeting her in the flesh one day. But the flesh-and-blood women that I met or even liked to spend time with did not come close to that vision of perfection that haunted my dreams. I thought that, if I had that woman by my side, I could achieve the impossible. So, I did not really fall in love with any of the girls I dated in India or came into close acquaintance with in Columbus, Ohio.

Things changed when I first saw that young Indian woman, a PhD student in pharmacology, in Columbus, Ohio. She had the same bodily features—that slim figure, that beautiful long neck, that same sharpness in her features, the same intelligent eyes, and a pair of thin smiling lips with red lipstick partially exposing the pearl-white teeth behind them. But she dressed differently from the girl of my dreams. Instead, she wore a rust-coloured sari with a golden border and a red long-sleeve crew-neck sweater, which accentuated her long, tender neck. The long sleeves of her sweater resembled those of the sweater that my dream girl wore, except for the colour. She wore a dot on her forehead and her long, curly black hair hung gracefully around her shoulders.

You never get everything you dream of, but this came terribly close to what I was dreaming about, and in many respects, much more. She was not just physically attractive; altogether with her intelligence, merit, self-confidence, and personality, she was the most beautiful woman I ever met. I fell in love at first sight, and we were passionately in love with each other. But as if it was too much of a good thing for me to have, the situation suddenly changed, and a family emergency called me back to India. I thought I had lost her forever. But sometimes fortune favours those who earnestly desire something. Two years later, we were back together as through a miracle, never to be separated again, and she became my wife and lifelong partner. She is Srimati. I still have the picture of her first appearance before me in our living room, and every time I look at it, I fall in love with her again for the first time.

## Sad News and a Return to India

While I was in the United States, Suratha, my IPS brother who was central Calcutta's deputy commissioner of police at the time, died in a car accident. He was only thirty-four years old. He was returning from the maidan in his jeep after a horse-riding exercise. A lorry hit him in the side, and he died instantly. The news was all over the front pages of all the Calcutta newspapers. My family, however, did not give me the news, as they were concerned that I would be too disturbed and possibly return home at once and leave my career behind. A few months later, when I was in the house of one of my friends, I saw a Bengali monthly magazine with my brother's picture in it and the news of his death. I immediately sent a telegram to Partha telling him that I was very upset that he did not let me know the news of Suratha's death and that I would be coming back home soon. Within a few weeks, I wrapped up everything, left Columbus, and returned to Calcutta.

On arriving in Calcutta, the first thing I did was to go to the home of Suratha's in-laws, where his wife Suchitra moved with her two little girls after he died. When I arrived, I saw a big party going on in the house. Suchitra's mother came to the door, told me that Suchitra could not see me at that time, and politely turned me away. I heard that Suchitra was getting married again, the groom was an officer who worked for Suratha. I was disgusted to see what happens in Calcutta's socialite circle. The tears of mourning Suratha in my eyes had barely dried, and Suchitra was off to marry again!

In Calcutta, I also had many encounters with Gayatry, but all my attempts to reconcile Partha and Gayatry failed. This relationship seemed to have ruptured beyond repair. I discovered, however, that Gayatry began to like me more than she did before, and my feelings for her were reciprocal. But there was no romance in our relationship. It was platonic love between two friends, and we wanted to keep it that way. I will describe Gayatry in greater detail in an episode in Book 2, *The Makings of PMC Group*.

Back in Calcutta, a few of my previous romantic relationships rekindled. I was now less inhibited in talking about sex than I was before. One relationship that I revived was with the daughter of the minister for land, whom I tutored before. The minister wanted me to marry his daughter, and my mother was also in favour of this arrangement. But seeing what had happened to Gayatry, I was not ready to marry a woman of my mother's choosing and ruin her life. Dating was OK with me, but not a permanent commitment.

Another interesting situation was with the Paramanik daughter whom also I tutored. She was now an MSc student at Jadavpur University. Apparently, she fell in love with a fellow student whom her parents did not like. They sought advice from Devi-di (Devi Chakravarty, head of the Department of Chemistry at Bethune College). Devi-di told her parents that the only person she might listen to was me. Her father asked if I would talk to her and dissuade her from her romantic relationship with her classmate. I agreed and was also interested to know how she was doing. She came and told me all about her lover. Their relationship was deep, and it would not be fair if she married any other man of her parents' liking. It would not be fair to her parents' choice or to herself. I agreed with her and told her to do what her conscience directed her to.

There are important moments in life that will never come back; these moments we must enjoy when they occur. I asked her if she recalled the day while I was tutoring her when she took me to a room in the inner compound of their house and closed the door. Clearly blushing, she told me then that no one would come there to disturb us. I behaved as if this was nothing unusual, as if it was another day of as-usual tutoring, and we got back to the task. I now told her that I knew then what she was hinting at. On that earlier day, my face was also blushing with emotion as much as hers, and I had stiffened inside my pants. But I suppressed those feelings. We lost a valuable moment that day, and we will never get it back again.

At this, she nodded her head in agreement. Then she asked, what about me now? I said that I am now less inhibited, but not ready for any serious relationship. I was still going through the trauma of a severed relationship, and my mind was not yet steady enough for new commitments. She put her hand on mine, pressed it softly, and asked me if she could see me again. I was so understanding and easy to talk to, she said, and she wished to see me often. I told her to feel free to come and talk to me whenever she wanted. She has visited me many times since that day, we went out for coffee or a drink, but we did not talk much about her love life again.

Things also were not going right with my career in India. When I returned, I took a temporary position at the Chittaranjan Cancer Research Centre in Calcutta as a scientific pool officer. This was a programme created by the Indian government to reverse the brain drain and provide temporary employment to Indian scientists who wanted to come back to India and find suitable positions. The research centre was housed in a beautiful building with beautiful offices, but it did not have any facilities to conduct research. So, even though I received a salary for coming to my office, I did not have any duties to perform. I thought of reviving my education chain, but that would have required me to take a teaching position. I thought of teaching at Calcutta University, but no openings suited my qualifications at the time.

I received several lucrative offers for industrial positions, but they were mostly in Maharashtra or Gujarat, states that were industrializing very rapidly. If I went to another state, I might have landed a desirable teaching position, but that would also mean moving away from my family. I had returned to India to stay near my family, but my professional opportunities did not accommodate that need. The minister whose daughter I taught thought that my upstanding reputation in society qualified me for a good political career. But I was not comfortable with such notions.

As I was mulling over what my next move should be, I did a few things to keep myself busy. At the invitation of All India Radio, I gave a talk about cancer. I also wrote two articles for the annual issues of *Betar Jagat*, an elite literary magazine of wide circulation. I gave invited lectures to several colleges, and they were all well received. I also began to visit the British Council library. Before I had left for the United States, I began to frequent the institution and developed a liking for it. In the course of my frequent visits to the library, I saw an ad in a scientific journal about an ICI fellowship. This fellowship was for aspiring postdoctoral researchers who wanted to expand their research experience by working on their projects at a university in England. I applied and was granted the fellowship. I thought it could be a more interesting stop-gap position than staying as a pool officer in India while considering my next permanent move. Even with the fellowship, I still had to find a university that was willing to give me a lab and research facilities. I wrote to several universities and received positive responses from a few. One interesting response, although not an offer, is worth mentioning here. It was from Dr M. Stacey, FRS, Mason professor and head of the Department of Chemistry, University of Birmingham. It was dated 6 February 1967. I just quote a few lines from that letter:

> Dear Dr. Chakrabarti,
> I am astonished to find that that after all your achievements a suitable post could not be created for you in India … I would have thought that you could create a department of some distinction … I really think that you ought to stay and persevere in developing some of your natural products for the ultimate good of India …Why not ask some of your sponsors such as Professor Newman to intervene with higher authorities on your behalf? …
>
> Signed, M. Stacey.

What Professor Stacey did not know was that, in India, local politics determine who or what is good for the country. When Dr Har Gobind Khorana wanted to return to India and applied for a reader's job, he was bypassed, and the job went to someone who never amounted to anything. Khorana went back to the United States and in 1968 won the Nobel Prize in physiology or medicine as an American. He went on to join Harvard University as a professor and established a distinguished research group there. India lost an opportunity. But did it really care? So, despite such encouraging letters and the compliments heaped upon me, I decided to go to the UK. I accepted an offer from the University of Hull in Yorkshire to do my research as an ICI fellow.

## In England, 1967–68

> My best postdoctoral research associate ever.
>
> —Dr N.B. Chapman,
> chairman of Department of Chemistry,
> University of Hull, UK, 1968

## *Research*

The very nature of discovery research is that it can often take twists and turns along the way towards progress. When I went to Hull, my primary goal was to solve an interesting problem in brazilin and haematoxylin chemistry, namely the structures of brazilein and haematoxylein, which I did not get a chance to fully investigate earlier. Brazilein and haematoxylein are shining, brilliantly red compounds with a metallic lustre; they form when brazilin and haematoxylin undergo mild oxidation such as by exposing them to air for a long time. I thought that the structures proposed in the literature by Micovic and Robinson (*J. Chem. Soc.* 1937, p. 43) were wrong.

The proposed structure did not explain an important property of these compounds, which is that they were only slightly soluble in water or alcohol. I thought that brazilein and haematoxylein were "charge-transfer complexes" between two alternative structures, one of which was rejected by Micovic and Robinson. The earlier researchers based their conclusions on insufficient evidence, presumably because the concept of a charge-transfer complex was not fully understood in their time. Anyway, setting aside the scientific jargon, determining the structures of brazilein and haematoxylein were my primary objectives at Hull when I went there.

At Hull, there was a convention that PhD students would present their research during lunchtime in the faculty dining room. At the time, almost the entire department was involved in synthesizing various derivatives of a heterocyclic compound called benzo[b]thiophene in the hope of finding interesting drug molecules. As I listened to many of these presentations, one common theme emerged. Their progress was severely hampered due to the time required to make a common starting material for their research. For example, a PhD student would spend her/his first year of research making enough starting material for the synthesis of the derivative molecules they were interested in.

One day I asked a PhD student and his supervising professors why it took so much time to make the starting material. In short, they answered that the reaction conditions were complex, the process required long periods of high temperature for each step, the reactions created a tarry mess, and the yield of the target product from the tar was very low. Preparation of enough starting material and its purification thus took an enormous amount of time. They showed me the process steps to impress upon me why it took such a long time. Professor Chapman, chair of the department, was also present during that discussion. Though Professor Chapman and I had talked before, those talks were mostly about administrative matters because I was working on my project with the ICI fellowship.

One maxim I always held is that the best way to think about complex matters is to think in simple terms. A corollary of this maxim is that to think simply, one must think in theoretical terms—in terms of basic mechanisms or concepts—that can be applied more broadly; this allows one to borrow from experiences in other fields. These maxims have served me well. Professor R.D. Haworth, FRS, as we saw, also observed my reliance on these maxims in my approach to research when he examined my DSc thesis.

When I was a child, I read a poem by Rabindranath Tagore titled "Discovery of the Shoe". In a slightly modified form, the story goes like this.

A powerful king assembled all his ministers and told them that he did not like getting his feet dirty whenever he set his foot on the ground. He wanted them to find a solution. At first, they all scratched their heads, but eventually they told the king that they had come up with a solution; the cobbler sitting in the far corner of the assembly room should be able to implement it. They said that they were going to have the cobbler cover the king's walking path with leather. The cobbler slowly rose and asked the king if he was allowed to say something. The king said, "Go ahead and say whatever you want, but I know what is in your mind. This is a big job, and you must be thinking about how you could accomplish it alone. But do not worry," the king said, "you will be able to hire as many people as you want."

The Cobbler said, "No, your majesty, that is not what I was going to ask. What I was going to say is, rather than covering all the roads with leather, why don't I cover your feet with leather?"

The king was pleased, and the shoe was thus invented. The lesson is that when faced with a complex problem, rather than looking for a complex solution, one must first try to find a simple solution.

When I went to bed on the night of our discussion in the faculty dining room, I thought of the mechanism of the reaction the researchers were carrying out. I saw a flaw in their way of interpreting the implications of that mechanism, and this misunderstanding might have been moving from one lab to another, with no one ever questioning the way their predecessors interpreted the mechanism. I thought that if my ideas about the mechanism were correct, there must be a very simple and easy way of preparing those starting materials.

The next day, I ran a pilot experiment and could not believe how beautifully it worked. I spent the next two days repeating the experiment with some variations and confirmed the identity of the product. On the fourth day, I asked all the faculty and the students from the dining room to come to my laboratory. What they saw was me slowly adding one chemical mixture from a burette to another mixture in a beaker. As I did this, they all saw a white solid precipitating as glistening crystals. I told the students to take the crystals and confirm that they were the same product that they had been taking practically a year to synthesize and purify. Needless to say, they confirmed this; the yield was 100 per cent.

Their task, which had required a year of their time, they could now complete in a matter of days and with far fewer chemicals and equipment. I then published two seminal papers.[1] These changed the course of research on this subject not only at Hull University but at many other universities and industrial labs. I became the talk of the department. Professor Chapman, who was also Lord Chapman, and who joined me as co-author on the papers, became one of my closest friends. Later, after I moved to the United States, he would come and visit me whenever he came to the country to attend various meetings.

## *Social Life in Hull*

When I was in England, I lived in the International House on Westbourne Avenue, Hull, Yorkshire. Because I was not sure how long I would stay at Hull, I did not want to rent an

1. (1.) Mechanism of Oxidative Ring Closure of Compounds of the Buta-1,3-diene-1-thiol Type with Halogens to give Thiophen Derivatives. *J. Chem. Soc.* (C), 914, 1970. (2) An Improved Synthesis of substituted Benzo-[b]-thiophene-2-carboxilic Acids and Related Acids. *Tetrahedron*, 25, 2781, 1969

apartment. The International House was a wonderful housing arrangement run by a husband-and-wife team—Mr and Mrs Whiting, whom we knew as the wardens. The Whitings were great hosts. We would have breakfast and dinner served every day, and cakes and pastries before bedtime except Sundays, when high tea would replace dinner. Most of the residents were from four countries—Nigeria, Germany, India, and Pakistan. The Nigerians and the Germans were mostly undergraduate students who relied on their families' financial strength. Most of the Pakistanis were government officers sent by their government for various types of training under the commonwealth arrangement between the countries. I was the only Indian there and the only one who did not fit either of the two descriptions.

Every weekend, the Whitings would throw a dance party where friends of the opposite sex from outside the International House were welcome. A few German girls would show up uninvited. They would be looking to meet single Indian or Pakistani men. Ever since World War II, Germany had an excess female population, and many of them came to England in search of husbands. I met one such girl who would maintain contact with me even after I moved back to the United States.

On an earlier occasion, I mentioned my futile attempt to learn guitar while I was a Sir P.C. Ray Fellow in Calcutta. That failure did not quite stop my interest in becoming a musical performer. There was a grand piano in the living room of the International House. I thought I should make another attempt to learn a musical instrument, this time the piano. I hired a German lady to give me lessons. It was another futile attempt. My friends would tell me that I spent more time looking at the teacher than at the keyboard. Jokes aside, I finally realized that I did not have a musical ear. This interest, but not the ineptitude, would later transfer to my children and grandchildren. My youngest son Raj became an accomplished pianist, and in 2020, his six-year-old daughter, Aaria, received a standing ovation at her piano recital when she played Beethoven's *Ode to Joy*.

## *The Love of My Life Returns*

While I was in England, Srimati, with whom I fell in love while I was at Ohio State University, sent me a message that she was coming to see me. She did not ask if it would be OK. She decided to come regardless. That boldness is what made this determined bachelor finally give up his determination. I took Srimati to meet Professor Chapman. Professor Chapman advised her not to tour the country like an American tourist, meaning seeing places only to be able to say that you saw them. He told Srimati that there were hundreds of years of history hidden in places like Hull and to think about them when she went to other parts of the city. His goal was to convince Srimati that I should consider staying at Hull. Anyway, we did not have much time and had to adopt the American way. We travelled by train and boat from London to Inverness and enjoyed every stop along the way. In the end, I proposed marriage to her—the time and place were yet to be determined.

One negative thing about living in England was that, although I was highly respected on campus and in any professional environment, when I went out shopping or for other purposes, I felt that, as an Indian, I was treated by many Britons as a second-class person. The situation may have changed somewhat now, but in those days, it was quite prominent. The situation was quite the opposite in the United States, where Indians were treated with high regard. The reason might have been that in England there was a large population of first-generation menial migrant labour from the Indian subcontinent, while most of the first-generation migrants from India to the United States were professionals. Even then, as now, there was not a single patient who had not been treated by an Indian doctor while visiting a US hospital.

## *Considering a Return to the United States*

After I finished the manuscripts of my seminal papers on benzo-[b]-thiophens (these would be published in 1969 and 1970 as mentioned earlier), Professor Chapman asked me if I would consider a permanent faculty position at Hull. I thought if I had to live outside India, I would rather live in the United States. First, I did not like the way ordinary Britons treated foreigners, particularly Indians. They had a term for us. They called all Indians "Pakoos", meaning migrant Pakistanis who performed menial labour in England. You saw them in rail stations, and you saw them in the airports. I felt uneasy living in a country whose citizens by and large did not respect the dignity of labour.

Another equally important reason was that I did not want Srimati to abandon her graduate studies. When Srimati came to visit me in England, she had already finished her coursework for a PhD in molecular biology at New York University and was in the middle of completing her experimental work. While we were engaged but living apart, I missed her keenly every day and felt the urge to go back to the United States. Because I did not consider any profession other than teaching, I wrote letters to several US universities seeking teaching positions. Most did not have positions open at the time but wanted me to keep in touch in case something did open up. Dartmouth had an opening; it was looking for an assistant professor in organic chemistry and invited me for an interview. But I wanted a job offer, not an interview. Such an offer came from Michigan Technological University (Michigan Tech) in Houghton, Michigan. When I applied for that teaching position, however, I never checked the academic ranking of the institution. That was not important to me. I had confidence in myself. The most important thing for me was that the university had modern research facilities and was willing to give me enough lab space to carry out my research. Michigan Tech offered both, so I accepted their offer.

I told Professor Chapman that I would be moving to the United States. He tried to convince me one more time to stay at Hull, but when I mentioned that I left my fiancée in the United States, he understood.

## Back to the United States

### *Assistant Professor, Michigan Technological University and Getting Married (1968)*

I returned to the United States in August 1968. After spending a couple of weeks in New York, where Srimati was working on her PhD at NYU, I moved to Houghton, Michigan, a town on the northernmost peninsula of Upper Michigan. I was offered a university faculty apartment for my residence. It was a beautiful two-bedroom apartment on the top of a hill with awesome views. After a few days, Srimati called me and said that she did not want to live alone. She decided to give up her ambition for PhD and would submit her thesis for a master's degree instead. She said that her mind was made up and she would be leaving for Houghton in a few days. When she came to Houghton, I put her in a hotel and applied for a marriage licence. Once we got the licence, we went to see a local justice of the peace to marry us. When we arrived there, a big sign was fixed to the door, saying: "Gone Fishing, will be back in seven days." We could not wait seven days. So, we went to the next county. That justice of the peace married us in front of witnesses that were his office staff. We both said "I do" to the vow he asked us to take.

We were officially married on 14 November 1968. Srimati did not have a wedding gown. There were no flower girls for her. I did not have a best man present. We were married without any friends or relatives at the wedding.

Later, we gave a reception to which we invited university faculty and some Indian families I had met on campus. I did not, however, let any of my friends or relatives in India know of our wedding, fearing an adverse reaction from my mother if she heard that I married without her permission or knowledge. I decided to tell her at an appropriate time. Fifty years later, I told Srimati that we should celebrate our golden anniversary with pomp and splendour and have a Hindu priest marry us. Srimati said since it has worked so well so far there was no need to try anything else, so we decided not to celebrate our golden anniversary.

The campus of Michigan Tech was very nice during the fall. The faculty also welcomed me very enthusiastically. I particularly remember several faculty members being excited to do joint or interactive projects with me. Among them were Leslie Leifer (professor), Vernon R. Sandal (associate professor), and David H. Kenny (associate professor). Professor L.B. Hein, chairman of the Department of Chemistry, gave a welcome party for Srimati and me that we appreciated very much.

Mrs Hein gave Srimati a nice pair of ice skates. Srimati, however, knew nothing about skating.

I enjoyed teaching, something I had not done for four years. My last teaching assignments were at City College and Calcutta University from 1960 to 1964. The responses I received from the students at Michigan Tech and the feedback from other professors were very positive and full of compliments. I felt good about that. There is nothing more satisfying than hearing from your students that you are their favourite teacher. I had an open-door policy, and I encouraged students to come to my office anytime if they needed help in understanding any part of my lectures. They were very appreciative of this policy. Most often they would not come to understand what I taught but to chat with me about their career goals.

### *Blue Beauty*

Realizing that it would be impossible to get around in Houghton without a car, we bought a used blue Chrysler New Yorker from the chef of the university cafeteria for $275. It was a big car with an impressive console with many push-button controls. We fell in love with that beauty. We would drive around to nearby cities and have a wonderful time. A few days after I bought the car, someone hit its rear bumper while it was in the parking lot of a grocery store. The insurance company settled the claim for $250. Since the car was drivable and the look of a dented bumper did not bother us, we kept the money and kept driving the car.

Our pleasant impression of Houghton began to change when winter set in and snow started to fall. We soon became familiar with subzero temperatures and snow accumulating up to the tip of road signs. Every car needed tire chains to drive on that snow. On New Year's Eve, we were invited to a party. One Dr Kakkar, who was also a professor at Michigan Tech and lived with his family in the same faculty housing compound as we were, was also invited to the same party. Dr Kakkar asked me to drive his family to the party because I had a big car. I agreed, although he knew the roads better than I did, as he had lived there for several years.

As I started to drive, Dr Kakkar gave me a piece of winter-driving advice. He said that if I ever applied the brakes to stop the car completely, I might not be able to make it move again. The rear tires would merely spin and create grooves in the snow; there would be no forward movement. So he advised me to never stop, not even at a stop sign. Of course, we were sure to encounter several stop signs along the way. At one of them, I had to make a right turn onto a highway. I asked Dr Kakkar to look for any approaching cars from the left before I took the turn. Dr Kakkar said that the coast was clear, so I took the turn without stopping.

As luck would have it, as soon as I took the turn, a car came straight through from the left and hit the left front fender of my car. My car spun around and came to rest in a snowbank, which saved us from further harm. The car that hit me ran away. Fortunately, my car engine did not stop and though we lost the left fender, the car was still drivable. Our youthful energy and intense desire to attend the party came into full play at that moment. I drove to the party and we all had a good time.

The next morning, Srimati and I assessed the car's damage. Aside from missing its front left fender, it was otherwise quite functional, so we decided not to call the insurance company. The price of the car had already been paid by the insurance company due to a prior incident. We thought that it would be morally wrong to get another payment from the insurance company. The car, however, developed another problem. In the cold weather, it would not start in the morning. We were told this was because of some leak in its electrical system. We found a solution: keep the battery disconnected at night and connect it in the morning.

With this car, we took long trips and went to see friends in Minnesota and Buffalo, New York. During our last trip, oil started to leak from the engine, and we had to stop every 50 or 100 miles to put fresh oil in it. Then, the power steering also failed, and it became a struggle to drive such a big car without power steering. It was time for us to part ways with "Blue Beauty", the name we lovingly gave to it. I called the used/junk car dealer nearby. He said if he could drive it to his lot, he would give me $50 for it. But if he had to tow it to his lot, I would have to pay him $50. The dealer was able to drive it to his lot, and he gave us the $50. We were as sad to lose Blue Beauty as we would have been to lose a member of our family. It served us well, we drove it for less than free, coming out $25 ahead.

Eventually, the severe winter in Houghton got the best of us. Even so, my friend Professor Leifer told me that you could not find any cleaner air anywhere than in Houghton. He also said that he gave up an opportunity to teach at Harvard to live in this place. He said that once I got acquainted with the snow, I would start loving the area. I, however, thought that for warm-blooded animals like my wife and me, it was much too cold to become comfortable with. But the final straw concerning our discomfort came when summer arrived. The intensity of the summer heat, at least on some days, was as severe as the intensity of the winter cold. Srimati got blisters under her feet after walking outside on her bare feet. That was it. I had to find another job in a somewhat more temperate part of the country. We also needed to buy a new car. I toyed with the idea of having a corporate job to make some money and then find an academic position in a more suitable place.

5

# Life in Corporate America

## *FMC Corporation, 1969–72*

(Ages 29–32)

Dr Chakrabarti was the best research scientist I have seen in the last ten years.

—Dr G.P. Volpp
Manager, R&D
FMC Corporation, 10 April 1971

You might be the brightest scientist here, but if you were given my job, you would fall flat on your face.

—Dr Sherman Reed
VP Central Research
FMC Corporation, January 1972

When I was looking for a corporate job in the summer of 1969, I had not yet formed a coherent plan for my future. All

I had was a loosely formed idea about what I would like to do in my job. I knew my strengths. I was good at research, and this was confirmed by the raving praises that my DSc thesis received from its examiners, by the success of my research at Ohio State University, and by my contributions at Hull, where my work changed the course of the department's research forever. I was good at teaching, as confirmed by the feedback I received from my lectures and guidance at City College, from the lectures I gave at the University College of Science, from the demand I had as a private tutor, and from the commendations I received for teaching at Michigan Tech.

I also had good communication skills, as I always received great praise when I gave formal talks or presented my papers at scientific meetings. I knew that a key to effective communication was to continually assess one's talk and adjust it to the knowledge level of the audience, especially to its knowledge of the topic. Effective talks are never one-size-fits-all. When teaching a freshman class, I would start from the most basic concepts, which I would skip while teaching a graduate class. For those higher-level students, I would tend to discuss how the subject had broader implications for development in the field. When presenting a paper before a professional group, I would begin by talking about what they were going to hear in the paper, pinpoint the gap in our knowledge, and what they would hear in my presentation about how my research addressed those gaps before talking about details. The approach I found most effective in professional communication was first to generate a focused interest and then to satisfy that interest with laser-sharp precision.

I knew that these strengths would be valuable in a teaching/research job, but I did not know how my skills and aspirations would fit in a corporate environment. All I knew at that time was that a corporate position would allow me to satisfy an immediate financial need and offer me time to think about my future.

After I decided that Houghton was not going to be the place where I would spend another year, I started to seek corporate research jobs. I wrote letters to the research directors of several top-rank chemical companies. The responses were better than what I had expected. Quite a few of those companies invited me in for interviews. The first interview I took was at the Central Research Center of FMC Corporation in Princeton, New Jersey. The main reason for selecting this as my first choice was its location.

## The Interview

At the interview, I was asked to be the speaker for that day at their weekly seminar series, which most of the researchers at the centre attended. My host was the assistant director of research, Dr Hugo Stange. I talked about my graduate research and my research at Hull. I had already attached a testimonial from Professor Chapman with my application. The talk went very well, as I could assess from the big applause I received upon finishing my talk. I then talked to a few senior people and research managers one-on-one. Hugo then invited several research managers to join us for lunch at a Princeton restaurant. I thought of Srimati. She came with me to Princeton. I had left her at the Holiday Inn across the road from the research center. I asked Hugo if it would be okay if my wife joined us. Had it been anytime later, when I was more savvy about corporate etiquette, I would have never made such a request. But Hugo was gracious and said that it would be a pleasure if she would be willing to join us for lunch. I went in Hugo's car, and we picked up Srimati on our way.

During the lunch, most of our talk centred around my work, particularly what I did at Hull. One major programme at Princeton concerned agricultural chemicals, and so the heterocyclic chemistry that I developed at Hull was of particular interest to the agriculture group.

## My Decision to Join FMC

After returning from lunch, Hugo took me to the office of the vice president and director of the research centre, Dr Sherman Reed, and introduced me to him. It was just a formality. We then walked to Hugo's office, where he offered me a job and told me that I could join one of the two groups overseen by the research manager. He then went on to recommend that I join the group led by research manager Dr Gert Volpp.

I then went to Gert's office, where he told me about his background. Born in July 1930, Gert was ten years older than me. He was a PhD summa cum laude from the University of Basel, where he studied under Nobel laureate Tadeus Reichstein. He then led a postdoctoral group under Nobel laureate Robert Burn Woodward at Harvard before joining FMC's Central Research Center.

I could not believe my ears when Gert said that he had worked in Woodward's lab. Woodward was my hero, and it was his total synthesis of cholesterol and strychnine that motivated me to choose the total synthesis of brazilin as the topic for my

DSc research. I thought I was looking at my hero through Gert Volpp, a stout five-foot-seven specimen of German stock with a sharp nose, extremely thin lips, a near-sculptured face, and penetrating eyes. When he spoke, his words were measured, and self-confidence glowed from his demeanour as he spoke. I was sold. I did not have to talk to anyone else. I decided to join Volpp's research group. Apart from Gert, I found so many other brilliant scientists at the FMC's Central Research Center that I changed my opinion about a job in industry. I saw how research in corporate America was moving the country forward. My respect for research in industrial settings increased thereafter.

## Change of Project: From Synthetic Pesticides to Detergent Builders

I joined FMC Corporation's Central Research Center in Princeton in August 1969. Initially, I was supposed to work on the synthesis of novel agricultural pesticides—an area of business identified at the corporate level to be strategic. But as soon as I started my work, another area of high interest piqued the research centre's curiosity.

FMC Corporation was a major supplier of phosphates (especially sodium tri-polyphosphate) to the detergent industry. In detergents, phosphates act as "builders" by making detergents work more efficiently. FMC's major customers for detergent phosphates were the manufacturers of laundry detergents such as Procter & Gamble. Concern about phosphate pollution in the nation's lakes, however, appeared to be leading to a prohibition against them.

Phosphates facilitate the eutrophication of lakes because they are essentially a fertilizer for algae. High phosphate levels in lakes, therefore, lead to algal blooms, which consume most of a lake's dissolved oxygen and thereby suffocate other aquatic life. With detergent phosphates representing 3 per cent of the corporation's sales, finding a replacement for phosphates became an urgent priority.

The pressure to create such a replacement only increased in light of a patent that had been issued to F.L. Diehl of Procter & Gamble (USP 3,308,067, issued on 7 March 1967). This patent covered a group of chemicals called polymeric polyelectrolytes, which appeared to be the only class of non-phosphate chemicals that worked competitively with phosphate-based detergent builders. Consequently, FMC was in a panic over the prospect that it might lose its phosphate detergent business if Procter & Gamble made their detergents using their builders based on the Diehl patent. A large group of chemists from both the inorganic and organic research groups at FMC was working on the project, but progress was slow.

Thinking that the field might benefit from an independent look from someone outside the field, Hugo Stange and Gert Volpp asked me to assess FMC's research in the area. I had never been involved with the chemistry of surfactants (the main component in detergents), let alone the builders that increase the effectiveness of the surfactants in washing something.

To make a worthwhile assessment, I had to fully understand not only the chemistry of surfactants and builders but also the physico-chemical phenomena that bind soil to cloth and that facilitate the release of soil from cloth. I also had to understand how water quality affected those properties. I wanted to see what made Diehl's patent unique and why no one could synthesize a non-phosphate builder without the patented process. I spent two weeks studying the chemical and physical properties of surfactants, phosphate detergent builders, polyelectrolytes, and even related chemicals called anti-redeposition agents (chemicals that prevent released soil from re-adhering to cloth). I asked Volpp to arrange a seminar where I would present a comprehensive review of the field and then receive questions from our resident experts.

I gave that seminar less than a month after I joined FMC, and all the scientists, managers, assistant directors, and Director Sherman Reed attended it. After the main talk, I broke down the task forward into three sections: 1) develop a new group of polyelectrolyte builders outside the scope of the Diehl patent, 2) develop a new field of soil-release chemicals that would not need built detergents for washing, and 3) design surfactants that would work well without builders. Reed, Stange, and Volpp saw awesome business opportunities in what I presented. Stange and Volpp said that it was the first time they got a comprehensive view of what they would need to address the problems in the field.

Later that day, Stange called me in his office. Volpp was already there. They wanted me to spearhead an exploratory group to pursue some of the things I proposed in the seminar. So, I hired three qualified junior chemists—Andrew Kirk, Tom Guralski, and Frank Scott—to help me in my experimental lab. I also had two other senior researchers cooperating with me—Dr Eckhardt Lindemann for biodegradability studies and Jerry Saldick for detergency evaluation. I was asked to devote 100 per cent of my time to the detergent builder project and abandon my work on the synthetic pesticide project. I also saw a challenge in developing a new field of inquiry.

Once I defined the scope of the project and prepared an outline of the jobs to be performed, progress occurred at great speed, much faster than even I had imagined. I carpet-bombed the entire field of polyelectrolyte detergent builders with new patents, leaving only an island of compositions to the Diehl patent. This brought a big sigh of relief to FMC business managers. Simultaneously, I also pursued the development of soil-release additives that would work with permanent-press finishes to make washing even more effective. For all of this, FMC rewarded me with two consecutive promotions—from research chemist to senior research chemist I and senior research chemist II over the next two years. During 1970 and 1971, I received the highest raises, in percentage, ever given to any scientist at the centre.

FMC also allowed me to wrap up some of the research I was pursuing at Michigan Tech. In 1971, I presented a paper on the Friedel–Crafts reaction of 1,3-dichloroacetone (a work I started at Michigan Tech but could not complete there) at the sixth north-east regional meeting of the American Chemical Society in Atlantic City—Abs. No. Org. 51. Srimati and I enjoyed visiting Atlantic City. It was our first trip to this city that was famous for hosting the annual Miss America Pageant.

## First Taste of the American Dream

To make me happy, Hugo Stange told me that FMC owned a residential house in the nearby city of Yardville, and if I wanted, I could buy it from the company at book value, which would be about seven or eight thousand dollars less than the market value. We bought the house in early 1971. We owned our own house for the first time in our life, on Fenway Road. Our mortgage payment was no higher than the rent we were paying for our two-bedroom apartment. Srimati also took a job as a research associate at the New Jersey Neuro-Psychiatric Institute near Princeton. We bought two cars—a new Bonneville and a used Pontiac LeMans. We quickly started to experience the middle-class American dream. We would invite our friends to our house, and they would invite us back to their apartments.

In 1971, Professor Chapman came to the United States as a visiting professor at Duke University. On his way to North Carolina, he stopped in New Jersey to spend a few days with us. He stayed with us in our newly owned house, and I arranged for him to give a seminar at FMC. We also showed him around. There was an embarrassing moment during the time we took him to see the various places nearby. One place we stopped was Washington Crossing, a historical site where George Washington's army defeated a garrison of Hessians who fought for the British in the Revolutionary War. At Washington Crossing, a video of that victory played repeatedly on a big screen. We noticed that the video show seemed to agitate Chapman. In the end, he said that "had it not been for a stupid mistake by a stupid British general, history would be different". We were embarrassed that we brought him there, but aside from that history lesson, Chapman enjoyed his stay with us and wrote a wonderful thank-you letter from Duke.

From the perspective of our professions, our work, our economic condition, and our interaction with friends, we felt that life was good.

## Trouble at Home: Tempest and Calm

While we were enjoying our professional and social lives at this time, turmoil was brewing in another aspect of our lives. In 1970, I sponsored four members of my family—my parents, Partha, and Ashutosh, my younger brother—to immigrate to the United States. I brought them to my apartment in Hightstown, New Jersey, where they met Srimati for the first time. My mother was furious when she found out I was married and refused to accept Srimati as her daughter-in-law. Her formal objection was that Srimati did not come from a Brahmin family—but I believe the real reason was that I married without her permission.

I had to rent another apartment for Srimati until I could solve the problem. To ease my mother's anger, I bought Partha and Ashutosh a brand-new car, but that did not help. Ashutosh and Partha, both being fellows of the prestigious London Institute of Actuaries, sought jobs in the insurance industry. But, as most of the largest insurance companies had their headquarters in New York City, driving a personal car and finding a place to park was more of a challenge than a benefit. So, I rented an apartment for them in the city and promised to pay the rent until Partha and Ashutosh got good jobs. My mother took all our furniture from our Hightstown apartment to their New York apartment. I did not object, hoping that that would calm her anger. But it did not, and that was not the end.

When Srimati came back to the apartment and saw that I had given away all the furniture, she started to show her rage against me. She said that she had carefully decorated the apartment and thoughtfully chosen the various pieces of furniture. How could I give them away and not care about her emotions? I calmed her down by buying the same brand and colour of furniture for the apartment. Both Ashutosh and Partha soon landed very good jobs in the city and they moved with our parents to a bigger and nicer apartment. So, the immediate problem was solved, but I was made an outcast by my family even though I performed my "duty" to provide my share of the family's expenses. I also had to visit New York once every week to take care of whatever needs the family might have during the coming week. Eventually, we established a temporary truce. None of my colleagues or our friends ever knew what a storm I had weathered.

## My Decision to Leave FMC

Though I was making great progress in my project, I decided to leave FMC because of a political development that I felt was unfair. In early 1972, FMC was reorganizing the research centre and in this process, one of the research scientists who worked in the inorganic chemistry department for several years but got his PhD from Princeton only three years previously was promoted to research manager. This surprised many of the senior scientists, and all of them thought that it was due to his connections at higher levels in the company. I protested to Gert and Hugo, telling them that if anyone deserved to be promoted to research manager, it was I.

They told me that they had no control over such promotions—if I wanted to take up the case, I should talk to Sherman Reed. I went to see Reed. He was initially very polite and told me that management skills are different than technical skills. He said that I could soon be considered for promotion to research fellow in recognition of my technical contributions. What made me fume with anger inside was when he said that I might be the brightest technical person at the centre, but that was not enough for a managerial position. As brilliant a scientist as I was, if I were to be given his job, he said, I would fall flat on my face.

I never felt more insulted in my life. Had my foreign origin disqualified me for a managerial position? In those days, there were not very many Indians in managerial positions in big corporations. I told Reed that I did not agree with him and that technical management is more than managing people; providing technical leadership should be the priority. With that, I left his office without making any more comments, thinking I would prove him wrong.

My interest in surfactants and their mode of action led me to consider joining a company that had a major surfactant business. I thought I could make an even more profound contribution in such an environment than I was making at FMC. Such an opportunity soon arose. GAF Corporation, one of the most prominent suppliers of specialty surfactants (meaning surfactants for high-end markets) had an opening for a surfactant research group leader. The position reported directly to the director of chemical research at the company, Dr Frederic Grosser. At that time, GAF was a big corporation with three divisions—chemicals, photography (especially colour films), and building products (especially roofing materials and sidings).

During World War II, the US government assumed control of all German properties on US soil, which GAF was back then. It had since been released from that control and was now a publicly traded company on the New York Stock Exchange. GAF's chemical research centre was part of their manufacturing compound in Linden, New Jersey. In the tradition of many German chemical companies, GAF's top executive—its chairman, Dr Jesse Werner—came up through its chemical R&D department. I thought it would be an interesting company to work for, so I applied for the advertised position.

I went for an interview with GAF at Linden, NJ, and they wound up offering me the job of leading their surfactant research group. At first, I hesitated to work at a manufacturing site that was different from the park-like setting of FMC Corporation's Central Research Center in Princeton. Realizing my hesitation, Dr Grosser mentioned that the company had just acquired the research centre of Uniroyal on a hilltop in Wayne, NJ, and that the chemical R&D department would soon move there. He told me to visit the place and call him back if I was still interested in the offer. Srimati and I went to see the new R&D location. It was a picturesque site—a sprawling complex overlooking the valleys, and at night, the campus had a clear view of the New York City skyline. We fell in love with Wayne, and so the next day I called Dr. Grosser and told him that I would accept the job but would need at least a month to wrap things up at Princeton before I could start.

On 31 March 1972, Dr Grosser sent me the appointment letter for group leader, Surfactants. I started on 15 May and initially reported to the Linden office, moving to Wayne in July. Linden was less than 30 miles from my house in Yardville, but Wayne was, unfortunately, more than 80 miles away.

In June, we put our house on Fenway Road up for sale, and we sold it within twenty-four hours. We bought this house at the beginning of 1971, sold it in July 1972, and made a profit of $10,000. In Wayne, we bought a larger, four-bedroom colonial house on Ratzer Road. It was less than a mile from my new office in Wayne.

FMC was sad to hear about my decision to leave. Gert Volpp gave a big departing party in my honour. This party was at the same restaurant where I had my hiring luncheon. I worked for two years and nine months at FMC. One chapter of my corporate life was over and another was about to begin. Dr Gert Volpp died on 8 February 2019, at the age of eighty-eight in his house in Princeton, New Jersey. In April 2019, his surviving daughter, Sophie Volpp, now on the faculty at UC-Berkeley, reached out to my assistant, Ms Patti Griggs, and wrote, "My father spoke of Dr Chakrabarti several times in the week before he died. It meant a great deal to him that Dr Chakrabarti had achieved such great success." She asked Patti if I would be willing to speak at Dr Volpp's memorial service later that month. I gladly accepted the invitation. Had I known that Gert was talking about me before he died, I would have surely visited him before he breathed his last.

# 6

# Life in Corporate America

## *GAF Corporation, 1972–82*

## (Ages 32–42)

Dr. Chakrabarti has demonstrated an outstanding ability ... in one year he has earned the respect of his group as well as his peers and members of marketing and manufacturing.

—Dr F. Grosser
Director, R&D, GAF
1 May 1973

Dr. Chakrabarti is rated as the top section manager in my department because of his aggressive, creative, and productive performance and leadership.

— Dr F. Grosser
Director, R&D, GAF
1 May 1975

> [Saw the news of your promotion to Director of Research] … If there is one thing I did at GAF, it was to identify talent. You are. And as I said to Ms. Moran [Exec. VP & Vice Chair, GAF], if I were ever to have a statue in my backyard with a vigil light at its base, it would be in the image and likeness of Paritosh.
>
> —John G. Hughes
> Vice-President
> Booz Allen Venture Management
> 22 September 1977

> This is, of course, based on Dr. Chakrabarti's work and is a very nice development.
>
> —P.B. Dalton
> President, GAF to Dr Werner, the Chairman
> 22 March 1980

I joined GAF Corporation in May 1972 as a group leader, surfactant research, reporting directly to Dr Fred Grosser, director of chemical research—barely two years and nine months after I started my first corporate job at FMC Corporation. Reporting directly to me were three senior scientists—Dr Lou Nehmsmann, head of synthesis; Mr John Griffo, head of industrial applications; and Robert Verdicchio, head of personal care applications. These scientists each had two or three technicians working for them.

During the first three months, my office was at GAF's manufacturing complex in Linden, NJ. At Linden, the company still maintained the old German system. I had a large office with a private attached bath. I also had a sink in my office—also typically European. There were also separate elevators for managers, which I was. This looked odd in the United

States, but at Linden, GAF was comfortable maintaining its old customs.

## Getting to Know the Company

It took me some time to get acquainted with GAF's organizational structure. GAF's corporate headquarters were in New York City on the fifth floor of 40 West 51st Street. I went there to meet the sales and marketing people—particularly Raymond Smith, VP of sales and marketing, Chemicals; Fred Krupin, director of marketing, Surfactants; and Jay McAndrews, director of sales, Surfactants. Smith showed me around the various executive offices. He showed me Chairman Jesse Werner's suite and told me that he had a private chef to cook lunch for him. He also introduced me to Juliet Moran, executive VP, and told me that she was a very powerful woman. I saw the glamour and excesses of the top executives of corporate America—something I did not see before and not while I was at FMC.

Smith, Krupin, and McAndrews took me out to lunch. Krupin told me that surfactants had once been the most profitable business unit in the chemicals division, but that it lately had become the least profitable. He outlined the priorities for R&D—chief among them being the quality of and cost to produce GAF's line of non-foaming surfactants, trade-named the Antaroxes®. He said that he had to decide whether to keep that line alive or to discontinue it. If a product line could not generate a 35 per cent gross margin, he said, corporate guidelines called for discontinuing it. The Antaroxes were on the chopping block according to corporate guidelines. He told me that if I could improve the production cost so that we can get back to a 35 per cent gross margin, I would be a hero at the company. At that time, I did not know what the real problem was but promised to look at it. Krupin said that the batch time was ninety hours and that no product could be profitable with such long a batch time.

## The First Success at GAF

As I was driving back from New York, I thought about how I helped to reduce the time required to make the starting chemicals for the graduate students at the University of Hull from years to weeks. I hoped that there would be ways to cut down the production cycle time of the Antarox products, but I was not sure if that alone could save the product line. I also knew that the first impressions of my ability were going to be important in how I would be treated going forward within GAF.

The next day when I went to my Linden office, I asked Dr Lou Nehmsmann, an imposing, six-foot-five figure, to come and see me. I asked him to explain why the cycle time of the Antaroxes was so long and if there were any other issues with these products. He said that there were two issues—colour and cost of production. The highly acidic condition under which the reaction occurred, he said, generated too many colour bodies, which in combination appeared dark brown, to be acceptable for sale. I asked him what colour was acceptable. He said the marketing group would accept a light brown colour. I asked him what he was doing to solve these problems. He said the only solution to the colour problem was to run the reaction under mild conditions, which in this case meant running the reaction at a lower temperature. The problem was that, when the reaction occurred at a lower temperature, it took more time to complete, and that increased costs. He said that there was no other solution if the marketing group insisted on having a low-color product. I told him to describe the chemistry in detail, and he did. While we were talking, an idea of what the problem was with the process occurred to me.

The idea was related to an experience I had while in Professor Newman's lab in Columbus, Ohio. It concerned distilling a pure compound from a tarry mass under a vacuum. I had described this experience before very briefly, and now I remembered the details. The boiling point of the pure compound I was trying to recover was around 195°C. I set up an elaborate arrangement—a hot-oil bath for heating, a distillation column, and a stirrer for the viscous mass that would only become more viscous as I distilled my product. I was prepared for the process to take several hours.

At that point, Professor Newman entered my lab. He said "Paritosh, remove all these arrangements for the time being. Let me show you what I would do as the first step with products like this."

He then used a Bunsen burner to heat the flask, and, without any column, flashed out as much liquid as he could. That liquid had a medium-brown colour and low viscosity; a tar remained in the distillation flask. He said that I could now use my arrangement to fractionally distill the brown liquid to obtain the pure product. I found that most of the brown liquid was my product, which was a water-white liquid that I recovered in high yield. The high yield resulted from not having to deal with the tar during the fractional distillation.

Apparently, my conventional set-up exposed the crude product for a long time to a moderately high temperature, thus promoting more tar formation, which made the distillation of the pure product increasingly difficult. After taking Prof. Newman's suggestion, the entire operation—flash distillation followed by fractional distillation—took one-fifth of the original time. In other words, the operation became less troublesome despite the (very short) exposure to the much higher temperature.

I thought that something similar might be happening with GAF's Antarox process. If my intuition was correct, what Nehmsmann was doing was exactly the opposite of what was required. The reaction involved some of the harshest chemicals known and generated copious quantities of hydrogen chloride, a highly acidic gas, which, when dissolved in water becomes hydrochloric acid. I suspected that the culprit was the long exposure of the reactants to the harshly acidic by-product.

I told Nehmsmann to set up a few lab-scale experiments that I would run myself. I knew that the only way to get a real feel for the reactions would be to run them myself. That way, I could observe the subtle changes that might occur. I ran several experiments at various temperatures—from 50°C (the existing process) to as high as 100°C. As a rough rule, reaction rates generally increase threefold for every 10°C. So, by running the reaction at, say, 90°C rather than 50°C, we should be able to reduce the reaction time eighty-one-fold. The reactions run at a higher temperature and for a significantly shorter time gave lighter-colour products. I told Nehmsmann to test the quality of the product and report the results to me.

The next day, both the analytical and synthesis groups came to me and said that the products met or exceeded all quality-control specifications, and the colours were from pale yellow to light brown—the palest colouring they had ever seen for this product according to their colour-scale rating. I then asked Nehmsmann to see me with the production manager. I told the production manager to make whatever modifications to the production equipment that were necessary so that the reaction would occur in one hour rather than in ninety hours, but at a temperature of between 90°C and 100°C. He assured us that very little modification of the equipment would be necessary. They then ran a production-scale preparation. The product met all specifications: the colour rating was much better than acceptable, and, more importantly, the calculated gross margin was much higher than the guideline of 35 per cent. The news spread quickly to the New York office, and Fred Krupin came to see me at my Linden office. He called me a genius and said that I had saved a product line from its death. He further said that, with that light colour, they should be able to sell even more products.

For many years, I was not allowed to reveal how I solved this problem. But now, because all this happened more than forty-five years ago and I am no longer bound by the company's confidentiality requirements, I can tell this story.

In research as in other life experiences, the key to creativity is to be able to apply experiences we learn in one area to another. In the above example, each experience—my lesson from Prof. Newman and the problem with Antaroxes production—involved a different sort of chemistry; the real creativity was finding the deep-seated relationships between the two. This required what we call intuition. No scientific discovery has ever been possible without first having an intuition. Of course, intuitions are fuzzy concepts, they always require modification and better definition through rigorous testing and retesting. I will further discuss this aspect of creativity in Book 3, where I will apply the principles of thermodynamics to come up with an economic arrangement superior to either capitalism or socialism.

## From Group Leader to Section Manager

The Antarox development already made me a hero to my boss, Dr Fred Grosser, and the surfactant business team. When we moved to our new research centre in Wayne, I soon realized that the surfactant department suffered from the lack of new chemistry and new products. So, in quick succession, I introduced several new and unique products, including a group of hybrid sulfonates that were a promising class of anionic surfactants with unique applications, a group of amphoteric surfactants and Igepon TC 99 (tradename for a surfactant). The marketing group even named one novel amphoteric surfactant that we developed after me—amphoteric pc (for Paritosh Chakrabarti).

In February 1974, less than two years after joining GAF, I was promoted to section manager. In recommending me for the promotion, Dr Grosser wrote the following to President Dalton:

> Since joining in May 1972, Dr. Chakrabarti has demonstrated an outstanding ability to utilize his exceptional technical knowledge and experimental technique to 1) solve several technical problems, some of longstanding duration, in the surfactants area and 2) develop several new products with significant sales and profit potential, as well as outline programs for several

> more new products ... he has also effectively directed the entire synthetic and applications efforts of the surfactant group. With this promotion, his group will consist of seven professionals, nine technicians, and a secretary.

I had a very productive time as section manager with the large size of my group, a size that would have been difficult to get had I stayed at FMC. Our product list expanded significantly, and we revised most of the existing manufacturing processes to assure the lowest-cost production and consistently superior quality. The surfactant section moved from the least profitable to the most profitable business unit in chemicals.

## GAF Starts a New Household Products Division

Our success with surfactants and their application in various household products prompted GAF to consider establishing a new division of household products. Some top-level marketing people were hired to launch this group. The idea was to compete directly with giants like Procter & Gamble. The responsibility for developing the product lines fell on me. I had to add a new group in my section dedicated to making packaged products to be sold directly to consumers. The marketing group would first run concept tests for various products, basing them on my input about our product characteristics. They then came back and gave us a list of product attributes they considered desirable.

My team would then develop the products as per the required specifications. The next steps were to conduct concept tests and then several layers of consumer tests. We developed three products—a superior anti-static softener, "Velvet Touch", for use in clothes dryers (marketed as a spray and an impregnated paper); a pre-soak stain remover, "Good Riddance", and a non-phosphate dishwasher detergent. The initial field test results were quite favourable with all these products. More about this division later.

## From Section Manager to Technical Director

Under my leadership, the surfactant group introduced many new products, new processes, and new product applications. These included alipal EP-115, biopal NR-20, antaron FC-34, agent AT-846, agent AT-811, emulphogene EL-985, igepal CA-950, gafanols, agent AT-855, the antron FC-34 process, the soramin CAZ process, gafamide CD-518D, alkanolamides, novel imidazolines, dowanol chloroacetates, new amphoteric surfactants to compete with Miranols®, and Antarox BL-330, 434, and LF-330. We filed over a dozen patents to protect those inventions. To help market them efficiently, I introduced a sales training course in which my team and I educated salespeople about the technical benefits of our products. My experience as a college professor came in handy in conducting those training courses.

I presented various papers at many national meetings, including the American Oil Chemists Society, Chicago, September 1973; the Society of Cosmetic Chemists, May 1974, Chicago; the Chemical Specialty Manufacturers' Association, May 1974; and Cosmo Expo, June 1975, New York. All these appearances helped to publicize GAF's innovations.

GAF's surfactant business became a shining example of how creative product and application development could rapidly change the character of a business. I would now be called upon by our film and building products divisions to help them whenever they faced any technical problems.

One experience comes to mind. When the building products group was designing a new production plant that would use fibreglass (instead of asbestos) as the supporting mat to make asphalt roofing, they faced a problem. Unlike asbestos fibres, fibreglass fibres tended to stick together, or tangle, when stirred in water. This meant that they had to use reaction vessels that were many times larger than what they had been using for asbestos to keep the fibreglass suspension below its tangling concentration.

Dr Kantor, vice-president of R&D at GAF, asked me if I would look at the problem. I was aware of the physico-chemical factors that caused the tangling problem. I thought the solution would be easy; we could use a group of dispersants called amine-oxide surfactants. The solution worked like a charm—no additional equipment was necessary for replacing asbestos with fibreglass. I filed four patent applications to fully cover the field. These patents—which were later issued as USP 4,178,203, 4,178,204, 4,178,206, and 4,179,331 in December 1979—would permanently change how fibreglass-based asphalt roofing shingles were made.

By 1977, I was a well-known entity in the C-suite. I wrote a report for company executives on new chemistry that I developed, and it came back with comments from the company's chairman. Dr Grosser had sent this report to the president, who in turn sent it to the chairman, Dr Werner, appending "this of course is Chakrabarti's work and is a very nice development". As Dr Werner had been a chemist before becoming a business executive, he asked me a few mechanistic questions about the chemistry I was developing, and I replied with a detailed mechanistic explanation. I was now in direct communication with the chairman at a professional level!

Early in 1977, Dr Werner, Ms Moran (executive vice-president), and Richard Fleming (president) invited me to meet them for lunch in Dr Werner's private dining room. It would be the first time I dined with the chairman and the president in a private setting. During the luncheon meeting, Dr Werner told me that the company was very pleased with my performance and that I would be promoted to the position of technical director. In that capacity, I would have all the section managers and Dr Grosser, who would be handling environmental compliance matters, reporting to me. I told Dr Werner that I appreciated his confidence in me very much, but I had just one minor request. I told him that I had such great respect for Dr Grosser that I would feel very awkward if he was reporting to me. Dr Werner said that he would ask Kantor to consider my request. So, effective 1 March 1977, I was promoted to technical director. The announcement read, "Dr. Chakrabarti replaces Dr. Grosser, whose new assignment will be announced shortly."

The following positions were now reporting directly to me:

1. Section Manager, Surfactants (to be filled)
2. Section Managers, Agricultural Chemicals (Dr Robert E. Graham and Dr. Michael Brown)
3. Section Manager, Acetylenic Products (Dr Eugene Hort)
4. Section Manager, Analytical Services (Dr Stan Frankowski)
5. Section Manager, Household Product Development group (to be filled)

Dr Grosser's secretary, Marianne, would now become my secretary. She was an outstanding person, as smart as she was efficient. It was a great help to have Marianne on my side. She knew all the people and how they interacted with the office of the director.

Various newspapers, trade journals, and magazines covered the news of my promotion. I received many letters congratulating me. One of them, coming from GAF's ex-director of the Household Products Group, John Hughes, who had recently become vice-president of Booz Allen Venture Management, read as follows.

> September 22, 1977
> Dear Paritosh
> It was a good feeling to see your "beauty shot" in a recent issue of Soap, Cosmetics, and Chemical Specialties. Congratulations on your promotion.
>
> If there is one thing that I did at GAF, it was to identify real talent. You are. And, as I said to Ms. Moran a few years ago … if I were ever to have a statue in my backyard with a vigil light at its base, it would be in the image and likeness of Paritosh!
>
> One of our subsidiaries is Foster D. Snell. So, if you ever get restless, just call.
>
> Congratulations.
> Cordially,
> John G. Hughes

My promotion from group leader first to section manager and then to technical director all came within five years of the day that I had my terse discussion with Sherman Reed, director of research at FMC, and left the company. I took a clipping of the announcement from *The New York Times* with my picture in it and sent it to Reed, with the note: "I did not fall flat on my face." I also sent a copy of my comment to Hugo Stange and Gert Volpp. Gert wrote back and said he showed my comments to all the other managers at FMC. They had a hearty laugh over it.

By then our two boys, Debtosh and Raj, were already born. We decided that it was time for us to move to a bigger house, so we built a new house of white stone with Corinthian columns on a hilltop in Cedar Grove, NJ. This was our third house—each bigger and better than the one before. Our little boys enjoyed the new house and its various amenities. We were living the American dream.

## As Its Chemical Division Prospers, GAF Unravels

We started to make great progress in all the R&D sections. I hired a new section manager, Dr Tally, for the surfactant section.

The manufacturing plant for acetylenic products (Reppe chemistry) was in Calvert City, Kentucky. I visited the plant with section manager Dr Eugene Hort and identified several opportunities to improve the various processes. We also established new programmes to develop new products and applications—new solvents, new applications for our Gantrez® and PVP polymers, new detergent additives, new corrosion inhibitors, and new chemicals such as propargyl and other acetylenic amines—based on our unique chemistry and capabilities in acetylenic chemistry.

I was not very happy, however, with how the programmes in agricultural chemicals were progressing. The programmes—

plant-growth regulators (proprietary GAF products), Blazer® (a toll production project for Rohm and Haas), manufacturing process development for Amiben® (a pre-emergence herbicide for Union Carbide), toll manufacturing of D.V. ester (a pesticide intermediate for FMC)—were disjointed projects, and I was not satisfied with the progress that was being made by its section manager, Dr Graham. So I hired Dr Michael Brown, a veteran agricultural scientist from ICI, England, to help Dr Graham. I also asked Dr Frankowski, the section manager of the analytical group, to work with the other section managers and form new product development teams.

In household products, we were making great progress, surpassing all expectations. I asked all R&D sections to participate in developing the products. Three products—an in-dryer fabric softener / anti-static in spray and impregnated paper forms (Velvet Touch®, designed to replace Procter & Gamble's Bounce), a pre-wash stain remover (Good Riddance®), and a non-phosphate machine dishwashing powder—were showing excellent promise in extended consumer trials. Rod Neuman, product manager of Household Products, could not have been more excited.

The non-phosphate dishwasher detergent created a sensation in the media with more than a dozen magazines reporting on it. Both *The New York Times* and *The Wall Street Journal* ran articles praising the development as an environmentally responsible product.

> GAF Tests Nonphosphate Dishwashing Detergent—A Breakthrough—Patent 4,203,585 describes … It was developed by Dr. Paritosh M. Chakrabarti, Technical Director for Organic Chemicals.
>
> —*New York Times*,
> 24 May 1980

> GAF Corporation Tests Non-phosphate Detergent ... GAF is hoping to complete evaluation of its newly patented phosphate-free dishwashing detergent by early 1981 ... The formula patented last month is an extension of the company's work in surfactant chemistry. It was developed by Dr. Paritosh M. Chakrabarti, technical director for organic chemicals at the company's administrative and research center in Wayne.
>
> —*Chemical Marketing Reporter*, 14 July 1980

Similar coverages appeared in many other local and national journals. The reason for such high interest was that until then, no effective machine dishwashing detergent could be formulated without phosphates, and phosphates were now being held responsible for the pollution of our lakes and rivers. The biggest fan of this product, however, was none other than the wife of Chairman Werner.

Everyone was excited about what was going on at the Chemicals Group. The management committee, comprising Dr Werner and the heads of all marketing and commercial development departments, came to the Wayne R&D centre to review our projects. Dr Kantor, vice-president of R&D, wrote the following note to me after the review meeting:

> April 22, 1981
> Dear Paritosh,
> Accept my sincere appreciation for your excellent presentation yesterday. The members of the Management Committee indicated that they spent

a worthwhile and interesting day reviewing our program.

The hard work that went into your presentation was clearly evident. Please extend my thanks to your associates who assisted you.

Sincerely.
S.W. Kantor, Vice President

We could hardly imagine that amid such raving praises of the progress that the Chemicals Division was making, things were not going well at the corporate level. A cascade of events and a set of strategy failures were unravelling the corporate giant. The crucial problem began when the company reported a $40 million pre-tax loss in its building products division in 1981. Cash dried up and some of the household product consumer tests were to be terminated or delayed. Two successive proxy fights by a little-known Connecticut real estate executive, Samuel Heyman, would soon defeat Werner's management team, take control of the company, and break it into pieces.

In the corporate world, things often happen fast. This applies to growth as well as to decline. It took five years for me to be promoted to technical director, and GAF's future looked brighter than ever. It took another five years for that fortune to turn sour and for me to consider leaving the company. Let me describe the history of the company, its evolution under Dr Werner's chairmanship, and what set the stage for my next move in a nutshell. The description below is a summary of a cover-page article, "Why GAF Did not Succeed", published in the 5 May 1982 issue of *Chemical Week* (page 42).

## GAF: A Case Study of Strategy Failure

After the Japanese attack on Pearl Harbor and the United States' entry into World War II, the US Treasury assumed control of General Aniline and Film, the US wing of the German corporate giant IG Farben (manufacturer of Zyklon B, the cyanide-based pesticide that the Nazi government used in gas chambers to kill millions). The company's board remained under the control of the US military until 1965. Dr Jesse Werner, who joined the company in 1938 as a research chemist, became the company's vice-president for research in 1959, and when the Kennedy administration came to power in 1961, he was promoted to president and CEO (rumour had it that his promotion was connected to his good relations with the Kennedy family). In 1965, the US government relinquished its control, and General Aniline and Film became a publicly traded company on the New York Stock Exchange. In 1968, the company officially changed its name from General Aniline and Film to GAF.

GAF became a highly regarded company with two formidable business divisions, chemicals and photographic products. Its chemicals business became the envy of the world—thanks to its mastery of Reppe (acetylene) chemistry, in which only two other companies, BASF and DuPont, had expertise. It also had a dominant position in the photography business with photographic films, cameras, and various reprographic products. Its photographic business was so dominant that Rensselaer, New York, where this business was located, became known as the GAF city. A leader in film technology, GAF, not Kodak, produced the film that US astronauts used to take pictures on the moon during the first manned landing there, Apollo 11 in 1969.

The company's successes, however, may have gone to Chairman and CEO Dr Jesse Werner's head. According to internal sources, Werner became very autocratic after he became the chairman and CEO. The seed of GAF's downfall may have been its acquisition of Ruberoid in 1967, which soon became GAF's building products division. The Ruberoid acquisition was part of Werner's conglomerate strategy of growth, whereby companies grew by combining various unrelated businesses. (I will show in Book 3, *The Wealth of People: A New Economic Framework*, why conglomeration, also known as the lateral integration of various businesses, is a flawed strategy.)

A year earlier, in 1966, the company had purchased the New York City classical music radio station WNCN. Speculations varied about why Werner decided to buy a radio station. According to one theory, it was his love for classical music. Another, more plausible, theory was that it was insurance against a takeover threat, particularly by foreign companies. At that time, any change in the station's ownership had to be cleared with the Federal Communications Commission.

One of the problems with the building products division was that, while GAF's other two divisions—chemicals and photographic products—were based on high technology, building products, which produced roofing and siding products, was decidedly a low-technology business. Wall Street rewards high tech and punishes low tech. Consequently, GAF's stock lost its high-tech premium on Wall Street. (I will show in the next chapter how a PPG-Scripps agreement that I negotiated while working for PPG greatly improved PPG's market valuation even before a cent was spent on the project.)

The more serious problem, however, was asbestos. Traditional roofing products were based on asbestos fibers.

With asbestos facing the threat of a nationwide ban, changing manufacturing processes to use fibreglass-based technology became a matter of extreme urgency that required massive investment. Although transitional technologies had already been developed (I have described them earlier), the additional expenses and increased operational costs caused the division to post a pre-tax loss of about $40 million in 1981.

The photographic business also faced an unprecedented challenge. While GAF management was busy fixing its building products business, photographic rival Kodak stole a march and introduced its Instamatic 110 camera while simultaneously re-entering the film development market with a unique technology that could be used to develop only its films. GAF considered this to be an anti-competitive move and sued Kodak. But by the time it took for GAF to win the battle of its antitrust lawsuit against Kodak, early in 1982, the war was lost. GAF no longer had a leading position in the consumer film market, Kodak had overtaken it.

When I joined GAF in May 1972, none of the above weaknesses were visible. GAF was a Fortune 200 company with a bright future. It had an unbroken record of paying dividends for thirty-eight consecutive quarters.

Autocratic as he was, Dr Werner was also a master at passing the blame for failure onto others. Between 1977 and 1982 he had three presidents—Richard Fleming (1977–1978, ten months), Phillip P. Dalton (1979–1981, twenty-five months), and Jay Olson (1981, five months). The chemical division was pleased with Dalton's leadership, but he lost his job on the flimsy grounds that he allowed a customer to visit the Linden Plant without Werner's permission. Dr Werner, who was to have retired in 1982, was given another five-year contract by a friendly board. At that point, Olson, who aspired to become chairman after Werner's expected retirement, resigned.

In 1981, things started to take a turn for the worse after building products posted that pre-tax loss of $40 million. The major shareholders revolted. They wanted GAF to sell its divisions individually to unlock their underlying values. The biggest challenge came from diminutive Connecticut real estate executive Samuel Heyman. Heyman, who owned only 4 per cent of GAF shares, launched a proxy fight. After withdrawing from an earlier challenge in exchange for certain promises from the company, he returned, this time winning the fight and seizing control of the company. GAF was eventually dismantled with only the chemicals business remaining at Wayne, although under a new name, International Specialty Products, or ISP for short. The film business became part of Fujifilm, and the building products became the new GAF. ISP, however, remained one of the most profitable specialty chemicals businesses in the United States.

## My Decision to Leave GAF

Early in 1982, Dr Kantor called me. He said that he and Jay Olson wanted to have lunch with me at the Harvard Club in New York. Olson had already resigned from GAF as its president. They suggested that the three of us should join forces and acquire one or more chemical companies. They said that my knowledge of the chemical industries would be critical in forming such a venture. We evaluated several candidates, including a private-label cosmetic company. None were attractive. With GAF in turmoil, I, like many other top executives, decided to leave the company. I had a highly attractive offer from ppg Industries, and I decided to accept it. Kantor took a faculty position at the University of Massachusetts, Amherst. Many other executives—including Louis G. Zachary, senior vice-president for chemicals—also resigned during that time.

## Concluding Remarks

As I mentioned above, GAF's chemical division was renamed and incorporated as ISP after the parent was dismantled. A *Chemical Week* article on 15 December 1982, reported that GAF's former chemicals business "ranked fourth among the top 100 U.S. chemical producers in operating return on assets … it is one of the soundest operations around". As I read that report, it occurred to me that most of ISP's products and processes carried my signature all over them. I wished that they had people who could move the unfinished programmes forward, but unfortunately, most of the creative people had left by that time.

Every grand idea, be it in science, business, or social matters, arises and matures in an individual brain but finds its implementation through a team. When the originator (or the womb of its maturation) is also the leader of the team, success is almost guaranteed. If any of the links in the chain—idea, leader, or team—breaks, the project falters. FMC's Sherman Reed missed this point when he told me that a brilliant scientist could not be a brilliant manager. It may not always be easy to find such a combination of skills in a person, but not trying to find one is a great management failure.

Sherman Reed missed an opportunity for his company on that day when he and I talked. I left FMC and joined to prove that point. My success at GAF was the result of being able to maintain that chain. Some of the projects that I started and that presented immense opportunities but did not have time to finish, however, had to die after I left for lack of a champion. For me, departing GAF was an opportunity to build the same successes, if not bigger ones, on another playing field. This time it would be at PPG Industries. In the next three chapters, you will see how that played out.

# 7

# Life in Corporate America

## *PPG Industries, 1982–86*

## (Ages 42–46)

Dr. Paritosh M. Chakrabarti has been appointed Director of Research and Development for PPG Industries' Chemicals Operation … In this newly created position, Dr. Chakrabarti will be responsible for research, development, and technology licensing efforts of PPG's Industrial Chemicals Division and Agricultural and Performance Chemicals Division.

—PPG Press Release, October 1982
*Pittsburgh Business News*
8–14 November 1982

Paritosh has performed commendably … his technical capabilities and leadership within chemicals have been distinguished ... through personal involvement and example he has increased the level of innovation throughout the organization.

—Robert D. Duncan
Group Vice-President
PPG Industries, Chemicals,
15 July 1985

Dear Paritosh,
The 1985 Cross Group R&D Meetings were the best yet. .... I thoroughly enjoyed myself and got a feel for some of the promising new areas in which PPG is working. It was a real treat to be able to attend and it was good to see you.

—James F. Junge
Chairman of the Board, Pitcairn Inc.,
Member of the Board of Directors, PPG Industries
7 June 1985

Paritosh,
The agreement just announced between PPG and the Scripps Research Institute is a significant milestone in PPG's technological effort. Your role as a "champion" of the project was a very important factor resulting in PPG's participation. I want to thank you for your individual effort ... in this significant accomplishment.

—Edward J. Slack
President, PPG Industries
21 January 1985

## A New Job Search

My interview with PPG Industries came in a rather strange way. In the middle of the proxy challenge launched by Samuel Heyman, as the dismantling of GAF looked almost inevitable and the resignation of Jay Olson as president practically confirmed it, my boss at GAF, Dr S.W. Kantor—who was vice-president of R&D for all of GAF—was looking for other opportunities. As the probability of building a new company in collaboration with Jay Olson fizzled, at Jay's suggestion, Kantor interviewed for a job at PPG Industries. PPG was looking for someone in chemical R&D who could bring a new vision to its chemicals group and change its business portfolio.

At the time, GAF's chemicals business was the envy of the chemicals industry. It was one of the most profitable, if not the most profitable, chemicals businesses in the United States. Most industry leaders knew about the excellence of GAF's chemicals business, but it would take a few months, until the 15 December 1982 issue of *Chemical Week*, to confirm their belief. It reported that GAF's chemicals business ranked fourth among the top 100 chemical producers in the world in operating return on assets. During his interview at PPG, Kantor was asked who ran PPG's chemicals R&D, and Kantor mentioned my name.

I was unaware of Kantor's interview at PPG when it occurred. At about the same time, however, I wrote to the presidents of a few large companies, including Earl Burrell of PPG industries, inquiring whether they had a suitable position in their organization for someone with my knowledge and experience. I included a brief, one-and-a-half-page letter providing the highlights of my background and mentioning why I wanted to leave GAF. Not that I was revealing anything he didn't already know. News of the proxy fight for control of GAF was well known within the C-suites of corporate America by that time.

With a double-digit unemployment rate and a gloomy economic outlook, there were not too many job openings at the time, particularly for positions at my level. Yet, because of GAF Chemicals' reputation and its record of rolling out new products at a steady rate as evidenced by articles in various trade journals and other news media, my letter generated quite a few positive responses. My letter to Earl Burrell, president of PPG Industries, was one among them. I received an invitation for an interview with the vice-president of PPG's Industrial Chemicals group, William (Bill) Harris. Burrell forwarded my letter to Vincent Sarni, senior VP, Chemicals, and Sarni forwarded it to Harris, suggesting the interview. The interview letter came from Robert (Bob) Williams, director of human resources for Chemicals at PPG.

## The Interview

When PPG invited me for an interview with them, I knew that they were an industrial giant with three groups of businesses—chemicals, glass, and coatings and resins. Its chemicals business was bigger than all of GAF with its chemicals, photographic products, and building products. My first interview was with Bill Harris, the powerful vice-president and head of the industrial chemicals division. He grilled me about what I did at GAF and before that. I went in as well-prepared as I could be, but I knew that I would not be intimidated by PPG's size. As the interview progressed, Harris became more cordial and friendly. We went to lunch at the Duquesne Club—a posh club in Pittsburgh—and were served in a private room.

During lunch, Harris mentioned that I will soon hear that PPG will get out of its joint venture with Dow Chemicals. Known as PD Glycol, the venture made ethylene glycol. I asked him if he had thought about repurposing the venture into making non-ionic surfactants and polyols rather than glycols, which were at the bottom of the profitability ladder. He said that he would have considered such a strategy if it had been presented to him earlier, but now it was too late. I could see that he was quite intrigued by my suggestion and seemed somewhat disturbed that they had not at least considered that as an option.

After we returned from lunch, Bob Williams, director of human resources for Chemicals came and told me that Vincent Sarni, senior VP of the entire chemicals group, would like to see me. Bob said that this was good news and wished me luck. Sarni asked several rapid-fire questions. The idea behind this interview technique is to gauge the interviewee's knowledge of a topic; if you do not know your subject well, you're not likely to respond instantly. His questions mostly concerned R&D strategies and my personal contributions to developing those strategies at GAF. One question that I was not able to answer to *my* satisfaction concerned GAF Chemicals' return on assets. I said that I was not sure, but my guess was about 21 per cent. He seemed to know those numbers for most chemical businesses and told me that my guess was close enough. When I left, he said that I would hear from them soon. Bob told me that my interviews were going very well.

When I returned home from the interview, I told Kantor about it. It was then that he mentioned how my name came up during his interview a few weeks earlier. He said that it was a big job with a salary that would be unthinkable at GAF and that PPG was conducting a wide search to fill that position. During my interview, I never talked about salary and neither did Harris nor Sarni. Apparently, Kantor knew more about the job than I did.

Despite what I had heard from Bob Williams and Sarni, I gave up hope of a quick response. So, I was quite surprised when I got a call from Bob, inviting me for a third interview—this time with Earl Burrell, president of PPG.

When I went to see Burrell, I was expecting another tough interview. This time I familiarized myself with the various financial terms and came prepared with the relevant figures. But he surprised me. He did not ask any financial questions. He was not even ready to grill me. He asked me one of the most open-ended questions I had ever heard. The first thing he asked, without even raising his eyes from a document he was reading, was, "What are your thoughts this morning?"

At first, I did not know how to respond to such a question. My first thought was that I must take this opportunity to direct the interview towards the way I wanted it to go. So, I told him about the discussion I had with Harris and Sarni and what my thoughts were about how to redirect the strategy of the chemical group at PPG to become more profitable. Then I turned his question back to him. I asked him if he had any thoughts on how we should proceed.

At this, he raised his eyes from the paper he was reading and looked straight at me. He said that his view was that there was nothing wrong with the strategy they had, but he leaves the decisions concerning future directions to his vice-presidents. He then talked about the various businesses within the chemicals group. Since he came up on the chemicals side of the business, he seemed to be familiar with details that many executives at his level would not know. In the end, we shook hands.

Bob Williams was waiting in the sitting room next to Burrell's office to escort me out of the president's suite. Bob told me that the interview with Burrell was just a formality. The final decision was Sarni's. Unless he was willing to offer me the job, he would not have sent me to see the president. Bob then told me about all the benefits at PPG, including their very generous relocation programme. I came home optimistic but not yet sure that they would choose an Indian for such a big job. My other thought was that we had built our dream house only a couple of years before in Cedar Grove, New Jersey. With unemployment in double digits and the real estate market collapsing, what I would do with the house if indeed I took another job in another city?

Within a week, I received an offer letter from PPG industries. It was better than the best I would have ever thought. My designation would be director of research and licensing, Chemicals. I would be reporting to Bill Harris. My starting salary would be about double what I made at GAF as technical director. PPG would buy my existing house at the appraised value. I would be given a "short service credit", which meant that the ten years I worked for GAF would be added to my service time at PPG in calculating my pension benefits. I would be allowed to live in a hotel with my family for three months at company expense until I found a place of my own. When I told Kantor about the offer, he said that he would have considered it to be a dream job for him, but they chose me over him and many other candidates. He wished me luck.

I joined PPG in September 1982. On the day I joined, Vincent Sarni saw me. He explained the organization of the

Chemicals Division. He was in charge of the entire operation. Two vice-presidents reporting to him—Bill Harris, VP of Industrial Chemicals, and Jack MacMillan, VP of Agricultural and Performance Chemicals. He explained that most of the sales and profit of the Chemicals Division came from the industrial group. The company created the performance chemicals group to develop new growth opportunities. He told me that my first task would be to look at the portfolio of the entire division and recommend how we ought to be organized to bring balanced growth between commodities and specialties. I should not be too concerned with internal divisions. All the site directors of the R&D centres would be reporting to me. In addition, the director of licensing, director of patent department, and the president of PPG International (a staff function located in Europe) would also be reporting to me. I would have a research manager and a senior secretary to help me manage those functions. He told me that PPG was a matrix organization and that R&D was also responsible to the business units. If, in the course of doing my job, I got any resistance, I should talk to Bill Harris about it. He wished me good luck and said that there was a lot of work to be done and to get on with it.

In announcing my appointment, *The Pittsburgh Press* of 8–14 November 1982 interviewed Bill Harris and wrote:

> Paritosh M. Chakrabarti has been named director of research and development for PPG Industries' chemical operations. In the newly created post, Dr. Chakrabarti has overall responsibility for the research, development, and technology licensing efforts of PPG's Industrial Chemicals Division and Agricultural and Performance Chemical Division.

It also confirmed what Williams, director of human resources suggested in my appointment letter but did not specifically spell out, that "chemical operations" meant all chemical operations—industrial, agricultural, and performance chemicals.

## First Four Months at the Job: Figuring Out Things Within and Outside PPG

We moved to Pittsburgh, and Srimati did not like living in a hotel for three months. Within two weeks, we rented an apartment in the city, at the company's expense, and enrolled our two boys in one of the city's elementary schools. We would soon buy a house in Upper Saint Clair—one of the two most desirable school districts in the Pittsburgh area. It was a California-style colonial, red brick and cedar, on Redfern Drive. Its backyard sloped down to a large, wooded area. Our two boys loved the big trees in the wooded area and thought of playing Tarzan from the vines that were hanging from the trees. We also moved the boys from the city school to Baker Elementary School in Upper Saint Clair. Debtosh was nine and Raj seven and a half.

When I joined PPG, I learned that I was replacing Wil Graybill, who was a placeholder for the research director's job. Both Bill Harris and Vincent Sarni told me to begin by visiting all the PPG Chemicals sites in the United States and abroad, as well as PPG's major business partners in the UK, France, Germany, and Japan. Wil Graybill was to travel with me and introduce me as the new research director as we travelled. After I came back, I was to write a strategy paper for review by the management committee, indicating the changes I would consider for the group.

Though my visits to most of the plants, R&D centres, and international partners went smoothly, I sensed quite a bit of resistance from the business managers, particularly those running the Agricultural and Performance Chemicals Division. On one occasion, one of the senior managers told me to stay away from Agricultural and Performance Chemicals—they had their own research director, Sandy Durrell, who came from Ciba-Geigy and was hired only a year ago. When Bill Harris heard about the incident, he was furious. He called the manager to his office. I later heard the story from Harris's secretary. She said that as Harris castigated the manager, the manager said that it had been a difficult day for him, otherwise he would not have said to me what he had. At this, Harris told him that if in the future he faced a difficult day, he should bang his head against the wall rather than insult the research director. From that day, I did not have any more resistance.

For my peace of mind, the first thing I needed to do was understand the chemicals business from its historical and technological perspectives. PPG entered the chemicals business in the late nineteenth century to integrate backward into soda ash (sodium carbonate), a key raw material for glass making. Later, caustic soda (sodium hydroxide, or lye) replaced soda ash as a source of alkali in glass making. So PPG made the bold step to incorporate an electrochemical process for co-producing chlorine and caustic soda; this was high tech for the times. Soon the chemical business flourished in its own right and PPG took advantage of the opportunity to produce the downstream products from chlorine, among them vinyl chloride (the raw material for PVC), and several chlorinated solvents, including the solvents used for dry-cleaning.

During the growth periods of the 1950s and '60s, PPG scientists developed world-class processes to make those products and licensed the processes all over the world. PPG pioneered the manufacture of optical plastic CR-39—another offshoot of chlorine chemistry that would be the basis of lightweight plastic eyewear that replaced glass. PPG's position in caustic soda led to the production of precipitated silica, which was a major component in rubber compounds. So successful was PPG's chemicals business that some of PPG's top executives came from its chemicals manufacturing line. In fact, Earl Burrell, PPG's president when I joined PPG in 1982, had been a manager at PPG's chemical plant at Barberton, Ohio.

Those were the heydays for the chemicals business; this is an industry that had long been considered recession-proof and where growth took care of management inefficiencies if any existed. Decisions were easy—build more capacity and let the scientists and engineers develop the processes for the next product to be made and the next plant to be built. It was time for the bold, only the timid failed. In this euphoria, the industry would build capacity more than the market could use.

Situations started to change during the early 1970s, overcapacity exerted an ever-increasing pressure on pricing. And then the oil crisis of 1974 (the year I was promoted to section manager at GAF) threw most of the industrial chemicals business into a tailspin. Management failed to comprehend, or conveniently tried to ignore, the implications of the new reality. It blamed R&D for not being creative enough to develop products and processes that could flourish as in the past. They increased R&D budgets and hired new marketing people, hoping to repeat the past by doing more of what their predecessors did. They developed processes for making hydrogen peroxide, titanium dioxide, and many other commodities only to discover that providing a quality return in the highly competitive commodity market was an illusion in the new market reality. Hence, the company turned to diversification and specialties in the late 1970s, even while clinging to the hope for a miracle technological innovation in the commodity business to solve its problems. It reminded me of what Earl Burrell told me during my interview with him—he did not think there was any problem with the strategy, only a problem of innovation and execution.

This situation was not unique to PPG, every major chemical player was talking about specialties in those days because commodity chemicals suffered a severe blow in that recession while specialty chemicals escaped unscathed. I came to PPG to help it leap forward from pure commodity play to a balanced portfolio with specialties occupying a major place.

As a next step, I reviewed all the R&D projects, their locations, and the mechanism of their funding from within the various business groups. At the time, there were about 600 scientists with Chemicals R&D (seven times the number that I had in my department at GAF) located at three research centres—Barberton, Ohio; Corpus Christi, Texas; and Chicago, Illinois. These centres were all located at company plant sites—reminiscent of the situation at GAF when I began there. The annual R&D budget for Chemicals R&D at the time was $60 million—this of course was in 1982.

The major R&D programmes were:

1) Developing new membrane technology to produce chlorine and caustic soda in collaboration with Asahi Glass of Japan
2) Developing various new chlorinated organics—what the company called its solvents business

3) Silica research with a primary focus on developing new grades
4) Phosgene chemistry—a business PPG acquired as a part of its diversification strategy
5) Brominated flame retardants—an offshoot of its ownership interest in Great Lakes Chemicals, a major producer of bromine
6) Agricultural chemicals research—a diversification effort involving over fifty people in R&D
7) Plasma technology for making anodes for aluminum production and titanium ceramics for automotive engine parts—an outstanding technological achievement for which the company received an IR 100 Award, a prestigious honour given for top industrial innovations
8) Electro-organic process research—an offshoot of the company's interest in electrochemical processes to produce chlorine and caustic soda.

## Presenting a New Vision for the Chemicals Group

After I had a chance to visit all the chemical plants, all the research centres, all the international collaborators, and reviewed all the R&D programmes—I was ready to make my recommendations to PPG's Management Committee. The process took about four months and Vincent Sarni was already getting impatient. When I sent an inter-office memo that I was going to make my presentation he replied with a terse, handwritten note on my memo, indicating that it was high time that I made my presentation and that he "had been growing beard waiting for it".

All the top executives—including Chairman Stan Williams, President Earl Burrell, Sr VP Vincent Sarni, VP Bill Harris, several other top corporate officers, and the heads of the other two business divisions, Coatings & Resin and Glass—attended my presentation. A detailed description of my proposal to the management committee and heads of the three business groups is beyond the scope of this book and it would also be an unwarranted public disclosure. Accordingly, I describe only the major initiatives that I recommended and a summary of why I made those recommendations. The essential points of my recommendation were as follows.

1. *Chlor-alkali Membrane Technology: Discontinue and Refocus*

   I told the committee that I would terminate all R&D related to the implementation of "membrane technology" to produce caustic soda and chlorine. I said that it was not because the membrane technology was not sound. In fact, if there were a need to build new production capacity, I would have recommended the membrane technology. But there was already an oversupply of caustic soda and chlorine.

   The purpose of PPG pursuing membrane technology was that its current asbestos-based diaphragm technology was under regulatory pressure, and there was every possibility that the use of asbestos for industrial purposes would soon be outlawed. Had it not been for regulatory and health concerns, the diaphragm technology that PPG scientists and engineers developed was a robust and very cost-effective technology for producing chlorine and caustic soda. It was for this strength that PPG was able to license this technology all around the world. At this time, however, people, including PPG's licensees, were racing to replace the asbestos-based diaphragm technology with a recently advanced "permionic membrane" technology. If PPG were to replace its diaphragm technology with membrane technology, it would have to invest heavily—I guessed it would be close to one billion dollars—to dismantle the current equipment and replace it with new equipment. I did not think it would be a good use of cash.

I told the members of the review committee that a better approach would be to develop an asbestos-free diaphragm that could be a drop-in replacement for the asbestos diaphragm and there would be no need for additional investment in equipment. I told the committee that, after discussing the matter with our resident engineers, I was confident that we would be able to develop such diaphragms.

2. *Organic Solvents Programme: Chlorinated Organics, Dismantle and Redirect*

PPG was a leader in the manufacture of several chlorinated compounds that were used in various cleaning and degreasing applications, including dry-cleaning, metal cleaning, and various other industrial cleaning applications. The purpose of the ongoing R&D program was to develop other improved chlorinated molecules with superior solvent properties. I told the committee that there was increasing environmental concern over the use of chlorinated solvents. Under the circumstances, trying to make improved chlorinated solvents is a misguided initiative. The origin of the solution, I told the committee, was to call this business unit "solvents business." If indeed PPG were interested in staying in the solvents business, R&D should be working on non-chlorinated molecules that could act as solvents.

But in talking with the business group managers, I got the impression that they did not necessarily compete in the non-chlorinated solvents business because they did not have any strategic advantage there. I told my audience that I agreed with that assessment and recommended that we milk the business as much as we could but not waste R&D dollars to develop it further. Having said that, I told the committee that there were certain chlorinated organics, the chlorobenzenes for example, that seem to have sustainable applications. We should look at those molecules and perform limited R&D to improve their production economics.

3. *Silica Research: Continue and Expand*

   PPG had a strong platform of precipitated silica products with many applications, including fillers in rubber tyres and sneaker soles. The value of the products lay in the function they performed, and it seemed that those functionalities could be improved by developing new grades. I recommended that the company should work on developing improved varieties and additional grades of precipitated silica geared for use-specific applications. I would describe another project with precipitated silica under "Discovery Research" later.

4. *Phosgene Chemistry: Low Strategic Importance, Support Incremental Projects*
   I told the committee that, understanding how the Bhopal disaster wiped out Union Carbide, I would not consider this to be a strategic business. We should support the business group with projects that could be justified by incremental profit.
5. *Brominated Flame Retardants: Continue*
   PPG's interest in this project arose from its ownership position in Great Lakes Chemicals, which was a major producer of bromine. As the project was currently designed, it was in good shape and I recommended continuance without much change.
6. *Agricultural Chemicals Research: Continue and Explore Differentiating Technology*
   This was a high-risk, high-reward initiative for diversification with over fifty people dedicated to the effort. If there was management commitment to enter the agricultural chemicals business, we should support it with all earnestness. My personal view, however, was that without a differentiating technology, it would be difficult to compete with companies that had already established strong positions in the market. Companies such as Monsanto already had a sizable agricultural chemical business and so could afford to spend significantly more resources to develop the emerging market of biotech-based products. We should be on the lookout for an opportunity to enter the field via the biotech route as we continue our current programme on conventional technology.

7. *Plasma Technology: Freeze and Look for A Strategic Partner or Divest*
   The project's focus was to make anodes for aluminum production and titanium ceramics for automotive engine parts. It was an outstanding technological achievement for which the company received the prestigious IR 100 Award. I, however, did not think that the project was something that PPG should continue on its own. If the company were to continue this project, it should try to get a strategic partner to co-invest in developing the technology further. Otherwise, PPG should put this technology on the shelf. At this, Sarni suggested that I should discuss the project with the head of Alcoa's technical department and assess their interest in the technology. He mentioned that if the technology were to be used to make anodes for aluminum production, Alcoa, a leading aluminum-producing company, should be interested. In addition, Alcoa had recently embarked on an advanced ceramics venture, and PPG's plasma technology should fit their ceramics venture better than PPG's unfocused interest.
8. *Electro-Organic Process Research: Discontinue and Explore Only Opportunistically*
   The project to produce common chemicals via an electro-organic process was an offshoot of the company's interest in electrochemical processes to produce chlorine and caustic soda. When a typical person buys a product, they care only that the product is the least expensive while meeting all their specifications. Accordingly, I did not see any

reason to continue this project unless one could demonstrate ahead of time that the process would be less expensive than the current process, taking into consideration additional capital expenditures that would be required. I had not seen any evidence of such a study. My recommendation was therefore to terminate the project. If someone could come up with favorable process economics for a certain product, however, we should revisit this question.

9. *Optical Plastics*

The first lightweight plastic material that replaced heavyweight glass was PPG's CR-39. CR-39 is a liquid monomer that polymerizes in prescription-eyeglass molds to provide lightweight plastic lenses. For decades, CR-39 enjoyed an almost exclusive market, so PPG did not bother developing any other grades of optical plastic. This allowed other companies to come up with differentiated products, particularly with high-refractive-index plastics that allowed thinner lenses for the same prescription strengths. My recommendation was that we should promptly develop other grades to supplement our product line, using what I called a "fast-follower strategy". I gave examples of how a fast-follower strategy could be enormously successful under certain conditions. I discuss this strategy in detail in Book 2, *The Makings of PMC Group*. To take advantage of PPG's strong brand recognition in the market for optical products, I also suggested that we should develop other companion optical products. One such product would be photochromic dyes, which I describe a little later.

10. *Swimming Pool Chemicals: Focus on Consumer Market*
As a producer of chlorine, PPG made and sold both sodium hypochlorite and calcium hypochlorite. In those products, PPG had an ideal opportunity to develop a swimming pool chemicals business rather than selling these products as commodity chemicals. R&D could provide applications and packaging solutions for the new initiative. R&D can also develop improved pool disinfectants based on bromine, in which PPG also had a position. We should work with the chlor-alkali business team to come up with product and packaging concepts. I considered this to be an area with a high probability of success. My experience in developing products for the household products group at GAF was helpful in making this recommendation.
11. *Establish a Discovery Research Department, Create New Business Platforms*
I told the committee that the chemicals group must establish profitable new business platforms if it was to flourish. To do this, I suggested that we should establish a discovery research group. This group should work only on projects that had an assured market opportunity. The only reason these projects were not yet established businesses was that there were technology barriers or not enough understanding of the platforms' critical nature that could make them business realities. I told the committee that before I presented the areas that could constitute a first list of projects, I wanted to establish a distinction between the terms *specialty chemicals* and *performance*

*chemicals*—a distinction that many in business did not understand clearly.

When I asked business managers what they understood by the term "specialty chemicals", the almost universal answer was that these were especially profitable chemicals sold in relatively small quantities. This is partly correct but mostly confused. A better definition of specialty chemicals is that they are specification materials, usually discrete molecules, with a limited market. They are more profitable than commodities because fewer companies are interested in making them, the primary reason being their limited market size.

For example, when a pharmaceutical company buys a pound of aspirin (active ingredient: acetylsalicylic acid) it buys the molecule of "defined composition and quality" from vendors who can sell it at the lowest price and yet make a good profit. If the market size for aspirin for some reason were to explode, and many more companies started to make it, it would become a commodity chemical and its profit margin would erode. A performance chemical, on the other hand, has a value related to its functional attributes. Performance chemicals are also sold by the pound, but the value of a pound depends on the performance that a pound of the product is expected to provide.

I asked the committee to consider a pound of detergent. What you buy is a certain amount of cleaning power in one pound of the product. If half a pound of another detergent provides the same cleaning power, you will pay the same price for half a pound. By definition, then, *performance chemicals are complex mixtures, and one cannot compare the composition of those chemicals by simple molecular specifications.* The market size of performance chemicals can be as large as those of commodity chemicals, and they never become commodities despite their large market size. The projects that I recommended for discovery research were mostly performance chemicals. With this slight digression, I presented a few projects as a preliminary list, and this list could grow if we were to match market concepts with clearly defined technical concepts.

a. **Surfactants**: The market for surfactants is quite big. But for a new competitor to succeed, particularly a new competitor the size of PPG, it must establish a beachhead of new and unique products. After such a beachhead is established, market access could readily be acquired by acquiring some existing businesses. I told the committee that I had specific ideas on how to establish such a beachhead. I did it once at GAF and could do it again at PPG. I then gave them a concrete idea of what that beachhead could look like and what market gaps they could fill.
b. **Photochromic Dyes**: While discussing optical plastics, I mentioned that PPG had an opportunity to use its brand recognition with CR-39 plastics to enter the companion optical products market. A huge market opportunity existed if we could make plastic lenses that allowed less light transmission when exposed to greater light intensity. For example, a

market could be created for an optical lens that limited the transmission of light to the eye when exposed to bright sunlight. As of the date I presented the concept, the only such product in the market was photo-grey eyeglasses made of glass.

These eyeglasses had lenses made of glass impregnated with microparticles of silver chloride. The size of the silver chloride particles is so small that they are transparent to the eye in ordinary light. When those lenses were exposed to strong sunlight, however, the ultraviolet component of the sunlight decomposes the silver chloride particles into silver and chlorine atoms, even though both these atoms remain confined to the space previously occupied by the silver chloride. In that decomposed state, silver turns the glass grey, just as silver emulsions do in photographic films. Unlike photographic films, however, when the intensity of the light decreases, the silver and chlorine (that remained in close proximity) recombine to form silver chloride, and the glass becomes transparent again.

The process is reversible over many, many cycles, but that technology could not be applied to plastics. The reason, I explained to the committee, was that elemental chlorine (which ultraviolet light creates by decomposing silver chloride) reacts with the plastic, leaving a permanently grey plastic that cannot reverse back to transparent.

The solution might lie in using organic photochromic molecules, which turn from transparent to coloured in the presence of ultraviolet light, with the extent of colour change depending on the intensity of light. The problem was that photochromic molecules turn into all shades of colour from red to violet, but not grey, while the optical market required that the change had to be between colourless and grey. I told the committee that we had developed a strategy to accomplish grey transition with organic molecules. But it was going to be a big challenge—a challenge I thought would be worth taking. I then explained the technical concept in layman's terms to the committee.

c. **Silica-filled Plastic Films**: Next, I talked about the potential of a silica-filled plastic film. Based on some work that was already taking place at PPG's Barberton Research Center, we identified the potential of creating silica-polymer films to provide a new business platform for synthetic paper. Such papers, if they could be successfully developed, would be water-resistant and hold a huge market potential.

d. **Biotech initiatives**: In the 1970s and '80s, biotechnology represented a new frontier of technological advances. To keep abreast of what was happening in that field, PPG established a small group of five chemists at the Mellon Institute. Sarni asked me to review the field and recommend what PPG should do in this area. I told him that I would come back after doing my homework.

12. *Establishing Funding Mechanisms and Improving the R&D-Marketing Linkage*
At the time I joined PPG Chemicals, the company centralized its research at the group level. Each strategic business unit (SBU) was allocated a fraction of the budget based on a formula derived from the SBU's assets and manpower. This disguised the true profitability of the individual SBUs, but the rationale for asset/manpower-based allocation was that the bigger businesses had the responsibility to carry a bigger burden of the cost for diversification. I recommended that SBUs fund whatever research directly affected their interests—items 1 through 10. That would create ownership of the R&D programmes by the SBUs, improve communications between R&D and marketing, and help in the seamless transition of technology into business realities. Discovery research—items 11a through 11d—should be funded at the group level. Discovery research would work closely with the commercial development department to maintain a sharp focus on the commercialization of the products of discovery.

## The Green Light to Proceed

After I completed my talk, I gave each of the committee members a bound copy of my presentation, which contained further details and materials in support of my recommendations.

The committee received my presentation very well; every member only praised the detailed analysis that supported my recommendations. Chairman Stan Williams held up the bound copy and called it the Chemical Group's blueprint for growth. This is the first time I met Chairman Williams. Sarni gave me the green light to implement the recommendations and suggested that I keep him and Harris informed on progress towards the goals regularly. He also suggested that I discuss my discovery research projects with Dr Marco Wismer, who was supposed to be present at the meeting as a part of the review committee, but for some reason was not able to come. I told Sarni and the other members that I had already discussed my entire presentation with Wismer, and he was especially supportive of the discovery research initiatives.

## About Marco Wismer

A brief introduction to Dr Wismer may help readers understand why Sarni suggested that I discuss my discovery research projects with him. Wismer was the VP of Science and Technology at the time. Although a single person in an organization never receives full credit for the success of any major project—it is always a team effort—if I were to single out one person for whom PPG's coatings and resins (C&R) group became the envy of the paint industry, it was Dr Marco Wismer. His team discovered what became known as "cationic electrodeposition", a technology that made modern automotive coatings provide long-lasting protection to the underlying metal from corrosion. This technology made PPG's automotive coatings the choice of all major automotive producers and PPG the leader in the field.

If there was something negative about Marco, it was that he was not a generalist and in his capacity as VP of Science and Technology, he did not provide technical leadership to either the chemicals or glass groups. This criticism notwithstanding, Marco was a believer in what he called "leapfrog" technology, which means taking a step beyond what people accept as the norm of the industry. Intellectually, Marco and I interacted well. Though I knew he could not provide much support for designing the chemical group's growth plan, his support was crucial in having any of my programmes move forward. Marco always provided that support.

In fact, Marco and I became good friends. He later confided in me that, even though he appreciated his promotion to the position of VP of Science and Technology, PPG excluded him from the financial rewards that other group VPs enjoyed, even though the C&R division turned in record sales and profit. Marco, who came from Eastern Europe and grew up during the Great Depression, valued financial rewards over any other form of recognition. It is sad that in this world, particularly in the corporate world, true contributors are often bypassed when it comes to sharing the fruits of success. Marco Wismer would retire in 1986 at the age of sixty-five. He died on 14 October 1996, when I had already left PPG to form PMC Group.

## No Lack of Resources

Coming back to my programmes at PPG, I had plenty of support and a clear mandate from top management to make the changes that I suggested. My organization also grew to give me the power to make the changes. My direct reports and responsibilities consisted of the following.

1. An Administrative Research Manager, Dan Wiley, who handled most of my administrative details
2. The technical directors of all the three R&D centres
3. The Director of Licensing
4. The President of PPG Europe
5. A highly efficient personal secretary
6. A 600-person-strong R&D organization
7. An annual R&D budget of $60 million (at 1982 rate)

## PPG: An Organization in Flux: 1982–84

In large US corporations, top management is always in flux. Hardly one year had passed since I joined PPG that an announcement was made that President Earl Burrell and Chairman L. Stanton Williams would retire in October and November of 1984, respectively. This precipitated a cascade of management changes going down to the business-group level.

In September 1983, Bill Harris became Vice-President of the chemical group. In his memo of 1 September, he announced that the following executives will be reporting directly to him: Vice-President, Agricultural & Performance Chemicals J.L. MacMillan; Vice-President, Industrial Chemicals R.D. Duncan; Director of Operations I.C. Klimas; Director of Research, Development and Licensing P.M. Chakrabarti; Director of Planning and Commercial Development G.J. Lazarchik; and Controller J.C. Davidson.

At that time, PPG had an unwritten convention that only those who had attended the Harvard Advanced Management

Program (AMP) were eligible for promotion to vice-president. When Greg Lazarchik, director of commercial development at PPG Chemicals attended the AMP in 1984 (AMP 83) speculation abounded that, with the imminent management changes, he might be promoted to group VP of chemicals, even though Robert Duncan had already attended the amp in 1980 (AMP 79). More about Lazarchik later.

When Lazarchik was still attending the AMP, another announcement of management changes took place. Starting November 1984, Vincent Sarni would become the chairman and CEO; Frank Breeze, Group VP of Glass, would become vice chairman; and Ed Slack, senior VP of Glass, would become president. The so-called Agricultural and Performance Chemicals Group was abolished, and all chemicals become a single Chemicals Group. In the Chemicals Group, Robert (Bob) Duncan became VP, and Bill Harris stepped aside to occupy the newly created job of VP of PPG International. For me, the upshot of all this was that, starting in 1984, I would not be reporting to Bill Harris anymore but rather to Bob Duncan.

## PPG Builds New Headquarters

There was another change taking place at around the same time. PPG's headquarters moved to a newly built landmark building called the PPG Building at 1 PPG Place. It is a forty-storey, glass-clad square building with a tall turret at each of the corners and four medium turrets midway between each set of corners—an architectural marvel designed by Phillip Johnson and John Burgee. The main building had five other small buildings around it. It would soon define the Pittsburgh skyline and become its identifying symbol the way the Empire State Building defines the New York City skyline and identity.

Members of the management committee—Vincent Sarni (chairman and chief executive officer), Frank Breeze (vice chairman and chief administrative officer), Ed Slack (president and chief operating officer), and Robert Mitchel (VP and chief financial officer)—had their offices on the fortieth floor of the new building. Dr Marco Wismer, VP and chief technical officer of PPG, could have had his office on the fortieth floor, but he preferred to keep his office in the C&R Technical Center in nearby Allison Park, PA. Later, when Dr Joe Rowe joined PPG as VP and chief technical officer upon Marco Wismer's retirement in October 1986, he had his office on the fortieth floor. The executives of the chemicals group were located on the twelfth floor, where the group VP, the director of manufacturing, controller of the Chemicals Group, and I would occupy the four corner office suites.

## Progress in Chemicals R&D

After I got the green light to proceed with my recommendations, I began to talk to the research scientists about the new arrangement. I told them that I would not sit back as director but would provide active technical leadership as well. I had blackboards installed in the offices I used when visiting the various research facilities. During my visits, I would use the blackboards to explain technical concepts. Researchers at PPG never saw the director of research ever discussing technical details. The research managers were also put on alert, and they had to do their homework before they faced me. I never ceased to be a scientist when I became the director of research of this large organization. I hired a few university professors as consultants to help our scientists solve technical problems in certain areas. Dr Melvin Newman, the professor under whom I did my postdoctoral work at Ohio State University, was one among them.

I told the researchers that when we succeeded with a project, we would jointly share the glory of our success, but if we failed, I would personally take the scorn of failure. Enthusiasm among the research department was vivid, and everyone was ready to contribute and make the new vision a reality.

We started to make measurable progress in all the areas that I defined in my presentation to the management committee. Within two years, i.e., by 1984, the progress we made in developing new products, new and improved processes, and new applications were being talked about both within and outside the Chemicals Group. Since progress in broadly defined areas are milestones on a continuum leading to a goal, and since the definition of the goal evolves with progress, I will talk about our progress in the next chapter. For now, however, Vincent Sarni, the newly elected chairman and CEO of the company, imposed another priority on me.

## Exploring Biotechnology

When Sarni became the chairman in 1984, he reminded me of the promise I made to report on possible opportunities in biotechnology. He told me that though PPG was making great progress, particularly in the Coatings & Resins and Chemicals groups, Wall Street still rated it as if it were a building products company, depriving its shares of a high-tech premium. We needed to change that image with some bold moves in technology. He said that biotechnology—an area that everybody talked about in those days as a promising emerging field—could be such a move. Genentech, the biotech company, was already making its name as the leading technology company. He asked me to look seriously into the feasibility of establishing such a technology platform within PPG.

In response, I summoned Dr Ron Betts, the PPG scientist who was leading a group of four scientists at the Mellon Institute who were dabbling in biotechnology. I asked him to generate a list of companies that were doing state-of-the-art research in biotechnology and a list of some prominent biotech scientists who were doing groundbreaking research in the field. I also started to do my own homework to generate my own lists. Within a month, we compared notes.

It appeared that other than pure-play biotech companies, Johnson & Johnson (J&J) and Monsanto were at the forefront of developing biotechnology for commercial exploitation. Monsanto had geared its programme towards developing agricultural and animal husbandry products, including genetically engineered seeds and bovine growth hormones. In addition to its in-house research, it established a five-year joint contract with Washington University to develop enabling technology in these fields. The champion of the Monsanto programme was Richard J. Mahony himself. Mahony was elected CEO of Monsanto in 1984. J&J was a pharmaceutical giant, but its decentralized structure did not offer much opportunity to explore biotechnology internally. It established several industry–academy cooperative programmes, of which the biggest was with the Scripps Research Institute in La Jolla, California.

I decided to get a much closer look at these two models. Sarni introduced me to Mahony at a chemical industry meeting that I attended with him. I spent an hour talking to Mahony. He said that I should read their annual report, where he wrote the "Chairman's Message to the Shareholders" on why they were focusing on biotechnology. I saw a Hamburg (business jargon for a sales executive turned CEO) who wanted also to pride himself as a scientist. Mahony introduced me to his chief scientific officer and asked him to provide me with all the counsel I might seek as we contemplated building a biotech platform. Monsanto's contract with Washington University intrigued me.

I asked Ron Betts to call the head of research at Scripps and invite him to present a paid seminar on biotechnology to our scientists. Dr. Richard Lerner, who was the chair of the molecular biology department at Scripps, accepted our invitation. In Dr Lerner, I saw a scientist of exceptional talent and a very ambitious entrepreneur. His seminar was very enlightening. I decided to visit Scripps to see their organization for myself and meet some of the scientists there.

When I visited Scripps, Lerner showed me around and introduced me to many of Scripps's research scientists; he also introduced me to Jim Church, the J&J VP who monitored Scripps's research progress in areas of interest to J&J. I was very impressed by what I saw at Scripps—both in terms of the scientists who worked there and by the state-of-the-art equipment and facilities they had. These were far better than many of the top universities I had visited.

Jim Church was the liaison between outside research institutions and J&J for all J&J research contracts. In Jim, I found a very engaging personality. He invited me to visit the J&J corporate headquarters in New Brunswick, NJ. Every time

I visited the J&J headquarters, Jim would send a company limo to pick me up at the airport. My discussion with Jim was very helpful in formulating our biotech programme. He told me that, according to its contract, J&J had the "first right of refusal" for any technology that Scripps developed that had applications in human health. Scripps was free to establish research contracts with other companies concerning matters other than human health. I saw an opportunity to tie up Scripps for the agricultural and animal health areas.

This seemed intriguing because PPG was already developing conventional herbicides through its internal research. I discussed the possibility of such a collaboration between Scripps and PPG with Dr Lerner and the director of Scripps Research Institute, Dr Franklin J. Dixon. The president of Scripps Clinic, Dr Charles C. Edwards, was also present at the meeting. They expressed their strong interest in developing such a collaboration.

After I returned from my visit to Scripps, I discussed with Sarni the opportunities that the Scripps Research Institute could provide. He asked me to move fast to establish this relationship. When I suggested that we could probably establish a ten-year agreement with an annual $6 million R&D grant, he asked me how long I thought it might take for any development at Scripps to become a business reality, I said that, given adequate commercial focus, it would take at least ten years. He responded that I should go for a fifteen-year contract.

After several negotiation sessions that involved my visiting Scripps several times, I reached an agreement. It was a fifteen-year, $120 million agreement. Upon payment of the first $10 million, Scripps would dedicate one research wing to PPG, and it would be called the PPG wing. The remaining amount would be paid in equal annual instalments over fifteen years. In return, PPG would get the right of first refusal for all developments in the agricultural area and other non-human drugs and the right of second refusal in all human drugs for which J&J had not exercised its right of first refusal.

I assigned Mark Levin, director of patents in Chemicals, who reported to me, to develop the legal document. One critical issue surfaced during the contract negotiations. Scripps's scientists enjoyed academic freedom. They receive their research grants from the NIH (National Institute of Health) and other government grant-making organizations and should be free to publish their discoveries in scientific journals. The contract called for all proposed publications to be submitted to us for clearance first, and we would decide within thirty days if we should file patent proposals before the discoveries could be submitted for publication.

PPG's board of directors promptly approved the contract. President Ed Slack and I flew in our corporate jet to Scripps to sign the contract on Friday, 18 January 1985. Praise for the agreement was swift and extensive. All the major US newspapers announced the deal either on the first page or prominently on other pages. Below are a few headlines that appeared the next day.

> Scripps, PPG to Seek Better Chemicals for Agriculture
>
> —*Los Angeles Times*

> Company to Back Research on Food—$120 Million to Be Invested by PPG
>
> —*The New York Times*

> World Hunger Targeted—Scripps, PPG in Biotechnology Research Venture
>
> —*The San Diego Union*

To manage the huge flow of manuscripts and promptly decide which ones to act on, I needed an expert biotechnologist as our resident manager at Scripps. After a worldwide search, we settled on and hired a renowned scientist, the right-hand man of Nobel laureate Francis Crick (co-discoverer of the structure of DNA), Jim Hicks, to be our resident director at Scripps. Hicks reported directly to me.

Most of the news articles—including the front-page articles in *The San Diego Union* on 19 January 1985—mentioned my name as the key architect of the agreement and quoted extensively from my interviews with them. Other academic institutions also started to take notice of our programme at Scripps.

Within a month of the Scripps announcement, I got a call from Professor Paul Berg of Stanford University, a noted biotechnologist and winner of the 1980 Nobel Prize in chemistry. He congratulated me for establishing such a high-profile R&D collaboration with Scripps and wondered if we could do something similar with Stanford University. He said that he had talked with Donald Kennedy, president of the Stanford Foundation, and that Kennedy wished to meet me in person to discuss a possible industry–academy collaboration between PPG and Stanford University. Kennedy came to see me at my office in June 1988; I will describe that meeting in the next chapter. The provost of MIT also visited me to promote liaison programmes between PPG and MIT.

*Chemical & Engineering News*, a weekly trade magazine that almost every chemist and engineer read, would publish several articles about our historic agreement, calling it PPG's bold move to become a major player in agricultural biotechnology.

All these developments illustrated that a company's products and technology are its brand. The Scripps initiatives created an instantly renewed corporate brand for PPG. From being listed as a building products company by Wall Street, it now became a player in high tech. PPG's share price ticked upward at the news. The value gain in the market following the announcement far exceeded our financial commitments to Scripps.

Within the Scripps organization, which included the Scripps Clinic and research departments other than molecular biology, my name spread rapidly. There were many scientists and physicians at Scripps who came from India. They reached out to me with congratulations, feeling proud that one of their countrymen had such clout at Scripps. I remember one couple in particular.

These two came to me and said that they were postdoctoral associates at Scripps. The man said that he was the son of Dr (Mrs) Devi Chakravarty, whom I knew very well while I was in India. She was the chair of the Department of Chemistry at Bethune College, Calcutta. I called her Devi-di and she used to recommend students that I tutored. The couple said that their term at Scripps was coming to an end, and asked if I could help them get an extension for another term. Soon I got an express letter from Devi-di, congratulating me for reaching such a height in my career but also requesting me to do what her son had already requested. I felt uncomfortable recommending anyone whom I did not personally know. So, I mentioned to Scripps Director Frank Dixon that if they were doing a good job, he might consider extending their appointment for another term. I told him that I knew the man's parents, but not him. Dr Dixon immediately extended their appointment for another term.

Thinking that I had great influence at Scripps, more people, particularly Indian scientists, would write to me, asking to arrange fellowships for them at Scripps. I felt very uncomfortable recommending people whom I did not know for jobs. I had to politely tell them this, but I felt bad that I could not help more people.

To be sure, some quarters within PPG resisted the programme with Scripps. Specifically, resistance came from Robert Duncan, VP of Chemicals Group, and from the leadership of the C&R Group. To highlight the difficulty encountered in concluding the contract, Richard Rompala, who would later replace Duncan as senior VP of the Chemicals Group, presented a caricature depicting me with a broken leg and the caption "It was rough climbing the Scripps mountain" at our annual management retreat as a slanted remark to Bob Duncan, my boss at the time, who opposed the project. One thing that I admired about Duncan was that he was always honest and open about his opinion. He would tell you what he thought about a subject even if he knew that you held an opposing view. For this, I respected him, even though I sometimes found that his opinions were not well thought out.

## Sarni Requests Comment on Progress toward Blueprint Goals: AMP Delayed

In June 1986, Chairman Sarni requested that I write him a letter indicating how I viewed PPG's progress in technology. I was not to confine my comments to Chemicals only; he wanted to know my views for all divisions. I presented my views in a six-page memo on 30 June 1986, touching on every aspect of PPG and the challenges that lay ahead.

Before I received this request, Sarni recommended that I attend the Harvard Business School's AMP. As I mentioned before, it was tacitly understood that when such a recommendation came from the chairman's office, it usually meant good news. I was happy to be nominated to attend the fall, 1986, session of the AMP. But shortly thereafter, I received a notification that, at the request of PPG, my enrolment to attend the programme would be deferred and rescheduled for the fall session of 1987 for "reasons of urgent business needs". My slim hope that completing the AMP presaged a promotion to VP was dashed. I had not connected Sarni's review of PPG's progress in various areas with the delayed request for my attendance at the AMP session. It did not occur to me, or at least I did not want to believe, that Sarni wanted certain people to be available if he wanted to discuss anything with them before the upcoming global conference on PPG's Blueprint for Progress. This saddened me, but I accepted the decision.

Unsure of what to read into it, I saw the following handwritten note from Duncan at the top of the delay notification. It read, "Paritosh, I appreciate your support on this *very much*. Let me know if you don't get prompt confirmation for the [1987] fall session." The emphasis was his.

## Wismer Retires, Rowe Appointed VP and Chief Technology Officer

In 1986, Marco Wismer retired. To prepare to fill that vacancy, PPG redefined the job requirements to attract appropriate candidates. President of PPG, Edward Slack, asked me for my opinion on what that job should look like. In a letter to him dated 14 August 1984, I provided a two-page memo outlining what should be the key requirements for the job.

An official search for filling the position began in 1985. After interviewing several candidates, the board eventually selected Dr Joseph Rowe, a renowned physicist. I was surprised by this selection. Dr Rowe did not understand many of PPG's technologies, particularly the organic chemistry-based products and processes of the Chemicals and the C&R groups. He had a better understanding of glass technology. So much for the advice I gave to Slack. It seemed that the board was more interested in Rowe's reputation as a scientist than his understanding of PPG technology. Rowe would replace Wismer on his retirement in 1986. Six years later, when Rowe retired, the office of the chairman gave my memo to the executive recruitment firm handling the search to develop a new job description.

## My Relationship with Chairman Sarni

I noticed that whenever Sarni needed any technical advice, he would reach out to me—not to his chief technology officer, and not to my other counterparts in C&R or Glass. He would also praise my scholarship and talent publicly. Of course, this behaviour did not escape the attention of the other executives, but I did not always feel comfortable being watched by the most powerful man in the company. Another thing about Sarni was that he encouraged his top executives to disagree with him when searching for a solution. This was evident from the way he welcomed resistance to the Scripps project from Duncan and the C&R group. He would not hide those disagreements but rather talk about them openly and forward those criticisms to me. I knew that when something succeeded, there would be no scarcity of people to take credit for it. But when something fails, corporations will always try to find a scapegoat. If the Scripps project faltered, I would be the first scapegoat. The resisters would say, we told you so, and the chairman could also say that I knew the arguments against mine.

Despite Sarni's public praise for me, something else started to worry me. In private meetings, he would always remind me that I must not let his praise go to my head. He was all business in those discussions. On one occasion, on which I was not fully prepared to respond to his questions, he was quick to tell me that the next time I came to discuss programmes with him, I must come fully prepared. If he ever got the feeling that I was taking my responsibilities lightly, he would not hesitate to terminate me.

I reminded myself that being successful in my responsibilities was no guarantee of stability in a company. The termination of Eugene Mossier—senior VP of C&R, the odds-on favourite to become the next chairman, and leader of a group that turned in record sales and profit—was a stern reminder of this. I also reminded myself of the termination of Phillip Dalton and Jay Olson, presidents of GAF, by Jesse Werner for flimsy reasons. Having said that I always felt that Sarni consistently had a very favourable impression of me. When I started to succeed in my own company, PMC Group, he wrote to me to say that he always knew that I had the talent to run a big company.

Two-year-old Deven on my lap watching Popeye on TV. Photo taken in February 2006

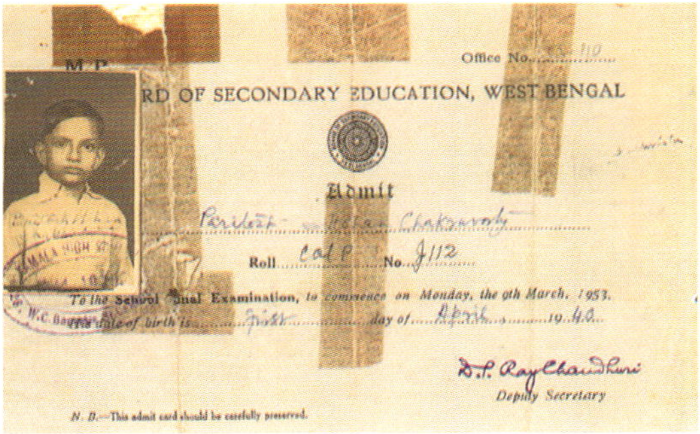

Office No. ...

RD OF SECONDARY EDUCATION, WEST BENGAL

Admit

Roll Cal P No. J112

To the School Final Examination, to commence on Monday, the 9th March, 1953.

The date of birth is First day of April 1940.

Deputy Secretary

N. B.—This admit card should be carefully preserved.

Admit card to appear for the 1953 final examination as a private student in school

Our first taste of the "American Dream" – owning our own house. We bought this house at 28 Fenway Road, Yardville, NJ from FMC Corporation in 1971. We sold it in 1972 when we moved to Wayne, NJ for my new job at GAF Corporation

*You never get everything you dream of, but she came terribly close to what I was dreaming about, and in many respects much more.* (Srimati, Columbus, Ohio, 1966)

Climbing the ladder of the "American Dream": The white split-stone house we built on a hilltop in Cedar Grove, NJ in 1979

Maggie Virostko's winning one-time promotion on occupational safety and health at the "Safety Awareness Day, Barberton Technical Center". Virostko, safety specialist with PPG Industries Inc, and Dr Paritosh M. Chakrabarti receiving the award.

PPG Chemicals R&D is recognized for its outstanding safety performance at the Space Car event. Photo taken in 1987

PPG R&D receiving the Prestigious IR 100 Award for 1984. The Federal 100 Award recognizes the most significant industrial development of the year. Paritosh Chakrabarti (centre) received the award on behalf of the PPG team.

Collegium Awards at PPG Cross-Group R&D Meeting, 1992. Chairman Vincent Sarni (centre) and Paritosh Chakrabarti (on his right) handing over the awards

Introducing Gerald Edelman (left) at PPG's Cross-Group R&D meeting, 1992, where he spoke on human consciousness. Edelman shared the 1972 Nobel Prize in medicine for his work on the immune system and the discovery of the structure of antibodies.

Paritosh Chakrabarti on the cover of technology consulting firm Arthur D. Little's *Best of the Best Colloquium on Products and Technology Management*

# 8

# Life in Corporate America

## *PPG Industries, As Vice-President, Chemicals R&D*, 1987–91 (Ages 47–52)

Paritosh M. Chakrabarti has been named Vice President in the Chemicals Group ... Neil Frick has been named Vice President in Coatings and Resins Group.

—PPG Press Release,
8 January 1987

The progress being made on safety, on product development, on research, and addressing opportunities gave me a good feeling about your Group.

—Vincent A. Sarni
Chairman of the Board, PPG Industries
(Letter to R.M. Rompala
Group VP, Chemicals, 23 May 1988)

In the first week of 1987, I received a call from the head of corporate human resources that the PPG Board had elected me a vice-president. He also said that Neil Frick, director of C&R R&D had also been promoted to vice-president. Soon there was a press release publicly announcing the news.

Companies set various policies concerning the title of vice-president. Some are liberal and give most of their senior executives vice-president titles. Normally, these are small to medium-sized companies. Others, particularly larger companies, are often very conservative in terms of giving someone the title of vice-president. The latter was the case with PPG Industries. Accordingly, the VP title was a very coveted one within PPG. Even in Pittsburgh's professional circle, when people heard that someone is a VP at PPG, they would treat that person with clear respect.

Pittsburgh and PPG were interesting in another way also. Real Pittsburghers are loath to move away from Pittsburgh. Similarly, PPG employees usually considered themselves as lifelong employees. Most senior executives at PPG grew up with the company. For instance, Edward Slack who became president in 1984, started in the company as a technician. This practice would evolve, though not completely, in Chemicals when Vincent Sarni became senior VP of Chemicals and later chairman and CEO. It was especially noticeable, however, when an Indian American who joined the company only about four years earlier was named vice-president.

There was not much surprise at the news of Neil Frick's promotion. Everyone knew that it was assured. Neil had been with PPG for most of his career. When Marco Wismar was promoted to vice-president of Science and Technology, Neil became the director of research at C&R. As long as

Marco kept his office at the C&R Research Center in Allison Park, however, the leadership of R&D in C&R rested on Marco. With Marco's retirement, C&R remaining the most profitable group in PPG, and enabling technologies driving the profitability of C&R, it was apparent that its director of research would be elevated to vice-president. But I was not sure about my case.

I was a newcomer to PPG. Delaying my attendance at the Harvard AMP for the fall session of 1987, even for apparently "urgent business needs" was not reassuring. I did, however, accomplish a lot for PPG during that short period. By 1986, just four years after I joined as director of research of the Chemicals Group, the contributions I made towards PPG's growth had become obvious. That progress changed the business portfolio of the group, a change that was noticed not just within the company but also outside. My work and opinions were featured in various newspapers, industrial magazines, and journals, including the front page of *The San Diego Union*, the *Chemical Marketing Reporter*, *Chemical and Engineering News*, and several other business journals. A Pittsburgh television station also featured me on the evening news. Even so, I was concerned that PPG, due to its conservative culture, might not give this title to a newcomer of Indian origin.

As soon as I heard the news of my promotion, I acted to ensure that we got tangible results from the collaboration I established with Scripps Research Institute. This involved giving a commercial focus to the project. I will describe it in Chapter IX, "A Biotechnology Vision and a Missed Opportunity". For now, let me get back to the bread-and-butter job of the newly elected vice-president of Chemicals R&D. Below is a roster of these activities.

## Progress in Research Projects: Pluses and Minuses

I present the areas listed below in the same order in which I presented my plan to the management committee when I joined the company.

- In the chlor-alkali area, the viability of the non-asbestos-based diaphragm was firmly established—pilot productions were conducted successfully. We terminated the permionic membrane programme and assured the company that, to remain in the chlor-alkali business, it would not have to invest $1 billion and adopt the membrane technology.
- In the area of chlorinated organics, the business unit told me that one of the high-selling products was para-dichlorobenzene (the active ingredient in mothballs). The problem, they said, was the co-product, ortho-dichlorobenzene, which the process delivered at a 40 per cent ratio, with the other 60 per cent being the para product. No market existed for the ortho isomer. They told me that, if I could change the ortho-para ratio to eliminate the production of the ortho isomer, they would give me a "Nobel Prize". They said that no one had ever been able to do that. When I achieved that goal, the strategic business unit (SBU) management organized a big reception and awarded me with a bronze plaque bearing the inscription: "To Paritosh M. Chakrabarti, 1985–'86, in appreciation of your contribution to PPG's chlorobenzene chemistry." They also presented everyone with a bottle of premium wine that they relabelled "Dichloroparatosh". I still have the bronze

plaque in my home office and have not yet opened the bottle of wine. This bottle is a constant reminder to me that quite often there are simple solutions to complex problems.

- R&D developed application-specific grades of precipitated silica. The business unit flourished and continued to do so.
- Several brominated organics as flame retardants were developed. But PPG decided to sell its interest in the business for reasons other than product technology.
- Agricultural chemical research continued its slow progress. With just one herbicide candidate to promote, field trials required a disproportionate amount of resources. The business unit's future was at stake, as I predicted it would be.
- At Sarni's suggestion, I discussed our project on plasma technology with the head of Alcoa and sold it to them. We had nothing to do with plasma technology anymore.
- Electro-organic process research was terminated after failing to identify products that could be made less expensively with this technology.
- R&D developed several high-refractive-index optical polymers. The progress in this area would, however, be dwarfed by the progress we made in the photochromic dyes under discovery research.
- With the help of R&D, the chlor-alkali SBU established a vibrant swimming-pool chemicals business.
- Where R&D shined the most was in discovery research. So spectacular was our progress that, within PPG and outside, the Chemicals Group became the centre of attention. Discovery research changed the nature of the Chemicals Group. I discuss these projects below as

individual cases—surfactants, photochromic dyes, and silica-filled plastic films.

### *Discovery Research: Surfactants*

We developed a beachhead for entry into the surfactant market by developing several unique surfactants. These were the only surfactants in the market that could simultaneously provide resistance to water hardness, withstand acidic conditions without hydrolytic decomposition, and remain functional at high temperatures. The crown jewel among them was a group of hybrid nonionic-anionic surfactants made practical by the chemistry I developed while at GAF. They held tremendous potential for underground applications such as the tertiary recovery of oil. With the memories of the 1974 oil crisis still fresh in people's minds, this invention assumed special significance. Emboldened by the progress made in discovery research, PPG acquired two surfactant businesses—Mazar Chemicals Inc. of Chicago (1986) and Ouvrie S.A.L of France (April 1990). This work created a new performance-chemicals platform. I would continue to guide the further growth of this newly established business.

### *Discovery Research: Photochromic Dyes, the Transition Lens Is Born*

We made phenomenal progress in this area. The ability to generate a photo-grey dye for plastic was spectacularly demonstrated by combining several chromophores in the same molecule. As of 1987, more work was still required concerning the long-term stability of the dyes. After much discussion regarding whether to sell the dyes or get into a new eyewear business, the office of the chairman approved the latter concept. PPG tied up with Essilor, and the *transition lens* business was established. It went on to become PPG's biggest business after automotive coatings.

Much of the credit for commercializing the photochromic technology goes to Greg Lazarchik, director, Commercial Development, for making the transition lens the new and separate business that it became. Without his uncompromising support and commitment, Transition® would not have become as big a business as it became. Here, trust and respect for each other's intellectual power played a major role, if not the only role that made Transition what it was destined to be—a global business with household name recognition around the world. The Optical Products business unit wanted to sell the photo-grey dye as a companion product to CR-39. But Greg sided with me, thinking that it would be a mistake not to take full advantage of such an enabling technology. Sold as a dye, the product would have commanded a $30 million market, but as the Transition lens, it eventually became a billion-dollar business.

The history of every major advancement contains stories of certain people. It may be helpful to my readers to understand who Greg Lazarchik was and why he did not get the recognition he deserved within PPG industries. Lazarchik prided himself as an MIT man. He did his undergraduate work at MIT before joining PPG Industries. He also had an exceptional musical talent. He was accepted at The Juilliard School, which he would have preferred to join, but his family convinced him otherwise and he went to MIT instead. As his career progressed at PPG, he became the director of Commercial Development, Chemicals. He had the potential and talent to become a group vice-president, if not the president, of PPG. But every time an opportunity arose for an upward move, he was bypassed and someone else got the promotion.

When an opportunity to become the vice-president of the Chemicals Group opened in 1985, Lazarchik was bypassed and the position went to Robert Duncan, whom Lazarchik dismissed as an intellectual lightweight. He found a new purpose when R&D successfully developed the "reversible" photo-grey dye, a feat that everyone thought was a technical impossibility. It was the breakthrough that made the invention a commercial reality. He immersed himself in the job and worked closely with me to see that no deficiencies were present in the product design. If I had to describe Lazarchik, he was possibly the smartest commercial man I ever met, but he was also openly contemptuous of people who could not think at his level. It was this latter characteristic that probably stopped him from climbing to the top of the corporate ladder.

## *Discovery Research: Silica-filled Plastic Films, Teslin®*

This was another area of spectacular success in discovery research. A fledging R&D programme to incorporate silica in plastic films was already in place when I joined PPG. I was intrigued by what I saw. I thought we ought to take this to the next level. Consequently, we developed a new type of "synthetic paper" with outstanding ink receptivity. The R&D progress led to pilot development, and another business—Teslin—was soon to be born. Here again, Greg Lazarchik's support in making Teslin a separate business unit rather than another product under the silica business was crucial for achieving the full potential of the technology.

## Relocating the Chemicals R&D Center

When I joined PPG, I found that C&R had a centralized state-of-the-art research facility in Allison Park—an affluent suburb of Pittsburgh. The R&D centres for the Chemicals Group were located at various plant locations, the primary one in Barberton, Ohio, within the confines of its largely abandoned chemicals manufacturing plant. As a result of this separation, we needed redundant support facilities, and the cross-fertilization of ideas across distinct business segments was inadequate. The locations of the Chemicals R&D centres also stood in the way of recruiting good scientists. I thought that consolidating the R&D centres at one location near Pittsburgh would not only give us cost synergy by eliminating duplicate support staff, but also help us recruit talented scientists from the neighbouring universities in Pittsburgh.

An opportunity arose in 1988. After the British firm Beazer took over Pittsburgh-based Koppers Inc., it no longer needed Koppers' extensive R&D centre in Monroeville. That was a sprawling complex with a 168,000-square-foot research building on 185 acres of picturesque land just 15 miles from the center of Pittsburgh. PPG bought this property at a bargain-basement price, completely renovated it, and moved most of the people from the other R&D centres to this new facility. The total cost of the project was $22 million, including the cost of relocating our employees—a fraction of what building it from scratch would have cost. Since we were creating new jobs, we also got a $3.75 million low-interest loan from the Sunny Day Fund.

Getting approval from the management committee for the funds to relocate the R&D centre was possible because of successes in R&D projects. The new center would receive praise from many people. Robert Duncan, group VP of chemicals wrote the following:

> Paritosh, I was very impressed with the job you and your team have done in terms of the relocation to Monroeville. The Center and Labs look much better than I thought they could. I'm pulling for you for the future. Keep the new products and technologies rolling out!
>
> —R.D. Duncan, 26 October 1989

## Leadership in Safety

Chairman Sarni wanted to be sure that PPG was considered the safest place to work. Each department and each location were charged with implementing proactive safety initiatives. We at PPG Chemicals R&D became a forerunner and received many awards from PPG and outside organizations for designing initiatives that became models for the industry. Some of the awards we received are listed below:

- The 58th All-Ohio Safety and Health Congress Award, highlighted on page 13 of the *Ohio Monitor* (picture shown)
- Our Buckle Up initiative (in compliance with the corporate plan) won the State of Ohio's Buckle Up Award.
- PPG Chairman's Award in Safety (picture shown)
- Letter of congratulations from the governor of Ohio for our outstanding safety programmes.

We proved that that R&D productivity and safety can go hand in hand without either suffering.

Most of the credit for our outstanding performance in safety was due to Maggie Virostko, whom I appointed as the safety coordinator for Chemicals R&D and charged her to take an uncompromising position when it came to the health and safety of our people. Maggie chaired several safety committees and made sure that every potential safety violation, however small, was detected before it occurred and its causes eliminated. She had my full support to implement the mandate. As a result of Maggie's single-minded devotion to her task, safety became a culture at PPG's Chemicals R&D

## Chairing the Cross-group R&D Conferences

One of the most interesting jobs that the VP of R&D had was to chair cross-group R&D conferences. These were mega-events attended by more than 250 senior scientists from across PPG's technical centres and most members of the management committee, including the chairman. Many of the board members were also present at those meetings. The responsibility to organize them alternated between the VP of R&D Chemicals and the VP of C&R. Dan Wiley, the research manager who helped me in administrative matters, would do the groundwork for me when the responsibility fell on me. I used to invite some prominent guest speakers from outside for these occasions. One such speaker I invited was Gerry Edelman, who won the Nobel Prize in physiology or medicine in 1972 for discovering the structure of antibodies. Later, he turned his research focus to consciousness. I found Gerry to be an exceptionally engaging personality who could discuss science and spirituality with equal command. It was a great experience to engage him in those discussions, particularly because of my personal interest in both subjects.

## Prestigious Appointments

In my capacity as VP of R&D, I also had responsibilities to promote PPG's image outside the company. I served in many prestigious positions, including the following:

- Member of a task force formed by Pennsylvania Governor Robert P. Casey to design the state's economic development strategy: "Investing in Pennsylvania's Future: The Keystone for Economic Growth—Science and Technology." The task force issued its report in January 1988 and published its strategy book next month.
- Member, Harvard-Princeton-Yale Club
- Member, Advisory Panel for Chem Week
- Member, Board of Directors: American Chemical Society Committee on Corporate Associates, 1989–91.
- Member, Carnegie Mellon University Board
- Member, Board of the Mellon Institute
- Distinguished Member, Carnegie Mellon Research Institute Advisory Committee
- Member, University of Florida President's Council
- Member, Industrial Research Institute
- Member, Council for Chemical Research
- Member, Microbiology Society
- Member, New York Academy of Sciences

I also travelled extensively to represent PPG as a guest speaker or chair of many global organizations.

## An Organization in Flux: 1987–91

When Ed Slack and Frank Breeze retired in late 1988, Sarni decided not to replace them. He assumed the posts of chairman, CEO, and president of the company. But there was a top-level hire during this period—Richard Rompala, president of Muller Brass, was hired as VP of Corporate Development in 1985. In 1991, Rompala replaced Duncan as senior VP of Chemicals, while Duncan became senior VP of the Glass Group. That meant that I would now report to Rompala. Such rotations were meant to prepare the top executives to compete for the CEO's job, which was expected to become vacant in 1993.

## Concluding Thoughts

Despite some of the setbacks that are inevitable in life, I did accomplish a lot for PPG from the time I joined until the end of 1991. Of course, I was rewarded with promotions, generous compensation packages, and the support of the chairman, none of which I ever asked for. But all that would not have mattered if I had not received the great support—I must say nearly 100 per cent support—for what I asked from my people. That kind of support is not possible unless a leader genuinely feels for his team and does everything possible for their well-being and gives them their greatest chance to succeed. But rather than merely talking about what such leadership means, let me quote a few of the many unsolicited letters that I received from PPG employees.

> In the past couple of weeks, I had time to reflect upon receiving the award [Chemicals Group Performance Award]. It is my understanding that you were very instrumental in making this award possible for me. In fact, I am told that you fought very hard to make the award a reality for each of the prospective team members … Oftentimes it seems that we tend to forget the special efforts that managers like yourself make to enhance an employee's well-being … Thanks very much.
>
> —Jerry Kinney
> R&D, Engineering, PPG Chemicals
> 3 May 1989

Kinney and several others received the Corporate Award for Outstanding Contribution at the Cross-Group R&D Convention that year. The award is decided by the PPG Collegium, a group of outstanding scientists from all three groups—Chemicals, Coatings and Resins, and Glass. Realizing that, without proper articulation, people from engineering do not generally get these coveted awards, I decided to personally present their case to the collegium that year, an unusual step by the VP of Research.

> During my career, there were many people I have been associated with. I would like to state that you are

> one of the finest gentlemen I have worked for safety in the safety field.
>
> —Maggie Virostko
> Safety Coordinator
> Chemicals R&D
> 31 May 1989

During my years as head of R&D at Chemicals, I put a special emphasis on the safety of our people. Dealing with chemicals and chemical R&D inherently carries an uncommon risk. Without constant safety awareness, employees may expose themselves to undue risk. Our safety programme became a model for all of PPG. We also received national recognition on many occasions for our safety accomplishments. Maggie Virostko was instrumental in keeping our safety programmes on track.

> Dear Dr Chakrabarti,
> At this time of the year, our thoughts turn to special people who are truly blessings in our lives—people like you. You will never know how much your kindness and understanding meant throughout this difficult year. We are taking life one day at a time, and with God's help we'll get through … You have such a fine blend of many qualities needed to be a good leader—your guiding spirit is an important part of what makes the Monroeville center so special … PPG is very fortunate to have you and the wisdom that you can impart … Thank you for everything.
>
> —Gene and Gail Beall, December 1992

Gene was a senior scientist at our Monroeville R&D Center. Gail was his wife.

There were many such letters that I received during my time at PPG Chemicals. Those letters were what made my job worth doing. These also tell us more about what leadership is, details that we can never learn by reading mighty books on leadership.

# 9

# Life in Corporate America

## *PPG Industries: A Biotech Vision, and a Missed Opportunity, 1985–87*

## (Ages 45–47)

As I was visiting Scripps regularly to review the research progress there, both Jim Hicks and I thought that the group was producing some excellent theoretical results by early 1986, results that had great implications for commercial products. In fact, a lead article in *Chemical and Engineering News*, on 16 February 1987, was headlined "PPG-Scripps Biotech R&D Linkup Poised to Pay Dividends". The article made its case by interviewing various people from the industry and at Scripps. But the wording of the headline came from comments made by Hicks and me in early 1986. The article quoted us: "According to Paritosh M. Chakrabarti, PPG Vice President for R&D, and James B. Hicks, [PPG's] Senior Managing Scientist for Biotechnology, the arrangement is now beginning to pay dividends in terms of basic research with potential commercial application."

As expectations for commercial dividends were rising, I thought it was time to put the programme on a sound business footing. I was already seeing the potential of building something like Genentech.

As some of the leading papers on the basic science of biotechnology began to emerge from Scripps—thanks to the funds from J&J and PPG—it dawned on me that the core technology was much too powerful to be confined to any single business area. Almost every other issue of America's most prestigious research publication journal, *Science*, had one or more papers from Scripps, and the journal would feature many more on its cover page.

The more fascinating the basic science that was coming out of Scripps, the more I became convinced that we had to design a business plan to maximize the power of the technology by allowing it to take us to wherever it led and not limit ourselves by directing the research toward the few applications that appeared most feasible in those early days. Otherwise, we would never be able to reap the full benefit of our collaboration. It was like a wheel in which the technology was the hub, and the spokes reaching out to the rim represented the entire universe of business. Focusing on just one spoke—one specific type of drug or agrochemical product—would limit the scope of the technology and deaden the spirit of innovation.

Furthermore, the matter was especially urgent to me, as PPG had just spent tens of millions of dollars trying to develop a single corn herbicide, Agent 844, and had concluded that it could not afford to spend any additional money for field trials. The business would thus soon be put on the market for sale.

Serendipity often misleads us towards wrong things. In the early 1980s, Merck's new cholesterol-lowering drug lovastatin had the potential of becoming a blockbuster with a billion-dollar market potential (and later realized that potential). Richard Lerner pointed out to me that Merck did not discover this drug but licensed it from the Japanese. The only credit that Merck deserved, he said, was that its scientists saw the potential and procured the technology with a licensing agreement before its competitors could. It was fortuitous that Merck's interest and the Japanese discovery coincided; the agreement would not have occurred if Merck had not also been working in that area. J&J apparently hoped that its collaborative research with Scripps would lead to something like Merck's success. PPG management's expectation was on even flimsier grounds. They imagined that a miracle agrochemical product would suddenly come out of the Scripps research. I knew that if we did not correct such misguided notions, the collaboration would soon lead to frustration.

I concluded that the reputation and image we built with the Scripps collaboration would be short-lived if we failed to put a proper commercial focus on the collaboration. I also knew that turning basic research into commercial products presented a challenge distinct from either purely basic or industrial research. Having been deeply involved in both kinds, I knew the kind of challenges we would soon face about what to do with what I called all the great "signals of science" that Scripps was generating. I thought that I needed to write a business plan about how to get maximum commercial benefit from the collaborative research that both PPG and J&J were doing with Scripps.

Before embarking on such an extensive undertaking, I wanted first to get the reactions of Scripps and J&J to the possibility of such a proposal. At Jim Church's suggestion, I visited J&J's headquarters at Johnson & Johnson Plaza in New Brunswick, New Jersey, on 12 February 1986. There, Jim introduced me to Robert Wilson, J&J's vice chairman. Wilson said that he had been reading about me in the media and heard a lot of good things from Jim. He wanted to meet me in person and hear my thoughts on how to enhance the common interests of J&J and PPG at Scripps. I described my thoughts about a potential joint venture (JV) between J&J and PPG that would explore all possible commercial paths.

The JV would take the signals of science coming out of Scripps and develop them into commercial prospects. As already mentioned, J&J had the right of first refusal to the royalty-based licensing of anything relating to human health, PPG had a similar right of first refusal for all other technology, and the JV could sell, license to third parties, or otherwise commercially develop anything for which neither J&J nor PPG had exercised its individual rights. The advantage would be that, before the companies exercised their rights, the commercial prototypes would have already been developed. The second advantage was that each company, because of its ownership, would get the financial benefits from an entire arena of biotechnology.

I told Wilson that the JV, if properly structured, could become the biggest biotech company in the United States, even bigger than Genentech. I explained to him that conventional business models do not apply to evolving technologies such as biotechnology. While conventional business models are "market-centric", meaning that investors search technology opportunistically from whatever sources possible, business models for evolving technology are "technology-centric". To be successful, they must serve all possible markets opportunistically. (For my readers who want to understand these two models, I explore them in detail in *Book 2—The Makings of PMC Group.*)

Wilson listened carefully to what I said and was very interested to learn more about my proposal. He wanted me to write up the details of my plan for consideration by both J&J and PPG. He also wanted me to visit their facility, Biotechnology Center Inc. (BCI) also located in La Jolla, which J&J had created to take advantage of their contract with Scripps. On 30 April 1986, I visited BCI and discussed its progress with Dr Friedman, who headed the centre. It appeared to me that Church and Wilson were not happy with that progress. I memorialized the minutes of those meetings in an interoffice memo on 3 March 1986. On 30 April 1986, I sent the memo to Duncan, Rompala, and Wismer, and forwarded a copy of it to Sarni. Later that year, I also discussed my thoughts with Dr Edwards (president of Scripps Clinic), Dr Dixon (director of Scripps Research Institute), and Dr Lerner (chair of the molecular biology department at Scripps). All seemed to be interested in the concept.

After returning from Scripps, I visited Church and again revamped the idea that I already discussed with Wilson and him. I asked Church to tell me candidly about J&J's experience in commercializing products from their collaboration with Scripps. He said it was very poor. He said that J&J did not have an organization that could take good science and translate it into a good product. They hoped that a fully viable commercial product would suddenly be discovered at the institutions they supported, that those products would be ready for clinical trials right away, and that the trials would be so successful that they would have a blockbuster drug.

Such serendipity had happened before, although it was extremely rare, perhaps just one other time as I discussed with lovastatin, a cholesterol-lowering drug. For J&J, investments in storied research institutions were not a big financial burden, so they continued to depend on hope. I told Church that hope may be positive thinking, but it could not be a strategy. I told him that I was already seeing some excellent science being developed at Scripps, but excellent science is not enough. You also needed a business focus, starting with a product development arm that could convert some of that science into potential product "leads". Yet even with that piece, the whole picture would still be incomplete, I told him.

We needed a commercial group by our side to take the leads to the next step of testing for market viability. That way, more viable leads could be developed. I told Jim that would be an expensive process, but without such an approach, we would be depending on nothing but luck. We again talked about whether J&J and PPG could join forces to build such an organization. The companies could then benefit in two ways—from exclusive rights to the product(s) in the respective areas of interest and the overall profit of the venture. Concerning orphan products, which neither J&J nor PPG was interested in developing, the venture could sell or license them to interested parties. Church thought it was a brilliant idea and that Wilson would also be interested in hearing more about it.

After returning from J&J, I went to see Sarni. I told him that it was time to convert the Scripps research venture into a business venture, starting with developing some of those signals of science into product concepts. I told him about my discussion with J&J, and Sarni told me that if I wanted to take this idea further, I should first write a proposal, circulate it to the key managers at PPG, and see what kind of reactions I get.

I was not quite satisfied with Sarni's response. I felt that he was pleased with what we did and he got what he wanted.

PPG's share price reacted positively to the news, and we were still enjoying the high-tech image and getting the high-tech premium on our share price. The fact that PPG had decided to sell its biochemicals (the internally developed herbicide) and potash (an ingredient in fertilizer) businesses might also have contributed to his detached response. He did not, however, reject my proposal and wanted to keep the door open. I saw that he was surprised at J&J's positive reaction to my proposal. Though I was not overly happy with the response I got from Sarni, I was not discouraged. I started to write a comprehensive business plan. I called it *A Biotechnology Vision*. I provide a summary of the plan below.

## A Biotechnology Vision

### *The Science, the Opportunities, and a Business Plan for Joint Consideration by PPG Industries and Johnson & Johnson (26 March 1987) by Paritosh M. Chakrabarti*

This was a comprehensive, 168-page document that outlined in detail the nature of the science, technology, and business opportunities of the venture, incorporated into a business plan that spelled out the competitive environment, management of the venture, valuation of the enterprise, and risk factors. The proposal was for the joint consideration of both PPG and J&J.

I knew that introduction was the most important part of any presentation. It must spell out in a nutshell what is unique about the plan and what one could expect in return for contributing to the venture. Business plans for such ventures are different from those that business executives usually see. They do not fit neatly into the structure of standard business plans. Because of the revolutionary nature of this emerging science, it would be necessary to write an introduction tailored to the revolutionary nature of the evolving field. Since the introduction looks as true today as it did all those years ago, I provide the entire introduction as I wrote it.

### *Introduction*

Einstein's theory of relativity was a piece of abstract and fundamental knowledge. From it evolved a cascade of basic findings, and their awesome power has been confirmed in mankind's command of nuclear force, its venture into space, its invention of the television, and many, many other phenomena.

Fundamental knowledge of such deep-seated implications once in a while brings a sweeping change to our technology. They cause a revolution. An avalanche of new inventions follows, each with a major impact on our society, our industry, and our business. Yet only a few can read the writing on the wall, and fewer have the courage to act during the early but most critical periods. Biotechnology is fuelling such a revolution now, and it will have an impact for the next 100 years or more.

Einstein's revolution started with the unification of matter and energy, and of space and time. The new biotechnology is based on the unification of life and chemistry. Its implications are as far-reaching as Einsteinian physics, and its impact on society could be equally as profound, though in an entirely unrelated field. It offers the best opportunities for solving critical needs in human healthcare, nutrition, congenital defects, environmental problems, chemical production, aging, and energy. We now have solid evidence to support such optimism. Knowledgeable sources place the value of biotechnology by the year 2025 somewhere between $50 billion and $100 billion. [In fact the global biotech market reached $141 billion by 2022.]

Developing a position to tap into a major source of such new knowledge is by itself a difficult task. Putting this knowledge into creating business opportunities is often a tougher challenge. For one thing, this knowledge does not fit conventional business ideas; those ideas are linear. A revolutionary technology like biotechnology, by contrast, is multidirectional. It stretches the limits of our expectations, creates new and totally unexpected markets, and has its own inner drive to create value. It calls for a new vision of a business—a vision that can only be born out of the opportunities it presents.

Both PPG and Johnson & Johnson have established excellent conduits to this science through individual contracts with Scripps. Together they cover the entire field of life sciences, which of course, biotechnology is all about. Both PPG and Johnson & Johnson have individual businesses that can be enhanced by biotechnology, and these were the primary factors that motivated these companies to get involved in this technology in the first place. The purpose of this proposal is to take this motivation one step further. It is to put the joint opportunities at Scripps, through a venture ("*The Venture*"), into the creation of extraordinary wealth, and at the same time further enhance the technology window to the parents' individual businesses.

Pursuance of high technology is not necessarily cheap. Many CEOs of large corporations are being told by their R&D directors and strategic planners that they will need to spend 12 to 25 per cent of their revenue to get into the high-technology game, compared to the conventional 2 to 3 per cent for commodity businesses, 4 to 6 per cent for the specialty chemicals business, and 6 to 10 per cent for the pharmaceutical business. The situation is even worse for those who want to enter fresh into such a new and emerging technology as biotechnology. The entry fee could be from tens of millions to hundreds of millions of dollars in negative cash flow before turning the corner.

The question is: Does it have to be this way? It seems that Thomas A. Edison answered this question for all of us when he said, "There is a way to do it better. Find it." This business plan is the result of a pursuit to find a better way. It not only promises to keep the technology expenses under control, but it also provides an independent opportunity for generating extraordinary profit out of such an investment.

A business plan to accomplish such lofty goals cannot be done casually, nor does it fit neatly into the chapters of a conventional format. Several critical factors must be considered, each interconnected to the other by the inescapable bondage of logic. First, one needs to be convinced that the point in time—in the evolutionary path of technology—is right for a major entry; even a slight miscalculation could result in major future frustrations. Among other factors, the power of the technology must be correctly assessed, and the opportunities that can be created by the venture must be visualized. The competitive strategies must be understood, the vision must be articulated, strategies established, and resources must be quantified. In addition, the parents must be convinced that the business projections are based on sound reasoning and that the plan has a decent chance of achieving its goals. Lastly, alternatives must be considered and tested against the proposed plan.

## *The Proposal*

The proposal I wrote had seven parts.

*Part I* traced the development of biotechnology from its primitive days. Though it began gathering steam in the 1960s with Holley, Khorana, and Nirenberg's Nobel Prize-winning "interpretation of the genetic code and its function in protein synthesis", two other discoveries were necessary to set the stage. These came in the 1970s with the discovery of restriction enzymes that enabled inter-species gene transfer and a method for the unlimited production of monoclonal antibodies in 1976. With those three tools, biotechnology was ready to become perhaps the most powerful and revolutionary technology in human history.

This technology, however, was highly interdisciplinary. Its sudden burst into prominence caught the interdisciplinary support areas by surprise, and it took a while for those areas to catch up and position themselves for the race. Thus, after a rough ride through the initial few years of turmoil, success stories began to emerge. The power of these stories and the lure of a noble cause soon also caught the imagination of ordinary investors and the objectivity of Wall Street.

The inevitable conclusion of Part I was that biotechnology was not an infant technology but was rather well into its explosive growth trajectory. The question was no longer whether history would be made. The question was who would be participating in the history it would make.

*Part II* provided an extensive review of current biotechnology and insight into the various aspects of its applications. It analysed areas of near-, medium-, and long-term potential. The major tools of the technology, recombinant DNA and monoclonal antibodies, were undergoing radical change, and a revolutionary wave of new developments was already gathering. The report analysed various aspects of these developments and their commercial implications. Every attempt was made to identify the areas where Scripps was leading the new development and areas where Scripps brought a major synergy.

*Part III* dealt with the biotechnology strategies of major corporations. I provided facts and figures for nine major companies. Monsanto was at the top of the list.

*Part IV* was the actual business plan. This part also identified additional financial commitments for creating the joint venture of J&J and PPG. I omit further discussion of this part because of company confidentiality.

*Part V* provided alternatives for PPG only, and I again omit further discussion of this part because of company confidentiality.

*Part VI* was a glossary of the unfamiliar terms that were used throughout the report.

*Part VII* described the risks involved and the rewards anticipated.

Before concluding my discussion of this report, I included the following observations.

The report was voluminous. It was meant to be a comprehensive proposal. But for those who might have found the technical matters too extensive, I identified the most densely technical sections by enclosing them in sidebars. The less technically attuned could then skip the sidebars and not lose the continuity of the theme. I provided the sidebar information for completeness and for those who could appreciate a deeper discussion of the subject.

Biotechnology was evolving faster than other technologies that had emerged in the previous decades.

I circulated the report widely among senior executives of all three groups at PPG and to the top executives at Scripps. I hoped that doing so would generate a consensus opinion of the plan. If such a consensus emerged, it would be easier for the board to approve the plan.

## Reactions to "A Biotechnology Vision"

Comments on the proposal soon started pouring in. Most of them were very positive, some ambivalent or on the fence, and a few negative. It also appeared from the comments that most of the proposal's recipients took the time to read it carefully. Taken together, their remarks were most valuable in determining the merit of the plan. I separate these comments into those coming from Scripps, those from J&J, and those from PPG below.

### *Comments from Scripps*

Dear Paritosh,
Thank you for sending me the biotechnology business plan, which I have carefully reviewed.

First, let me say that it is one of the most thorough and interesting documents I have ever come across concerning the new biotechnology and how one optimizes research to obtain products. A document like this emphasizes to us at Scripps your commitment and, most importantly, a thorough understanding of the nature of biotechnology and how it can interact with the corporate world. I am, of course, unable to comment on the nature of the venture vis-à-vis PPG's business interests, but it would seem to me that the plan that you outlined has the potential of being one of the most exciting in the industry ... I congratulate you for putting the joint venture on paper in such clear terms and hope that your colleagues at PPG will understand its true significance.

—Richard A Lerner

Director, The Research Institute of Scripps Clinic

27 April 1987

Dear Paritosh,

Thank you for letting me see a copy of your well-thought-out and carefully presented Biotechnology Business Plan. Insofar as I can judge the matters of the business world, markets, etc., it seems eminently logical and may well describe the kind of business vehicle we need to get things moving here ... I do have some concern, however, about the tone of your considerations given to RISC [the Research Institute of the Scripps Clinic] in your plan. In almost all cases where your new entity would relate directly to RISC, the precise conditions you present are no better than, and usually a bit less favorable than those that now exist, with our two separate Industrial Agreements ... I hope we have a chance to talk about this in the near future, since I think we should do all we can to promote your proposal.

—Frank J. Dixon, MD

Director Emeritus

Scripps Institute of Scripps Clinic

14 April 1987

Read the plan … A touch of genius.

—Jim Hicks, April 1987

## *Comments from Johnson & Johnson*

I just received over the phone (201-524-6762) preliminary comments from Jim Church regarding the biotechnology proposal. Jim said that he was so impressed with the report that he read it three times. He described it as magnificent and asked me if I would autograph a copy of this proposal for him the next time I was at J&J. He has sent it to Bob Wilson with his personal observations and with a recommendation that J&J take serious note of the points I made in the proposal. Jim also mentioned that he has talked to both Frank Dixon and Richard Lerner about the proposal … and both of them, he said, J&J will be ready to discuss it formally in two to three weeks.

—P.M. Chakrabarti<br>Memo to File<br>Subject: Discussion with Jim Church regarding the biotechnology proposal<br>14 April 1987

I called Jim Church. I asked him whether his management has reviewed the proposal yet. He said their chairman, president, vice chairman, and a few other top executives have reviewed it and were extremely impressed with the concept. He also mentioned that Richard Lerner was coming to visit on May 12 and will be discussing the concept further with J&J's top management ... He did not, however, know what the ultimate decision at J&J would be, but he reconfirmed that he will be willing to push it along with me and do his best to get it sold within J&J.

—P.M. Chakrabarti
Memo to File
Subject: Discussion with Jim Church regarding the biotechnology proposal
30 April 1987

### *Comments from PPG (in chronological order received)*

Paritosh, thanks for getting me copies of the documents outlining the events leading up to the potential for a joint cooperation with Johnson & Johnson for the whole of the life sciences arena. The idea really excites me, particularly the aspect of establishing an entity that is not constrained by specific end-use markets, as in the case with our existing arrangement at Scripps ... Paritosh, I applaud your efforts in developing this new more expansive opportunity for the chemicals group. It truly does have the potential to position us favorably in biotechnology. The organizational structure you suggest is clearly the most appropriate and has the best chance of succeeding. Obviously, with any new endeavor there will be problems along the way, but nothing I foresee that is not manageable. You have my full support, and I would be glad to assist you getting this deal together however I can.

—Howard I. Roe
Commercial Development, Chemicals
20 March 1987

P.M. Chakrabarti and G. J. Lazarchik:
We had several very exciting meetings and discussions with the Scripps Management Group while on the West Coast last week. I received excellent feedback from virtually every member of the Chairman's Council, and for certain, the level of excitement in regard to Scripps is at an all-time high within our company ... I feel there is a good opportunity for PPG in terms of forming a joint development company with J&J. Further, as I briefly mentioned to both of you, there is a possibility, after forming this company, to take it public and in so doing, generate significant revenue for PPG, while at the same time not losing the benefit of the technology we desire to commercially develop.

—R.D. Duncan
Group VP, Chemicals
1 May 1987

Very exciting concept—an awesome opportunity but also an awesome risk for PPG given its conservative culture mentality. Corporate sponsorship (rather than Group) would be more likely to provide long-term support that would seem essential for success.

—Jim Farst
Director, Chemicals Strategy
4 May 1987

Mr. Frank Breeze, Vice Chairman
By the end of July, the offering memorandum on the sale of biochemicals business [Herbicide Agent 844] will be ready to send. This, along with the public

information on the sale of potash business, will mark our intent to exit the agricultural market.

[Regarding the Scripps project] It seems to me that we have to do the following. Determine Johnson & Johnson's interest in structuring a venture. Paritosh believes that a venture similar to the one he describes in his paper would be of great interest to Johnson & Johnson and that Scripps would be willing to dedicate exclusively all of its biotechnology efforts to such a venture ... Personally, I am somewhat intrigued with Paritosh's proposal. As a recent cover article in *Fortune* points out, pension fund managers now manage funds of such scope that it is difficult for them to find investments that will make a material difference in their portfolios. Thus, I believe that PPG and Johnson & Johnson could in fact approach an investor like Prudential to act as a passive investor in a venture company that Paritosh described. That would only incrementally increase PPG's exposure and may in fact not increase it at all if the proper agreement was made ... If we were able to structure something with Johnson & Johnson, I think we could gain from mutual affiliation. If seen in that light, Paritosh's proposal is reasonable.

—John J. Horgan
Corporate Development
13 July 1987

Dr. P.M. Chakrabarti,
The proposal is excellent in its thoroughness, sincerity, and vision. I now wonder whether our attempt at Scripps was a minor step when we should have taken a bold leap such as the one proposed here ... PPG needs

major steps such as this to transform itself into a $10 billion company.

—John Maaghul
Director, Fiberglass
18 August 1987

## The Fate of the Proposal

The reactions from managers within PPG and Scripps were mostly strongly supportive with comments. There were a few comments such as "it is not a business for PPG". Sarni kept his opinion to himself. I told Sarni that, based on my conversation with J&J, if PPG approved the plan, J&J would join. To discover J&J's level of interest, Sarni asked Bob Duncan to meet with J&J management. At Duncan's request, I set up a meeting with Wilson. Duncan and I travelled in our corporate jet to Newark, and J&J sent us their helicopter to take us to their headquarters in New Brunswick. J&J gave us a great welcome and confirmed what I told Sarni—if PPG were agreeable, they would consider combining both J&J and PPG programmes at Scripps to create a new joint venture. In Duncan's report to Sarni, he said a 50-50 venture, which the proposal called for, would provide a lopsided benefit to J&J. The costs would be shared equally, but the emerging products would overwhelmingly be in the human health area. He also mentioned that the venture would distract Paritosh's attention, and he won't be able to give his full regard to PPG's in-house research programmes.

Duncan's action was a diplomatic way of not supporting the project. His comment about J&J being a bigger winner reminded me of a joke that Professor Alexander Klibanov of MIT told about the mentality of some of his colleagues regarding research grants: “God, I do not mind if you did not give any more wealth. In particular, please do not give my neighbour more than you gave me.”

PPG took up the issue at a meeting of the management committee. John Horgan was the most vocal supporter of the plan. But Sarni told the other members that he did not think he would get board approval for this project, particularly because two of PPG businesses—biochemicals and potash—were now on the market for sale.

Sarni called me and congratulated me for the excellent job I did and particularly to have J&J concur with the plan. But he explained that the climate at PPG was not right to undertake such a big venture now. I should continue to support the programme as is for now, and we could revisit the plan in a couple of years. He told me to reach out to J&J and explain our position.

Though I do not have concrete evidence to support my view, I thought it was Sarni himself who did not want to bring the proposal to the board of directors. He knew that his retirement date was quickly approaching, and he was going to ask the board for an extension of his term. He did not want any major proposal to clash with his request for the extension. If he got it, he might then have brought the proposal to the board at a later date.

Though the proposal did not go forward the way I expected it would, it changed management’s perception of me. They no longer thought of me merely as a superior scientist and research executive, but now they also recognized my business acumen.

What bothered me the most about the biotechnology business plan was not that the plan failed to bear fruit. Instead, I felt that PPG agreed to the Scripps programme not so much for its belief that biotechnology was a worthwhile technology in which to invest, but rather that getting involved in a high-tech collaboration with a world-class research organization would change Wall Street's perception of the company. When J&J heard about PPG's decision, it started to send me feelers to see if I would consider leading J&J's global research organization. That is another story that does not deserve much attention in this writing.

## An Epilogue

I would grow further in my job at PPG but would eventually leave to build my own company, PMC Group, in 1994. After I left, there was no champion for the Scripps programme. Most of the supportive top executives left for lucrative jobs, such as CEOs of other companies. Some of the up-and-coming, next-tier executives such as Don Bogus also left because their bosses left. All that let three people—Duncan, Leboeuf, and Dempsey—dominate the management committee. Dempsey was the newly hired interim CEO of PPG. None of them knew much about technology, and Duncan did not go against the opinions of the other two. In the end, PPG exited Scripps—the incentive was a tax write-off.

After I started PMC Group, Dr Lerner called me and asked me if I would like to visit Scripps and see what was going on. When I went there, I saw that the place was sizzling with talent. K.C. Nicolau, who would later get the Nobel Prize for his synthetic work, was there. Another Nobel laureate, Barry Sharpless, had also moved from MIT to Scripps. There were many other brilliant scientists. Richard Lerner's unusual skill to convince people about the value of Scripps was mostly responsible for attracting those brilliant scientists. Another factor was that Scripps also had some of the most advanced equipment that even the biggest universities could not afford. That equipment, which Scripps bought with PPG and J&J money, was a magnet for attracting world-class talent.

Lerner arranged for a group meeting of all the top scientists with me in a large conference room. They said that they had heard about me and my vision. Some of them also read the document I wrote. They asked me if I would reconsider starting the venture. I knew that their collective networking was powerful enough to easily raise the necessary funds. I told them that I had already started the PMC Group, where I had 100 per cent control. I did not think I had the time to lead another venture like the one I proposed. Things had changed since the proposal. I was not interested in being dominated by venture capital firms.

As I left Scripps, I was sad to realize what a huge opportunity had been lost by PPG because of Sarni's overly cautious approach and the stupidities of Dempsey, Leboeuf, and Duncan. They did not have the vision to do what it takes to build something great. Technology does not automatically spill out products. One needs to focus on products and drive the technology towards those concepts. History will never record those lost opportunities.

# 10

# Life in Corporate America

## *PPG Industries: Chief Technical Officer (CTO), 1992–94*

## (Ages 52–54)

When Dr Marco Wismer, the legendary inventor of cationic electrodeposition, retired from the position of chief technology officer (CTO) for PPG in 1986, the company went outside to hire Dr Joseph Rowe, a multitalented physicist, to be the next CTO. By 1992, Joseph Rowe himself was scheduled to retire.

Both Wismer and Rowe had their shortcomings. Wismer never got out of his comfort zone of coatings and resin technology, nor did he try to project himself as the custodian of PPG's technology outside of PPG. Joseph Rowe came with great global recognition, but he lacked knowledge about PPG's central technology platforms. By 1991, the PPG board recognized some of those deficiencies of the top office holders. The company hired Heidrick and Struggles to launch a global search to fill the position vacated by Rowe's retirement. It appears that corporate HR unearthed a copy of the letter I wrote to Ed Slack in 1984, in which I described my ideas concerning the qualifications for the position. PPG ignored my advice at the time and hired Joseph Rowe, who did not meet most of the criteria that I outlined. Now, however, it seemed that the company was rethinking my advice, though I was not sure. I thought they paid attention to my advice because the job specifications that Heidrick and Struggles used in the job search were similar to what I described in my letter. I show the specifications that were sent to several candidates below:

> **PPG industries inc.**
> **Research and Development**
> **THE POSITION**: Vice-President and Chief Technical Officer
> DUTIES: Reporting to chairman and CEO, this individual is accountable on a global basis for providing leadership and strategic direction to the corporation's technological and scientific thrust. PPG dedicates over 3 per cent of its almost $6 billion in sales to research, development, and the advancement of technologies. Four major R&D centres focusing individually on chemicals, coatings and resins, flat glass, and fibreglass are in the Pittsburgh area; they are supplemented by nine other facilities in the United States and abroad. More than 2,000 people are involved in research, development, and engineering; they report administratively to the business units and functionally to the CTO. Initial emphasis will be placed on the enhancement of R&D productivity and forward thinking on research, leading to the emergence of a centralized discovery research function.

**THE ORGANIZATION**: PPG is a global producer of flat glass, fibreglass, coatings and resins, chemicals, and medical electronics. Headquartered in Pittsburgh, the company employs more than 33,000 people. The world's leading supplier of automotive and industrial finishes, PPG maintains significant competitive positions in its major lines of business.

**THE PERSON**

**PREFERRED MINIMUM EXPERIENCE:** fifteen years

**EDUCATION:** PhD in materials science, chemistry, or engineering

**OTHER CHARACTERISTICS:** A creative self-starter who has worked well in a matrix organization providing motivation and discipline in diverse technological environments. Outstanding communication skills are a must. Will combine boardroom presence with laboratory curiosity and most importantly, leadership.

**EXPERIENCE:** A proven track record of identifying new product opportunities, enhancing productivity through technology input, and prioritizing current R&D programmes while supplying the vision for discovery research. Will have a solid business orientation and demonstrated management skills. Will enjoy customer interface and will have global outreach to academic, private, and public sector technology resources. Target companies include Monsanto, 3M, GE, DuPont, Dow, Exxon Chemical, BASF, Hoechst, Bayer, AKZO, Merck, and Pfizer.

Corporate HR explained to Heidrick and Struggles that, before any candidate's credentials were presented to the board for consideration, the candidate should be interviewed by all the senior

VPs of the company. A summary of those interviews, along with the search firm's recommendations, should be presented to the board for consideration. The board may then decide whether it wanted to interview the candidate. It was to be understood, however, that the board generally will go along with the chairman's, meaning Sarni's, recommendation. As the firm conducted its global search, it was also to consider possible internal candidates.

Naturally, I wanted to be considered for the position. All the senior VPs soon knew that I was the only internal candidate who was being considered for the job. Though I entered 1991 with a stellar reputation within PPG, I faced some resistance as well. Bob Duncan openly told me that he would not back my candidacy. He said that he had nothing against me but thought that the position of the CTO was a redundant job. The R&D director of each division should be the custodian of that division's technology. The CTO only put additional bureaucratic burdens on them. Rompala also told me that he heard one of the board members express an opinion that my accent could be a barrier to the job. There were also peer rivalries. There was already speculation, based on how close I came to having the biotechnology venture approved as the fourth division of PPG, that my ascent to the CTO position would not stop there. I would probably be aiming for the next move, the CEO's position, if I got CTO.

I decided to launch a full-fledged campaign for the job. Knowing my opponents was helpful because I could plan how to counter them. I thought the best way to start the campaign would be to explain to my audience my personal views on how one should go about finding the right person. This would be a generic description of how to interview a prospective candidate for any senior-level position in a company. I would then explain how I might fit under those criteria. I also had a strategy to disarm those who questioned my accent as a disqualifier.

Once I decided on the strategy, I started to prepare my presentation material. I took my presentation to every member of senior management, even to those whom I knew would oppose my candidacy, knowing that Heidrick and Struggles would compile the opinions of all those individuals. The purpose of my presentation was twofold—first to educate by laying out the criteria and then to describe my strengths against those criteria. I knew that most people, no matter how high a position they held, were poor at interviewing candidates for a top job. I was convinced that my approach would have a distinct advantage over the candidates who merely came and answered the interviewer's questions. I tested my approach by making my first presentation to William J. Davies Jr, partner of Heidrick and Struggles, who was the firm's main liaison for this search assignment.

I first presented a picture, shown below, with three overlapping circles. I called it "the circles of success".

## The Circles of Success

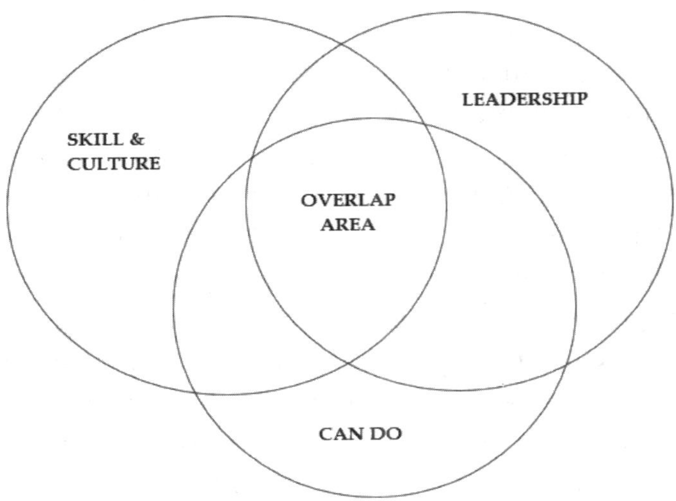

The circles represented three basic and broad criteria: 1) skill and culture, 2) leadership, and 3) a can-do attitude. I told my audience that a candidate, even with 100 per cent competence in any two circles, would fail if that person had zero per cent in the third. What we needed was an overlap of the three. The larger the overlap area, the better suited the candidate would be for the job. I then explained each circle separately.

## *Skill and Culture*

Skill means both breadth and depth of knowledge of a specific field. For PPG's CTO, it would mean knowledge in all three branches of chemistry and chemical engineering—organic, physical, and inorganic. Those branches cover all three major businesses of PPG—chemicals, coatings and resins, and glass.

As much as knowledge of the field of operation is important, so also is understanding an organization's culture. Each organization is unique, even as each person is unique. When you want a particular person to perform a particular task, it helps if you know that person's preferences. Similarly, when you want to accomplish anything in an organization, it helps if you understand the organization's culture. I told my audience that when I started as the director of research at PPG about ten years ago, I took four months to visit the company's various sites, learn about the company's global partners, and study its people before presenting my vision and strategy to the management committee. I faced Mr Sarni's ire for the time I took, but his anger melted away when he saw the product. The progress we made in Chemicals R&D would not have been possible had I not learned about the culture of PPG.

*Of course, knowledge of culture is not a guarantee of success, but not knowing it is a guarantee of failure.*

## Leadership

Leadership does not just mean cheerleading. It means helping people with skills to solve problems and leading by example. Providing advice does not make a leader. Advice is cheap—when people are lost, they do not need advice—they need a leader who can show them the path. Leadership in technology also means the ability to conduct gap analyses and focus on the areas where wide gaps exist between what is known and what could be the theoretical limit. Books on leadership rarely tell you what the secrets to success are. One cannot learn to be a leader by reading books on leadership.

I told my audience that I would like to beg their indulgence by elaborating on what I meant by leadership because it is the single most important criterion that defines whether a candidate for the job will succeed or not. With that, I started to explain my definition of leadership.

- Leadership starts with knowledge—an insatiable urge to learn about science, philosophy, and beliefs to discern truth from falsehood.
- Leadership requires a relentless pursuit of excellence.
- Leadership is sharing knowledge with others. It is about being able to convince people and always remain open to new perspectives.
- Leadership is the ability to articulate one's views and give voice to the legitimate views of the unheard.
- Leadership is courage—the courage to act on one's convictions, the courage to resist injustice, the

courage to protect others who are willing to act on their convictions, the courage to persevere in the face of adversity, and the courage to sacrifice petty self-interest to protect the greater interest of the plurality.

- Leadership is believing in people and building a bond of trust among people.
- A leader is not colour blind when building a team. Leaders have clear vision. They see strength and beauty in the diversity of black, brown, yellow, and white people in the team.
- A leader shares the glory of success collectively with the team but bears the scorn of failure alone.
- Leaders are humble; they can bring themselves to the same level as that of the plurality. Leadership is about respect for others, even one's opponents, and learning from opposing views.
- Leaders are compassionate. They feel others' pain and are willing to bear the pain of others.
- Leadership is about getting things done. It's about accommodating alternative views without sacrificing one's conviction.
- Leadership is not about reading books about leadership but about reading about leaders—leaders such as Martin Luther King, Nelson Mandela, and Abraham Lincoln—and trying to discern what mental qualities gave them the strength to pursue their convictions in the face of seemingly overwhelming obstacles.
- Leaders anticipate storms, adjust their strategies during stormy times, and resume their previous strategies after the storms pass.

In short, leadership is not about superficial things like style but rather about internalizing certain values and strengths and acting with strength according to those values.

I told the board that those were the elements of leadership that guided my life and will continue to do so. I felt that it was important that the board know about those views. That way, if they selected me for the job, they would do so knowing what kind of a leader they would be getting. I then thanked the board for allowing the brief digression and got back to the rest of my presentation.

### *A Can-Do Attitude*

This has to do with self-motivation. It means conviction, vigor, and intolerance for the status quo. It means an urge to succeed. Some people are extremely knowledgeable but lack the drive to succeed. What we needed was an attitude absolutely committed to success. All endeavours encounter resistance, but leaders with a can-do attitude are never dissuaded by resistance or failure. They find clues to success even in their failures. The playwright Samuel Beckett put it this way: "Ever tried. Ever failed. No matter. Try again. Fail again. Fail better."

## From Generalities to Specifics

Next, it was time to move from generalities to specifics. I divided this part of my presentation into three parts: 1) How I made the difference, 2) Linking to the blueprint goals, and 3) Disarming the source of the "accent" comment.

### *How I Made a Difference*

With evidence and examples that I mentioned in previous chapters, I demonstrated how I made a positive difference at PPG in the three areas just discussed above. I specifically discussed the following topics.

- My research and work philosophy
- Programmes for the existing businesses
- Vision for discovery research
- Communication skills—routine communication and internal and external communications
- Motivation
- Leadership
- Reputation as a scientist
- Track record at PPG and before
- Education
- Family—a case history of how to promote a culture of excellence

### *Linking to the Blueprint Goals*

PPG had already published its blueprint for growth. It was adopted at a giant global conference a couple of years earlier. Employees from around the world were invited to participate and debate before the blueprint was adopted. But now, the time for debating the blueprint was over. It was time for every department to pull in the same direction to accomplish the blueprint goals. So I described how, if I were to be selected for the job, I would link my initiatives to the blueprint goals.

| PPG's blueprint goals | Technology goals |
|---|---|
| Profit goal: Rank among industry leaders | • Gap analysis and programmes to close 20 per cent of all identified gaps<br>• Accelerating cycle time and improving energy efficiencies<br>• Safe operations to eliminate environmental costs |
| Growth goal: 4 per cent real growth | • Gaining market share in core products<br>• Generating new opportunities<br>• Establishing beachheads for new business<br>• Focused discovery research |
| Productivity goal: 3 per cent improvement each year | • Continuous effort to weed out marginal projects<br>• Structured nurturing of good ideas<br>• Translating customer needs into technical opportunities<br>• Relentless efforts to eliminate process inefficiencies |
| Social responsiveness | • Supporting education reform<br>• Participating in shaping the nation's technology strategy<br>• Voluntarism<br>• Involvement in community matters |
| Health and safety | • Leadership in behavioural change<br>• Safe technology |

Lastly, I described my strengths with concrete examples of how I achieved goals in each of those areas and provided specific ideas about how I planned to motivate the other two groups—C&R and Glass—to do the same. In total, it was a crisp one-hour presentation.

## *Disarming the Source of the "Accent" Comment*

While addressing the board, I wanted to put to bed any misgivings about my "Indian accent". I mentioned that I had heard that some board members were concerned about my accent. Perhaps, I said, those concerns originated in the fear that, if I ever became CEO of the company, my accent would prevent the investment community from clearly understanding me whenever I made a presentation to them. So I told the board that, as I was thinking about the issue, the idea occurred to me that I was the only one here who spoke with the *correct* accent, and everyone else seemed to have the wrong accent. At this, the members broke down in laughter, and I knew I diffused the issue.

Then I said, "Seriously, I agree that I have an accent that is different from most of yours. But on a very objective basis, I can tell you that I have been a teacher, and I have made more presentations to professional bodies than any other of the senior executives."

I went on to say that I had also interacted with people from more cultures and more countries than most senior executives. Frankly, I never heard anyone complain about not understanding what I talked about. On the contrary, many commented that they thought that I had a very pleasant accent. It may also not hurt to be reminded that PPG is an international company, 30 per cent of its revenue comes from countries outside the United

States, and the mother tongue of the people of those countries is not English, or they do not speak English with US accent. Of course, you will know after my presentation today if you have problems understanding what I present.

The accent issue being put to bed for now, I proceeded to the rest of my presentation.

I finished the talk with a comment regarding a misguided notion that many in the business community held, and that notion was that a good scientist could not be a good businessman, as if those two attributes were mutually exclusive. I told the "fall flat on the face" story to the board. This involved the comment that Sherman Reed of FMC Corporation made during my encounter with him in 1972 and the subsequent *New York Times* article about me that I clipped out and sent to him. The *NYT* article spoke of my rising to the position of director of research at GAF in less than five years after I left FMC. The biggest reason for such rash judgements, like Sherman Reed's, is that people do not look at the overlapping circles that I presented at the start of my talk.

After the talk, one of the board members said that it was one of the best presentations he had ever heard from any job candidate, let alone a candidate for CTO. They all thanked me, and I left after acknowledging their thanks and thanking them for their patience in listening to my presentation. By the time I got back to my office, people were already saying that I impressed the board members beyond their expectations. When I saw Duncan, he said, "Paritosh, please do not take my objections to the job personally. It was not against you—I was against the job of CTO. If you ever become CEO, I will be the first to give you my full support." I was surprised by the last comment.

The board seemed to have understood my emphasis that the CTO should have intimate knowledge of the company's technology platforms and be responsible for setting company-wide priorities for major technical programmes while making sure that such programmes aligned with corporate growth strategy.

On 14 August 1992, the chairman of the board, Vincent Sarni, sent out the following announcement:

> TO: ALL OPERATIONS
>
> I am pleased to announce that Paritosh M. Chakrabarti has been elected Vice President of Science and Technology effective September 1, 1992. He will work closely with Dr. Joseph E. Rowe, Vice President and Chief Scientist, until Joe's retirement on September 1, for a smooth transition of the corporate technology office.
>
> Paritosh, who has been Vice President of Research and Development for Chemicals since 1987, will play a key role in assuring the provision of the needed technology to support PPG's global market leadership in coming years. He will provide leadership and direction to the Company's technical and information systems thrust. Additionally, he will be responsible for establishing priorities and resource commitment for Group R&D portfolios, as well as for coordination and functional direction of the Group R&D and Engineering Departments.
>
> Vincent A. Sarni

The second paragraph was taken from the presentation I made to the board of directors. For the first time, the position of CTO became more than a ceremonial job. I moved from Monroeville to a fortieth-floor office in the PPG Building next to the chairman's, the one that was previously occupied by

President Slack. By now, there were only three executives on that floor—the chairman, the CFO, and the CTO.

I received many letters of congratulations. I very much valued the one that came from James F. Jungé, chairman of Pitcairn Inc., one of the oldest and most prominent family shareholders of PPG. This was not primarily because it came from Jungé but because of his understanding that technology does not stand still, and to remain a viable force, any major corporation must also be on the lookout for enabling new technologies. Jungé's letter is reproduced below:

> December 9, 1992
> Dear Paritosh
> I read with great pleasure about you becoming Chief Scientist for PPG Industries.
>
> While I am no longer on the Board of Directors, I continue to be tremendously interested in PPG maintaining its position of excellence. To do this, we must, of course, stay on top of what is going on in science, not only at PPG, but in the world at large.
>
> I can think of no better choice to help PPG to maintain this position.
>
> Best regards,
> James F. Jungé
>
> cc: Mr. Vincent A. Sarni, Chairman, President, and Chief Executive Officer

A new chapter began in my life. PPG was a giant among giants with seventy-five manufacturing plants globally. Its Chemicals Group was flourishing with three new major business segments—the Transitions lens, surfactants, and Teslin membranes—added to its already big platform. Its Coatings and Resins Group was the number one supplier of automotive paints in the world. Its flat and architectural glass business was the largest in the world, and its fibreglass business was also the biggest. The glass and fibreglass businesses, giant as they were, were also old commodities and had begun to represent an erosion of the company's overall profit margin. My job would be not only to maintain the company's growth initiatives but also to bring in new and emerging technology platforms that could become new businesses. That growth also had to be balanced with the global economy because 30 per cent of the company's revenue came from foreign operations.

My first job as CTO was to appoint a director of research for Chemicals R&D. In consultation with business leadership, I selected a high-potential R&D manager from C&R, Gerry Gruber, to become the director. This appointment sent the signal that we are not going to treat our technical departments as segregated islands or silos.

My next decisive action was to recommend that PPG terminate one of its most expensive glass research programmes. PPG spent more than half a billion dollars in developing a new glass technology. Though the technology produced a unique class of super-clear glass, the demand for such high-tech glass was very limited. Based on technology gap analysis, I became convinced that even if we did all the possible process improvements, the cost of producing that glass would remain significantly higher than our conventional flat-glass technology. At the 1992 management retreat, at Sarni's request I made the case for terminating that programme. Duncan, who was the group VP of Glass at the time, grudgingly accepted the recommendation, though he was upset that the recommendation had not come from his organization.

## Promoting Social Responsibility and Voluntarism

As responsible members of the community, every corporation has the moral obligation to promote the well-being of the community to which it belongs. One way of doing this is to encourage employees to donate some of their time through voluntarism. I made the promotion of this responsibility a part of my job. To begin with, I started to devote some of my time to helping the communities in which PPG technical activities were present and also encouraged our local R&D managers and staff to do the same. The following letter from our chairman is one example of many such initiatives from my office:

> April 19, 1993
> to: P.M. Chakrabarti
> subject: Langley High School
> Attached is a letter from the principal of Langley High Scholl, Daniel Belisario. In his letter, he commends you personally and a number of our PPG team for the work that you all are doing at Langley High School.
>
> Let me add my congratulations and thanks also. I want to take this opportunity to thank you and our PPG team associates who have worked so hard to help the Langley High School partnership.
>
> I hope that we can continue this effort and find more of our team to participate.
>
> Vincent A. Sarni

# 11

# Life in Corporate America

## *PPG Industries: Evaluating My Prospects for CEO, A Clash of Priorities, My Decision to Form PMC Group, 1994*

## (Age 54)

Barely six months after I was elected CTO, I got a call from a search consultancy firm, telling me that I was on a short list of internal candidates to be considered for the CEO's job when Sarni retired in August 1993. They would of course also look at outside candidates. I met with a representative of the firm and had a pleasant discussion. There were five names on the shortlist: Richard Rompala, Robert Duncan, Ray Leboeuf, Peter Heinze, and myself. Rompala was senior VP of C&R, Duncan was senior VP of Glass, Ray Leboeuf was CFO, Peter Heinze was recently hired (April 1993) away from BASF and was now senior VP of Chemicals, and I was the newly elected CTO. The most likely candidate was Richard Rompala, and either Leboeuf or I was the least likely. Neither Leboeuf nor I had operating experience. Rompala was hired in 1985 as VP for Corporate Development and he had been rotated between Chemicals and C&R as group VP. Duncan was the longest-serving insider, having started as a technical service technician and rising through the various ranks of management.

I thought that if I were to be in the play and decided to compete for the job, I should launch a serious campaign. I never lost in a competition where there was face-to-face interaction. I also had developed a reputation for being a proverbial "dark horse". What was certain, however, was that if an internal candidate were to be chosen, it would be per as Sarni's recommendation.

Chairman Sarni, however, could not decide on a successor. He thought that none of the five on the shortlist was ready for the job. Some had been in their top job for only a little while, and those who had been there long enough were not necessarily the best candidates. Rumour had it that Sarni wanted to get an extension of his term in office. The board apparently did not want to extend his term. It decided to hire someone from outside for a limited time so that the newcomer could select the next CEO from the internal list. A proud man, Sarni went along with the board's recommendation and said that he would see that the right person was hired from outside as interim CEO.

Sarni recommended hiring Jerry Dempsey as the next CEO, and the board agreed. Dempsey was the CEO of the garbage-hauling company VMX Environmental. The news of Dempsey as the choice for interim CEO almost provoked a revolution within PPG. Rompala was openly critical of the choice and said that it would be an insult for him to report to someone like Dempsey. Heinze thought he was deceived by being promised opportunities for upward movement. Duncan and Leboeuf were non-committal, and I was perplexed that, if operating experience was the criterion, someone like Rompala or Duncan would have been better qualified than Dempsey.

Whenever PPG hired someone from outside for a very high executive position, it was customary to have one of our senior executives meet the individual at the airport. In this case, however, everyone whom Sarni asked to meet Dempsey at the airport opted out on the pretext of being too busy on that day. Sarni then asked me if I would be willing to pick Dempsey up from the airport. I could not say no to Sarni—I had too much respect for him to come up with any false or lame excuse. I went to greet Dempsey at the Pittsburgh airport and brought him to the Duquesne Club. We had some pleasant talk during our ride from the airport to the club.

The next morning, Sarni called both Dempsey and me to his office. He talked admiringly about my contributions to the company and expressed hope that Dempsey and I could work together to further fortify our R&D strategy. He made a point to speak about the Scripps programme and hoped that we would be able to foster that relationship. Dempsey nodded in agreement. That August (1993), Sarni officially retired but remained a member of the board of directors. His new office was on another floor of the PPG Building. Dempsey did not know much about PPG's operations. He had to depend heavily on Leboeuf for running the business. Duncan also gave his loyalty to Dempsey.

Rompala was the first to exit. He called Dempsey "a lightweight" and refused to report to him. Before 1993 was over, Rompala took a job as president of the paint company Valspar, with a guarantee to succeed the retiring CEO in six months. Many of the high-potential, second-tier managers also left for lucrative offers from other companies. Heinze remained at the company but grudgingly so. In 1996, Heinze left PPG to become the president and CEO of the specialty chemicals company ISP. I tried to do my job but missed my close relationship with the chairman.

As 1994 began, I knew that if I wanted to get the CEO job, I had to start a serious campaign. The prospective list of internal candidates now numbered four—Duncan, Leboeuf, Heinze, and me. I had just appeared on the cover of Arthur D. Little's Best-of-the-Best Colloquium as one of the top ten "Practitioners in Product and Technology Management" in the world. I knew I would get Sarni's support and maybe that of a few other members of the board. I also knew that if I decided to launch a campaign, I would not do so half-heartedly. Mine would be a fully thought-out and fact-based campaign, and I would do it to win.

It was decision time, and I was torn between two options. One had all the certainties but also internal conflicts. The other was loaded with uncertainty, but I felt my heart telling me to follow it. If I decided on option one, I would put 100 per cent of my energy into a campaign for CEO. If I accepted option two, I would start planning to launch my own company. In the first instance, if I lost the campaign, I would still have my job as the CTO. But if I failed in the second, I would lose everything. The two options also presented the most profound clash of priorities—between what I thought was right and what PPG would require. I reflected on my family, my life, and the values and priorities I cherished in everything I did.

## Reflections on My Family

I had been blessed. When I left Columbus, Ohio, in 1966, I thought that I lost the love of my life forever. Yet I got her back in 1968, and we were married. The brief separation strengthened our marriage. By 1994, we had twenty-six wonderful years together and had the most extraordinary experience with raising our two boys, Debtosh and Raj. They were born a year and a half apart. When they were little boys, they were almost inseparable. They both read storybooks when they were in bed before falling asleep. Each would ask the other what page he was on. They wanted to read the same page even though they were in separate rooms. Of course, things changed as they grew up. So many memories of their birth and childhood came alive in my mind.

### *Debtosh*

As he was our firstborn, Debtosh was bathed in Srimati's and my love and affection. He also thought that his parents belonged to him and his brother only. When he was two years old, one of Srimati's friends from the neighbourhood used to come and talk to her. If the friend stayed more than an hour or so, Debtosh, who could not yet talk, would come, hold the friend's finger, take her to her shoes, and show her the door. His mother was his, and he would not share her with anybody else. When Srimati folded the laundry and put the clothing and linens away, Debtosh would take them out again and spread them out on the floor. Srimati would then playfully assume an angry face and chase him away. Debtosh loved those games. Srimati would tell me these stories when I came home from office, and we both cherished every moment of those tales as she narrated them.

One day when Debtosh was a junior at Upper Saint Clair High School, Srimati called me at my office. She sounded devastated. She was crying and told me that everything bad that could happen had happened. The principal of the school had called her and said that Debtosh and some of his friends were caught drinking beer in a hiding place behind the school. I immediately came home and saw on Srimati's face her belief that her child had gone bad and would not be able to go to a good college. Debtosh was crying too and said that what he did was a mistake, but that he would commit this mistake again!

We learned to accept such events as a child's typical growth experience. Of course, he excelled both in his studies and sports. Soon after, the *Pittsburgh Press* listed him as an All-Star Achiever, one of ten area students selected annually as most likely to succeed in life.

I remember another incident involving Debtosh. Out of the various colleges that had accepted him for enrolment, Srimati and I chose three as a short list—MIT, U Penn, and Cornell. Debtosh, however, did not like any of our choices. None of the friends he hung out with were accepted at those colleges. He was brainwashed into thinking that only nerds went to those elite colleges. He wanted to go to Penn State where his friends were going.

Both Srimati and I were worried, so I devised a plan. I called MIT's dean of admissions and explained our situation. I asked if he could suggest some students, who did not look like nerds, who could show Debtosh around the campus. The dean replied that many students have this misconception about MIT, but the faculty and staff there encouraged students to participate in all kinds of fun activities. He said he would have a few students take him around.

Convincing Debtosh to go and talk to the students, however, was another problem. I knew that he loved cars, so I told him that I had an idea. I would rent a Ford Mustang for him to drive around if he would agree to check out MIT and meet some of the students there. He did not have to enrol at MIT, there were no preconditions. He could only win if he agreed to my proposal—go with me to Cambridge, drive a sports car, visit a few students, and come back. He had nothing to lose, so he agreed. We went up to Cambridge. Debtosh met a few students at the DU (Delta Upsilon) Fraternity. For lunch, they fed him lobster. They then took him around and showed him all the fun activities at MIT. When it was time for him to come back, I looked through the window of my hotel suite and saw Debtosh, all smiles, walking back. Srimati and I were on the phone the whole time. She was worried that Debtosh would say no to MIT. I told her that he looked happy as he was walking back. We kept our fingers crossed. When Debtosh walked into the hotel room, he said he would love to come to MIT—it was a cool place. I called Srimati and told her to keep the champagne chilled for our celebration when we got back home.

### *Raj*

We had a much easier time with Raj. He excelled in school, very much so. When he was a junior in high school, he became a sensation when his science project took first place among 900 participants at the International Science and Engineering Fair (ISEF) in Orlando, Florida. We heard about it when the Associated Press called us to give us the good news. Raj was still in Florida. He would soon be named to *USA Today*'s list of the country's top twenty high-school graduates. Several other laurels were still to come—an all-expense paid trip to London to attend the Youth Student Conference, an invitation to do four weeks of research at the prestigious Weizmann Institute in Israel, being named as a member of the Academy of the American Institute of Advancement and being one of the two students to receive an invitation to attend the Nobel Prize ceremony in Sweden in early December of 1991. Raj was accepted for admission at all the top schools in the nation, and he decided to go to Harvard.

During the time our two boys were at MIT and Harvard, Srimati wanted me to buy an apartment in Cambridge so that she could go and stay there whenever she felt like seeing the boys. As I think back to how things were for Srimati, Debtosh, Raj, and me in 1994, I feel that our memories of those times are priceless, and no amount of money or prestige would be able to replace them. We were blessed to have such wonderful kids, and if I had achieved nothing else than that, I would have no regrets in life at all.

## Reflections on My Life

I remember my childhood. Born during World War II, with a vivid memory of an armed robbery at our ancestral home, with Hindu–Muslim riots raging during India's independence movement that split the country into an Islamic Pakistan and a secular India, being uprooted from one place to another and having no opportunity to attend elementary or secondary school, my displaced family of ten huddled in a partitioned single room in Kolkata, entering college at the age of thirteen, graduating with an MSc from Calcutta University ranking first in first class with a gold medal, becoming the youngest ever DSc from the same university, teaching at the City College, doing postdoctoral research at the Ohio State University and the University of Hull in England, a brief stint as a professor at Michigan Technological University, falling in love with Srimati, losing her and then getting her back, advancing through corporate positions at FMC Corporation and GAF corporation, and similar advances at PPG, reaching to a height second only to the CEO—all these memories confirm that life has treated me well.

Life could have been different. I could have stayed in India. I might have become wealthy working for the industries there, I could have entered Indian politics and ended up a corrupt minister, or I could have remained in US academia, dreaming about getting the Nobel Prize and becoming depressed over failing to reach that goal. I could have walked any of those paths without any guarantee of where it was ultimately going. As I turn these memories over in my mind, it dawned on me that whatever I did, I did with honesty and sincerity and with a clear conscience and love for my family and those who I encountered along the way.

I did, of course, face resistance and prejudice. There was the systemic prejudice embedded in the misguided notion of FMC's Sherman Reed that a brilliant scientist and a brilliant manager were mutually exclusive traits; I suspect that by "a brilliant scientist" he may have meant "an Indian-American scientist". There was also racial prejudice expressed in the comment that my accent was a barrier to becoming the CEO of a conservative company. And then there was the comment by the PPG manager to stay away from his area of business.

Those are the incidents of resistance and prejudice that come to mind, but I overcame that resistance and won over rival peers by helping those who wanted to stop me. I also made decisions without quite knowing how these decisions would affect my future, but I made them in good conscience—always, without fail. Refusing to decide was not an option for me—that is for the fearful, not the bold and courageous. In the end and in the aggregate, things have worked out for the good, despite the occasional tough experiences like turmoil at GAF during the proxy fight for control of the company. Many executives, including me, decided to leave the company then, but there was never a clash between my personal values and the values I pursued in my job.

Now, however, I found that I was confronted with the prospect of such a clash.

## A Clash of Priorities and a Clash of Values

As I thought about the prospect of becoming a CEO, I wondered for the first time in my life: Who would be my boss? What I realized was depressing. My boss would be the board of directors, who considered maximizing the interest of the company's shareholders as their only job. But who are these shareholders? For the most part, they are institutional investors or private equity companies. And what are their priorities? To maximize return on their investment. And how? By increasing the share price at any cost. And what was their time span? In most cases, *now*, but never to exceed seven years. So what is the primary job of the CEO? To please those shareholders. But what about the employees? They did not matter if they could not help the CEO get what he wanted.

I remembered my experience at GAF Corporation when a real estate merchant, Samuel Heyman, who knew nothing about corporate governance but happened to own 4 per cent of GAF's shares, took control of the company. I remembered how Chairman Werner made Heyman back out from his first proxy challenge with a green back and how, armed with this additional cash, Heyman returned the following year and snatched control of the company from Werner's management. I remembered how, after Heyman snatched control of GAF, he dismantled the storied company and sold off the pieces to create enormous wealth for himself and kept only the chemicals business under his control. And then even that piece, which had been hailed as the crown jewel of all the world's specialty chemicals companies, was milked of its value and eventually sold off, marking the end of a long and productive history.

I remembered how GAF, the once pioneer and undisputed leader in color photography lost its leadership and destroyed the prominence of the city of Rensselaer and how the dream of the Chemicals Group to become another Procter & Gamble became a casualty in the fight between Werner management and the private equity firm whose goal was to maximize its immediate financial interest. I saw how three successive presidents—Fleming, Dalton, and Olson—became casualties of petty conflicting interests of the board and how many top executives who came to make GAF a great company had to leave. I remembered how those among us who worked tirelessly to create sustainable value for the company were undermined by a few who did not mind destroying all values to line their own pockets and then disappear.

I also remembered why Chairman Sarni wanted me to get PPG into biotechnology. His goal was to boost the share price, and he got that. My goal was to create sustainable value, but I did not get that. Sarni might have been torn by internal conflicts, but he did not have an escape. He sympathized with me but finally did what the shareholders would have wanted him to do—get a boost in the share price.

Part of an imaginary dialogue between him and the shareholders might have gone something like this. The shareholders may have said, you did a good thing by getting the share price up, but do not spend money for the long-term health of the company. That would decrease your reportable profit, and we will not be here when the company would reap the long-term benefit of that strategy. Our time span is short. We do not care about the future. Give us what we want, now! It was good that you promised to spend $120 million in fifteen years. You got much more back than that in the jump in the share price. We loved that. Now, do not do any stupid thing that your VP of Science and Technology wants you to do. We will punish you if you do.

As I was providing leadership and guidance to the R&D groups at the companies for which I worked, I also thought of helping people outside the company. I endowed a chair at my alma mater and donated personal time and resources to improve other people's lives. I gave lectures at schools, colleges, universities, and professional organizations. In my invited talks to business schools and economics departments, I offered my thoughts about business models and economic growth models. Inspired by my talks, a PhD student in economics dedicated his thesis to me with the comment, "Dr Chakrabarti provided a shining example that business thoughts and intellectual thoughts can coexist peacefully in the same mind."

In those talks, I remarked on the importance of abandoning obsolete technologies and replacing them with new ones that could build sustainable value for business and society at large. My efforts helped create an enormous amount of societal value. For those efforts, the storied technology consulting firm, Arthur D. Little, named me as one of the top ten corporate value creators in the world. I thought *these values would clash with the values that I would be required to provide to satisfy the appetites of a small group of institutional shareholders*. I thought that now was the time to stand for what I taught and practised and preached.

As I looked at my experiences at FMC, GAF, and in everything that I did at PPG from a corporate perspective, I saw that they all indirectly served the same purpose, to increase the share price *now*! And as I did so, I found that likening a corporation to a person was hypocritical. People have morals. Corporations, by and large, do not. I could no longer be a part of an amoral entity. I had strong moral values. They made me what I am. They were the reason those employees wrote me the thank-you letters that they did. They were what drove me to donate my time to voluntarism. They were what made me a philanthropist, and soon I started to feel sorry for the Dempseys, the Leboeufs, and the Duncans of the world.

They are puppets, perfectly happy to execute other people's narrow interests at the cost of larger societal interests. I could not be happy doing what they did. My personal priorities clashed with the priorities of a typical CEO, so I decided not to compete for the CEO's job. CEOs of companies like PPG do not execute morally right actions. They execute the wishes of a select group of greedy institutional shareholders. For lack of a more forceful term, I would call them chief appeasement officers. They are great at deceiving employees with their clever words. Rather than becoming CEO of PPG, I would better spend my time realizing an alternative model for a corporation—one that has a soul.

I knew that I was smarter than many of the people for whom I worked. I knew that making money is not wrong but doing it in a foul or deceptive way was wrong. I knew intuitively that our version of a capitalistic economy had become immoral. I knew that this immorality created immoral investors. I knew that, if I did the right things, I could grow my company. I wanted to prove that both top-line and bottom-line growth could go hand in hand, and both could become a moral force for doing good in society as much as they benefitted the shareholders. I thought shareholder values must be intimately linked to societal values. *And as I saw how much my values clashed with typical corporate values, I saw the irony in calling corporations "public" companies.*

I called Srimati. She was at the apartment we bought in Cambridge, MA, to see the boys. I talked to her about my thoughts—about the risks and benefits. The risk, I told her, was that if I started my company and failed, we would lose everything; we wouldn't be able to leave anything for the boys. On the other hand, I told her, if I stayed at PPG and became CEO, we would become rich and famous.

Srimati quietly listened to what I had to say, then she spoke. She said that living the life of the rich and famous cannot be a goal. The goal should be to live lives that we could be proud of. She encouraged me to follow my instincts and let my conscience be my guide. She said not to worry about the boys. They were getting the best education the country could offer. They would do well in whatever they wanted to do. As for herself, she said, win or lose she would always be by my side all the way. With Srimati as my best friend, I had nothing to fear.

I decided to resign from PPG and concentrate on building the PMC Group.

## Epilogue

The history of corporate America is the history of its champions. When a leader or a champion is lost, the future takes a new turn. Programmes that may have progressed with fervent speed during the champion's tenure may now suddenly come to a halt or are discontinued. Companies typically adopt new directions under new leadership. When Heyman took control of GAF in a proxy fight and started to dismantle the company, the priorities of the Werner administration and my dream of building another household products business like Procter & Gamble disintegrated with it. When Sarni retired as chairman of PPG industries and I decided to build my own company, the priorities that I had set for PPG with Sarni, which included building another biotech giant to rival Genentech, also evaporated. (In 1990, Hoffman-La Roche acquired a majority stake in Genentech.)

When I left PPG, the list of prospective internal candidates for the chairman's job shrank to three—Duncan, Heinze, and Leboeuf—and the least likely of the three, Leboeuf, wound up becoming the next CEO. Anticipating what was going to happen, Heinze left PPG in 1996 to become president and CEO of the specialty chemicals company ISP. Dempsey and Leboeuf would take PPG out of its enviable position with the Scripps Research contract. As various leaders succeeded each other, PPG would sell off its chemicals and glass businesses and become a monolithic company involved only in paint. It has, however, remained a profitable company.

Reported profit, of course, does not always give a correct indication of a company's health. Companies often sell off good, but depreciated, assets at elevated market prices to beef up immediate profits, increase the managers' bonus pool, and boost the share price. But in doing so, they sacrifice the company's potential. Time will tell how successful PPG will be as a monolithic paint company, but my prediction is that it will soon experience a significant profit squeeze as opportunities for growth vanish and the company faces fierce competition, particularly in its low-technology product segments in paints.

# 12

# About Book 2
## *The Makings of PMC Group*

The makings of PMC Group was too elaborate a process to describe adequately in a chapter or two here, so I dedicated another book—Book 2: *The Makings of PMC Group*—to that affair. As I finish writing this chapter, PMC Group's story continues to grow. It has already become a billion-plus-dollar chemicals and pharmaceutical corporation. It is among the fastest-growing companies in the world with manufacturing plants in most of the industrialized regions of the world—the US, Europe, India, and South Korea; its products serve every corner of the world. This chapter and Book 2 ends in July 2022, though a few things in it, particularly those described in Chapter XV extend to my eighty-third birthday on 1 April 2023.

Every serious matter comes alive when we can relate it to our everyday experience. If we can do that, the task does not appear as foreign as it would otherwise. In line with the above thinking, I began each chapter of Book 2 with an experience from my life. Even our childhood experiences remain relevant as we age, as those experiences often parallel the circumstances we face in mature life. We know that any decision we make involves uncertain outcomes, just as in childhood. But when we can connect our past circumstances to the present, we can benefit from knowing in hindsight how our decisions transpired. Some of the experiences I describe go back to my early childhood when I was barely five years old, but the patterns evident in those experiences also match events that happened decades later. One reason for me to include the episodes is to give my readers the confidence that embarking on a new venture is not as scary as one might think. Everyone will be able to relate the experiences I describe with occurrences in their own lives. Illustrating these relationships was the main purpose of starting each chapter with an episode. The other purpose was to make the chapters more "reader-friendly". I hope my readers will agree with me on both counts.

Below I provide a chapter-by-chapter summary of that book.

## Chapter I. Reflection on the Decision

Every lofty endeavour is born out of motivation, and the stronger the motivation, the loftier the endeavour becomes. In the previous chapter, I described the reason I decided to resign from PPG Industries and form my own company—one with business and social purposes—a corporation with a soul.

In the opening chapter of Book 2, I describe this motivation in detail. The driving force behind my decision to form PMC Group, to which I already alluded, was my deepening concern about the failure of top global corporations to generate new growth. Corporate America's neglect of social responsibility in a single-minded drive to please the near-term appetite of a select group of institutional shareholders was also responsible for a steady loss of jobs. I was convinced that those strategies, although enormously successful in the short term, were dangerously flawed at the core. They were not only endangering the health and well-being of the corporations but also the very future of the United States vis-à-vis the global economy. I felt the need for a new model of a corporation—one that would avoid those pitfalls and set the standards for future corporate behaviour.

## Chapter II. A New Vision and Credo

This chapter starts with an episode that occurred when I was twenty-two years old. It describes Gora, an exceptionally beautiful and talented nineteen-year-old girl, who married the son of a tycoon when she had only three months left to sit for her chemistry major examination for her Bachelor of Science degree. At the request of a senior professor whom I respected highly, I agreed to tutor this girl so that she could pass the final examination. She not only passed but did so with high distinction—first-class honours. However, her husband, the spoiled son of a wealthy tycoon, did not allow her to continue her education. Her departing message to me was, "I know you will succeed well in life. I hope one day you will be wealthy enough to put the vane arrogance of the rich and wealthy into shame, but do so with high ideals."

This chapter is about the vision and the credo documents of the corporation I was about to build. I remembered Gora's departing message as I began to compose these two documents that were to guide me throughout the process of building PMC Group. I articulated the vision as follows.

My vision for PMC Group was for it to become a model twenty-first-century corporation—a corporation with a soul. I wanted it to grow rapidly, create societal value and jobs, promote social responsibility, and generate the profits necessary to perform those functions well. I wanted to show that the top and bottom lines of corporate growth can go hand-in-hand with the creation of jobs and the discharge of social responsibilities. I describe the model in detail and show how a corporation can experience phenomenal growth while upholding moral principles and discharging its social responsibilities. I decided to create PMC Group to embody and carry my vision forward.

To supplement this vision, I also established the values that PMC Group will adopt as it becomes the corporation it aspired to be. These are the values, the credo of PMC Group, that the company would adopt and be judged by.

- Commitment: To innovation, quality, and service
- Focus of commitment: Customer
- Citizenship: Global
- Loyalty: To society, employees, and shareholders in that order
- Unassailable factors: Health and safety of people
- Prized assets: Integrity of people working as teams

- Style: Lean and agile
- Treasured philanthropy: Promotion of education

Corporate laws treat a corporation as a person. If PMC Group adheres to its credo, it will be a moral entity and worthy of the status of a person. We commit to measuring our success by tracking the progress we make in three areas—sales and profit growth, job creation, and contributions to education and culture. We provide irrefutable evidence that promoting education and culture is the most worthy of all social causes.

## Chapter III. Strategic Considerations and Business Models

In this chapter, I discuss corporate strategy and various business models. It starts with the episode of Srimati starting a small printing and publishing company in 1984, when I was the director of chemicals research at PPG Industries. The lesson from that experience was that the gestation period for a start-up could be very long before it becomes profitable.

I talk about the S-curve that most business ventures follow. The lower flat part of the curve could be quite long in many cases, indicating very slow progress. Similarly, the upper flat part represents the very slow rate of progress after a business matures. The obvious strategic consideration for me, I was already fifty-four years old, was that I could not afford a long period to develop business infrastructure. My strategy was to buy existing businesses that already had a business infrastructure and convert them into more successful businesses by imposing the values that I already outlined on them.

I also discuss various business models and two of them in particular. The first is technology-centric and the other is market-centric. The technology-centric model applies to businesses that are strong in a core technology, and they try to expand their businesses by finding additional markets for the technology to serve. In a market-centric model, a company establishes a strong presence in certain markets and then tries opportunistically to acquire other technologies that can serve the same market. My primary strength is in technology, so I decided to adopt a technology-centric model for PMC Group.

In addition, I talk about the leader's and follower's advantages as part of business strategy. I describe how the follower's advantage could—with a series of modest innovations, a set of stacked S-curves so to speak—eliminate risk and be as powerful as a leader's advantage. A few years after I started PMC Group, I talked about the follower's advantage at an invited talk at the economics department of Purdue University, which was hosting an annual national conference on agribusiness—Food System 21. The chairman of the convention, Purdue economics Professor Michael Boehlje, was so impressed by my presentation that he decided to incorporate the follower's advantage in his curriculum for Purdue's graduate and MBA students.

I go on to discuss the role of corporate management teams and how to recruit a winning management team. I discuss the pros and cons of conservative and liberal financial structures, concluding that I could build the corporation I aspired to only through a conservative financial structure.

I end the chapter by summarizing the key pillars of PMC Group's business strategy:

1. Acquire existing businesses.
2. Continuously innovate technology: Replace existing products with those providing improved functionalities and introduce new products using the same core technology.
3. Combine synergistic acquisitions under the umbrella of existing companies.
4. Build an A-1 management team.
5. Give local management teams the freedom to operate and hold them responsible for results.
6. Maintain a conservative financial structure: Retain 100 per cent ownership in the companies.

## Chapter IV. Purchase Price Determination and Financing Considerations

If PMC Group were to grow by acquisition as its base strategy, we must know how to determine a fair price for an acquisition. Chapter 4 is about purchase price determination and how to finance an acquisition. I describe financial models such as net present value (NPV), internal rate of return (IRR), return on equity (ROI), and other methods. In the end, I distill them down to a simple formula involving multiples of earnings before interest, tax, depreciation, and amortization (EBITDA).

## Chapter V. The Beginning: Polymer Products Company

This chapter describes the official beginning of PMC Group with my first acquisition, the Polymer Products business from PPG Industries. This business is now the PMC Polymer Products Company Inc. (PPCI), a Pennsylvania corporation, under me. I describe how I essentially doubled its EBITDA from \$3 million to \$6 million during the first year of its operation. Since this was my first acquisition, I detail the elaborate process through which one acquires a business or company. I did not repeat this process with the acquisitions that followed, as subsequent chapters will show. I also describe how we grew PPCI both organically and inorganically with the acquisition of other synergistic businesses and integrating them under the umbrella of PPCI.

## Chapter VI. Accelerated Growth, 1995–97: Crystal, PMC Film, Lenco, and Pro Corporation

This chapter describes the period from 1995 to 1997, an era of exponential growth for PMC Group. It starts with an episode from when I was only five years old and how that experience mirrored my experience five decades later as I ventured into acquiring four US companies—Crystal Inc. PMC; PMC Film Canada Inc.; Lenco Inc. PMC; and Pro Corporation—within a short three-year period. I describe each acquisition separately and the opportunities and challenges that each presented. Following the pattern established in Chapter V, I also describe the companion acquisitions that expanded the platforms of these companies. During 1995–97, PMC Group garnered extensive media coverage with dozens of newspapers talking about the success of our morality-based strategy.

## Chapter VII. PMC Group Headquarters

The phenomenal rate at which PMC Group was growing called for establishing a headquarters to coordinate the diverse activities of the Group's various holdings. Here I describe our acquisition of a fourteen-storey corporate building within a stone's throw from Philadelphia's City Hall. We named this building PMC Group Building, and we became a corporate citizen of Philadelphia along with many multinational companies, banks, and law firms that had their headquarters in Philadelphia.

Our decision to establish our headquarters in Philadelphia, however, was short-lived. The primary reason was the rising cost of commuting and parking in Philadelphia and the burden that presented to our clerical staff. The other major concern was the safety of our employees. As we started to expand globally, many of our employees needed to stay at the office into the evening. Crime during the evening hours became a big concern. Our female employees were afraid of walking to the parking lots after dark. The 9/11 attacks also left people worried about working in tall buildings in major cities. The factors that made Philadelphia a preferred venue for corporate offices thus began to turn against it. In 2004, we relocated our headquarters to a beautiful all-glass building with abundant parking spaces on Route 73 in the heart of the corporate centres of Mount Laurel, New Jersey. This building, also named PMC Group Building, has since remained our global headquarters.

Our original headquarters building at 1312–1314 Chestnut Street in Philadelphia has not changed its name, although we sold it. The new owner considered the building's name as a point of recognition that would not be easy to replace. As one drives along Chestnut Street in Philadelphia, one wonders what relation that building might still have with PMC Group. The answer is none.

## Chapter VIII. Entering Europe and Building a Food-and-Related Process Chemicals Platform: PMC Ouvrie S.A.S.

Here I describe our first venture in Europe with the acquisition of Ouvrie S.A.S. in France from the world's largest chemical company, BASF of Germany. I describe how, starting from a rather modest base in Lesquin, France, it moved to a much bigger location in Carvin, France, to become the world's biggest specialty defoamer company. I describe how we achieved this goal not only through internal developments but also with three additional strategically important acquisitions—Delchim, the global defoamer business of Cognis, and the global protective-colloid business of Solvay Chemicals. Ouvrie now is organized under a broader holding company, PMC Group France.

## Chapter IX. Entering India: PMC Rubber Chemicals India Private Ltd

In this chapter, I describe our entry into India through the acquisition of ICI UK's rubber chemicals manufacturing plant and several associated assets.

The genesis of this acquisition goes back to December 1999, when the chief minister of West Bengal, Jyoti Basu, honoured me with a plaque at that year's global Bengali Conference held in Calcutta. At the end of the convention, the chief minister and several other prominent business leaders asked me not to forget my country of origin as I expanded my business globally. They already knew that I endowed a chair at the chemistry department of Calcutta University, but they wanted me to help invigorate India's, particularly West Bengal's, manufacturing sector.

Following that discussion, I hired the storied Investment Bank of India, ICICI Securities, to conduct a countrywide search for a substantive manufacturing business. After conducting due diligence about several targets, we zeroed in on ICI UK's rubber chemicals business in Rishra, West Bengal.

We concluded the acquisition in December 2005. The acquisition included ICI UK's massive holdings in West Bengal, which included the following:

- ICI's global rubber chemicals business, including its sprawling manufacturing plant
- Two residential compounds with several bungalows in each for executive homes. Each compound was located on eight walled-in acres.

- A fully staffed guest house with a private kitchen and a company chef for preparing meals for the officers and business guests
- A multi-storey, multi-apartment residential complex for the blue-collar employees
- Two prime apartments in the prestigious Woodland Centre of the posh New Alipore area of Calcutta
- Forty acres of excess industrial land around the plant
- A garden house with two jetties on the bank of the Ganga

The world later learned that the divestiture of ICI's massive investments in West Bengal was part of its global liquidation process.

This business did not, however, add much to our global sales or generate much profit for the Group. It did, however, present us with a huge opportunity to discharge many of our societal responsibilities that I outlined in our credo. I discuss them in Chapter XVII, Our Report Card.

## Chapter X. Building One of the Biggest Oleochemical Platforms in the World: PMC Biogenix USA and PMC Biogenix South Korea

In this chapter, I describe how we built one of the biggest oleochemical businesses in the world—a business we named PMC Biogenix, Inc. It started on 29 January 2008, with PMC Group acquiring Chemtura Corporation's global oleochemical business. By 2008, PMC Group owned seven companies—Polymer Products, Crystal, PMC Film, Lenco, Pro Corp,

Ouvrie, and PMC Rubber Chemicals. But in 2008, most of these businesses did not individually generate more than $25 million in sales. The acquisition of Chemtura's oleochemicals business, with its $185 million in annual sales, was our single biggest acquisition till that point. It nearly doubled our annual revenue in a single step. This also offered us the opportunity to later acquire Akzo Nobel's primary amides business in South Korea.

We were lucky to have closed this deal when we did, because if we had been delayed by only a few months, we could not have closed it, as later in 2008 all hell broke loose in the financial market with the onset of the Great Recession. With this acquisition, we not only made a quantum jump in our growth trajectory, we also acquired some of the oldest and most respected tradenames in the industry—Hystrene®, Industrene®, Kemamide®, Kemester®, Kemstrene®, Lubrazinc®, and several others. Though Chemtura's oleochemicals business was our single biggest acquisition until 2008, we soon shattered all records with our next acquisition, which I describe in the next chapter.

## Chapter XI. Building One of the Largest Plastic Additives Businesses in the World: PMC Organometallix

This chapter is about building the biggest organotin-plastic-stabilizer business in the world with a commanding market share around the globe. In the entry, "Trinity", of Harvard philosopher W.V. Quine's "intermittently philosophical dictionary", *Quiddities*, he extolled the virtue of *three*. He starts with stories such as The Three Fates, The Three Magi, The Three Musketeers, The Three Bears, and The Three Little Maids. He then moves on to quote the metaphysical categories that come in three—Immanuel Kant's "unity, plurality, and totality" for quantity and "reality, negation, and limitation" for quality, and Hegel's "thesis, antithesis, and synthesis". Concerning Christianity's trinity, he wrote: "Father and Son makes good substantive sense, but there is something tenuous about the Holy Ghost, suggestive again of trinity for trinity's sake." Quine continues, "The stability of three comes down to the brute and homely fact when we look upon the three-legged stool and contrast its firmness with the wobbly four legs or the toppling two ... Again, there is the rigidity of the triangle" [Quine 1987, pp. 210–12]

Whether the number three is magical or not, it so happened that we built our biggest business platform, PMC Organometallix, by combining three global organometallic businesses—those from Arkema, Dow Chemicals, and LANXESS. This trio made our billion-dollar goal possible.

After we concluded the purchase of Chemtura's oleochemicals business in 2008, the bottom fell out of the credit market. As the financial markets began to feel the severity of the Great Recession of 2008, corporate mergers and acquisitions came to a grinding halt. During this time, we made minor product-line acquisitions to strengthen our existing businesses. But as soon as the credit market rebounded in 2012, we got back into action.

We acquired Arkema's €180 million tin stabilizer business in October 2012. The business included not just Arkema's Thermolite® stabilizers but also their Fastcat® catalysts and fine chemicals. This was one of our most complex acquisitions, involving dozens of lawyers and auditors from several continents.

We quickly followed the Arkema acquisition with the acquisition of Dow Chemical's global polymer stabilizer business (also tin-based) with sales of more than $100 million in February 2013.

The third major piece of PMC Organometallix business came from the acquisition of LANXESS's organotin business in December 2019.

The combination of the three global businesses from three global giants gave us an awesome opportunity for internal innovation on three fronts—technology, manufacturing, and marketing. PMC Organometallix—with its triple trinities—became the most admired company of its kind in the world.

## Chapter XII. Building a Pharmaceutical Platform: PMC Pharma India, PMC Isochem France, and PMC Copperhead USA

This chapter describes how we built a pharmaceutical platform within PMC Group. Acquiring pharma companies is very expensive. First, it is hard to find profitable pharma companies that are for sale. Second, if one is for sale, it usually commands a much higher EBITDA multiple than a comparable commodity or specialty chemicals companies. Yet by 2017, with our robust portfolio of profitable specialty chemicals companies, and particularly after Raj agreed to give up his rapidly rising career as a professor of chemical engineering at Carnegie Mellon University and join PMC Group, I thought it was time for us to build a pharma arm in PMC Group. Because of the difficulty of getting into the business primarily through the acquisition route, we adopted a hybrid strategy—to buy only fully staffed manufacturing infrastructures and then invest heavily to develop the business through internal changes.

The process started with PMC Group International buying the assets of Yegna Manojavam Drugs and Chemicals Ltd (YMDC) of Hyderabad, India, in November 2017. YMDC was one of the largest fluoroquinolone drug manufacturers in India. However, the falling price of these drugs and the company's overextended responsibilities to creditors threatened its continued operations. After buying the assets of the company, we reincorporated the business as PMC YM-Pharma Inc., and embarked on a major expansion effort to build its manufacturing and clean-room facilities so that it would become a substantive manufacturer of active pharma ingredients (APIs) and drug intermediates in India. Since, according to Transparency Market Research, India commanded a $12 billion share of a global $135 billion API market in 2015, and Hyderabad was the pharma capital of India, we thought if we were to become a global producer of bulk drugs, we ought to be in India.

On 4 December 2017, within two months of our acquisition of YM-Pharma in India, we announced the acquisition of the pharma business of Isochem SAS of France. This was a fully integrated pharma business, comprising research, product/process development, regulatory approvals, pilot-scale studies, and full plant-scale production of drug intermediates and APIs for major pharmaceutical companies worldwide. Its products served many medical specialties: oncology, neurology, cardiovascular medicine, gastroenterology, and infectious and rare diseases. These facilities, with a combined footprint of 40 acres, occupy three sites—Gennevilliers, Pithiviers, and Vert-le-Petitt—within a 60-mile radius of Paris. The facilities are all cGMP US-FDA-audited plants for manufacturing pharmaceutical products. We renamed the company PMC Isochem SAS, and with its nearly 250 employees it became a wholly owned subsidiary of PMC Group France, PMC Group International's wholly owned holding company in France.

Though the acquisition of Isochem SAS gave us immediate recognition as a global player in the pharma market, we realized that it came with two weaknesses. The first was that right before our acquisition, it had lost an important customer. Isochem was the prime manufacturer of the intermediate for Sofosbuvir—Gilead's HIV and Hepatitis C drug. Due to the gradual erosion of markets for this drug, Gilead decided to discontinue its production. The loss of this business was a major blow to its profitability. The second weakness was that its prior owner—the private equity firm Aurelius AG—neglected much-needed capital investments in the manufacturing facilities. We could, however, remedy those deficiencies. They only meant that we would need to invest substantive capital during the coming years. The most positive aspect of this acquisition was that it held the potential to make PMC Group a leader in the pharma market. The Covid-19 pandemic would, however, lengthen the time for these changes to occur.

On 22 February 2021, we announced our third pharma acquisition—Copperhead Chemicals—an 875-acre US FDA-qualified facility in Tamaqua, Pennsylvania. Copperhead is the sole US manufacturer of the cardiac drug nitroglycerine.

The acquisition of Copperhead Chemicals also gave us access to another important market—the manufacture of explosives and energetic materials for the defence industry. Among the customers of Copperhead for energetic materials were companies that make US DoD munitions, such as BAE Systems, Aerojet Rocketdyne, and Northop Gruman. Copperhead also sells its energetic products to munitions and explosives manufacturers in foreign countries that have good relationships with the United States.

## Chapter XIII. Lucky Failures

This chapter is about two failed efforts. If they had been successful, we might have lost either some of the value elements upon which I promised to build PMC Group or our full financial independence to operate the company as we thought was right. It is for this reason that I call this chapter "Lucky Failures".

The first was a brush with the private equity firm, Kohlberg, Kravis Roberts, and Company, KKR in short. In August–September 2001, John Saer Jr, a partner of KKR contacted me to enlist my help in his attempt to buy PPG's chemicals business and more broadly to help KKR to build a major chemicals division within its portfolio of businesses. KKR's $25 billion acquisition of RJR Nabisco in 1989 in a hostile takeover bid was at the time the largest leveraged buyout in history and made it the most dreaded name in corporate board rooms. It even led to a book by Bryan Burrough and John Helyar, *Barbarians at the Gate,* which later was made into a movie starring James Garner. I spent considerable time with John Saer to help build a strategy for KKR's interest in the chemicals sector, but for various reasons, the efforts were not successful. If those attempts had been successful, whether I liked it or not, I would have been inadvertently sucked into the orbit of KKR and lost the vision for which I resigned from PPG and decided to build PMC Group.

The second lucky failure was our 2006 failed attempt to acquire Uniqema Company, headquartered in Gouda, Netherlands, from UK-based ICI. Uniqema, a wholly owned subsidiary of ICI, boasted thirteen manufacturing locations around the world and employed 2,500 people globally. In 2005, it reported revenue of $1.08 billion (£626 million) and EBITDA of $84 million (£49 million). In 2006, we did not have the resources to consummate such a deal without a financial partner. So we chose Citicorp Venture Capital Equity Partners (CVC), the venture capital arm of Citigroup, to be our partner. It was a complex arrangement in which we proposed to acquire Uniqema by a 50-50 joint venture between PMC Group and Citicorp Venture Capital. CVC would raise the cash for the acquisition. Our contribution was to be PMC Ouvrie, with a value of EBITDA x 9. CVC was to put a similar amount in equity. The rest of the purchase price was to be a loan from Citigroup.

We were very excited about the prospect of acquiring Uniqema. It would have instantly helped us achieve our billion-dollar dream. With our partner, we spent an enormous amount of time conducting our due diligence and made countless trips to the UK and the Netherlands. We became the top two bidders for the company. Ultimately, our competitor bested our offer of $688 million by $17 million and snatched the company for $705 million.

At the time, losing the Uniqema deal after spending so much money and time seemed to be a great setback. However, as I look back now, it was good that we lost. If we had succeeded, we would have lost PMC Ouvrie, which would continue to grow at 15 to 20 per cent per year. We would have also lost our absolute financial independence. With time, we would build

PMC Biogenix on our own to become a serious competitor to Uniqema. We would also achieve our billion-dollar goal without diluting our complete control of PMC Group. So, I consider the failure of the Uniqema deal to be a lucky failure.

## Chapter XIV. Failed Attempts and Personal Tragedies

This chapter describes the numerous tragedies and failures that I faced while building PMC Group. It should also dispel the belief expressed by many that it was pure luck that I succeeded in building PMC Group as a global corporation without sacrificing our morality-based agenda.

The chapter describes several deaths in my family and provides details of dozens of failures that I encountered during the twenty-eight years of building PMC Group. It shows that failures should not dissuade one, but rather we should use them to provide the zeal and motive force to move forward.

## Chapter XV. The Exits

No business strategy can be cast in concrete. In Chapter III, I discussed two business models, market-centric and technology-centric. I mentioned there that PMC Group would follow a technology-centric model. We, however, tried to test the market-centric model to see if, in special cases, we could make it work for us. Our subjects were plastic transparency and precision injection moulding businesses. Though these businesses generated good profits in the beginning, they did not work for us as well as the technology-centric businesses. As we built PMC Group's other platforms, these two businesses lost their strategic importance to us. In Chapter XV, I describe our exit from the plastic film and injection molding businesses to focus our attention on the other companies in our fold.

## Chapter XVI. Vitality: Going Forward

In this chapter, I describe how I see PMC Group's future unfolding after I am gone. I start with the observation that nothing is permanent and that PMC Group will also disappear one day. But its immediate future is bright. To explain why, I describe my two sons, Debtosh and Raj, who are responsible for running the PMC Group companies.

Debtosh, an MIT graduate in chemical engineering and an AMP from Harvard Business School, was my constant companion as I built PMC Group. He is president of PMC Group, NA, which has two of our biggest business platforms under its management, PMC Organometallix and PMC Biogenix. Our polymer products company and Crystal Inc. PMC also belong to PMC Group, NA. Debtosh is one of the most astute businessmen that I have encountered in my long corporate life. I am confident that PMC Group, NA's best days are still ahead under Debtosh's able management.

Raj, a summa cum laude graduate with highest honours in chemistry from Harvard University, and a PhD from Princeton, was a rising star as a professor first at Purdue University and then at Carnegie Mellon University before joining PMC Group. While in high school, he won the first prize at the International Science and Engineering Fair, was listed as one of *USA Today*'s top twenty students in the country, and was invited to attend the Nobel Prize ceremony. A Harvard Detur Prize winner and a finalist for the Harvard Society of Fellows, Raj is a scientist par excellence. His patented discoveries during his PhD work became one of the top five royalty producers in Princeton's history.

Raj is president of PMC Group International, under which comes PMC Ouvrie, our single biggest company in Europe, and our pharma companies—PMC Isochem, PMC YM-Pharma, and Copperhead Chemicals. PMC Rubber Chemicals India Pvt. Ltd also belongs to PMC group International. Raj is not quite in sync with a follower's strategy. A strong believer in the leader's strategy, he has independently developed a portfolio of leading drug molecules, diagnostic products, and health service products that hold the promise of changing healthcare and becoming a big pharma company. Raj will probably become the biggest promoter of the soul of PMC Group.

My conclusion is that, although like all other phenomena, PMC Group will one day cease to exist, that day is far in the future. Its immediate future is bright and full of vitality. We can expect some dramatic advances for the Group in the decades to come.

## Chapter XVII. Our Report Card

In Book 2, Chapter II, I described our credo—the value elements that guided us as we built PMC Group. These elements were commitment to innovation, quality, and service;

focusing our commitment on the customer; global citizenship; loyalty to society, employees, and shareholders in that order; the unassailable factors of the health and safety of people; the prized assets of integrity and people working as teams; a swift and prudently aggressive style; a lean and agile profile; and the treasured philanthropy of promoting education. In this chapter, I recount our progress towards those values and rate how we faired in each of them.

In our previous chapters, as we described the building of our various business platforms, I described our progress along several of our value elements—the innovations, focus on quality, and service to customers—that made each of our companies shine in their respective businesses. Our accomplishments, of course, would not have been possible without stringent adherence to the highest standards of business ethics and integrity. We have also affirmed our global citizenship by putting our businesses in every corner of the world and maintaining our manufacturing presence in the free world's most prominent regions—the US, Europe, India, and South Korea. We have proven the swiftness of our style by the phenomenal rate at which we grew. In all these categories, we far exceeded our initial expectations and gave ourselves ratings of A-plus.

In this chapter, we focused particularly on the remaining three value elements.

1. Attaining prominence as a business, which includes name recognition of its founder,
2. Loyalty to employees, including attention to their health and safety,
3. Loyalty to society, in the form of philanthropy in addition to promoting education and fostering intercultural harmony

Under the first item, we list dozens of newspaper articles highlighting our success, including features in *Forbes* magazine; my recognition as one of New Jersey's richest fifty residents by *NJBiz*, New Jersey's leading business journal; the various lectures I gave to international forums; and dozens of prestigious organizations and task forces where I occupied prominent positions. In this category, I gave us a score of A-plus.

Under the second item, we did splendidly well except for two casualties in India during the Covid years. In one case, the death certificate indicated Covid-19 as the cause of death. In the other, an employee was exposed to ammonia gas and could not get adequate medical attention because of the Covid emergency. Since the fatalities occurred on our watch, we could not absolve ourselves of our responsibilities. So I gave us a score of A-minus.

In the third area, we far exceeded our initial expectations. Our contributions in this space are too numerous to count. Though Book 2 touches on some of our philanthropic activities, Book 4 provides a far more extensive narrative. An abridged listing of them includes the endowment of a chair, the Paritosh Chakrabarti Professor of Chemistry, at Calcutta University; providing Chakrabarti Foundation Scholarships to college-bound children of our employees; establishing the Paritosh and Srimati Chakrabarti Indian Cultural Center in Evesham township, New Jersey; sponsoring a Srimati and Paritosh Chakrabarti Mancha, a stage for cultural performances at the Tagore Hall of Ananda Mandir in Somerset, New Jersey; being the biggest benefactor of the relief organization, Bharat Sevashram of New Jersey; the donation of the historic Bose House to Belur Math in West Bengal "for the construction and development of a cultural and educational center" with two museums to promote the unifying cultural, political, and religious messages of Swami Vivekananda and Netaji Subhas Bose; and creating entrepreneurial chains by focused donation to deserving people committed to building a better future for themselves and a commitment to helping others with similar donations when they succeed.

## Chapter XVIII. A Day of Retrospection

It is 1 April 2023, my eighty-third birthday. I am reminiscing about my entire life, starting with the day I began to form sustained memories until my eighty-third birthday. It also marks the formal end of my memoirs.

The weather forecast for 1 April 2023 was for storms with intermittent sun, cloud, rain, thunder, prospects of a tornado, and calm. Normally, I do not take my birthday off, but this time I did. I decided to laze around for the entire day and think about the collection of events that marked the eighty-three years of my life. As the mood of the day changed, various memories appeared in my mind. Some did not appear in any of the four memoir books, but they did on that day and gave my memoir a completeness that would not have happened without the collection of thoughts on that day.

The most important takeaway from that exercise was that our lives are a collection of events as varied as the changing weather on a stormy day. Yet when we count everything in life—the good and the evil, fortune and tragedy—we emerge as a clear winner with good overpowering evil and fortune overpowering the tragedies in much the same way calm prevails at the end of a day of tumultuous weather. I hope that this chapter will also help my readers see that the events of their lives are not much different from those of mine and realize that we are all made of the same fabric of destiny. When we live a life of adventure, as I did, we can never avoid adversity. The way to live life is not to dread adversity but to look at its bright side; it provides the thrill, allure, and worthiness of any adventure. Success would lose its definition if there were no failure.

13

# About Book 3

## *The Wealth of People: A New Framework for Economics*

My reason for resigning from PPG and forming PMC Group was a reaction to the fact that big corporations were losing one of their basic tenets—their moral responsibility to uphold and promote the broad interest of society. As I began to build PMC Group—a Corporation with a Soul, one that held its moral responsibilities at the core of its values—I began to question if a single corporation, however successful it is, would change the behaviour of others. I began to realize that our flawed economic frameworks lie at the root of unfair corporate greed.

If we were to change corporate behaviour, and in fact if we were to achieve socioeconomic justice, I reasoned, we must first focus on building a just and yet efficient political economy. Such an economic framework should be able to generate copious national wealth and assure a fair distribution of the same to the society's stakeholders. Viewed from these objectives, both capitalism and communism (or socialism) are flawed economic arrangements. Capitalism creates wealth but distributes it poorly. Communism and socialism purport to provide equitable distribution but fail to create wealth. The first time I openly expressed these views and offered a solution was during a lecture I gave at Purdue University.

While delivering a keynote lecture in 1997 at a session on innovation at the National Conference of Agribusiness hosted by Purdue University, I first expressed the idea that a fair and robust economic arrangement could be devised using the laws of nature as templates. During my talk, which received a gratifying response, I condemned the way big corporations operate today and highlighted the strategy I was adopting in forming PMC Group to remedy the pitfalls. After the convention, I joined several of the conference's attendees, including the faculty members from Purdue's economics department, at an informal reception. The discussion turned to economic theories.

"Unless the basic economic theories are replaced by something better," I told the group, "a full-fledged assault on the issue of immorality won't be possible." When a faculty member insisted that I elaborate, I said, "The main frameworks of economic theories grew from certain ideas—like those of Adam Smith and Karl Marx—about human nature at a certain juncture of socioeconomic development in England and Europe, and as such, they carry with them the personal biases of the originators of those theories. For a framework to be unbiased and sustainable, it must have the rigour of a scientific process. Today's economic theories do not have that." Then I talked briefly about how one could devise such a new framework using the laws of nature as templates.

The audience appeared quite interested in my thoughts, and one audience member suggested that I write a book articulating my ideas. Talking about a subject was one thing, I reasoned, but writing a book about it was quite another. However, the thought stayed with me. The details of such a book gelled over the next twenty-five years.

In *Wealth of People*, I examine two scientific principles: 1) the laws of thermodynamics, the second law in particular, and 2) Darwinism. Both are relevant to equality and inequality. The first principle, one of the fundamental laws of physics that rule the vast inorganic universe, strives to achieve equality in death, figuratively in the graveyard of entropy. The second tries to maximize inequality in natural selection with the law of the living world that represents the tiniest corner of the tiniest part of the universe.

Book 3 of my memoir series is about developing a new framework. Below I provide a chapter-by-chapter summary of that book.

## Chapter I. Structural Components of Modern Political Economy: Terms and Concepts

Here I introduce the structural components of modern political economy. I describe in plain language basic concepts like money, money supply, GNP-GDP, the velocity of money supply, monetary policies of nations, monetarists, Keynesians, econometric models, presidents' economic policy decisions, the role of gold in an economy, international balance of payments, foreign exchange and foreign exchange rates, the IMF, the World Bank, central banks and their role in the economy, credit, and stocks and bonds. I also offer a commentary on stock market crashes. Readers will become familiar with key economic terms and concepts, making it much easier for them to follow the rest of the book.

## Chapter II. Origins of Modern Economics and the Socioeconomic Climate

I trace the origins of key economic theories to the biographies of their originators and the socioeconomic climates in which they were born and worked (the eighteenth to early twentieth centuries in Great Britain and the nineteenth century in Europe). My focus is on the pioneers of the field: Adam Smith (1723–90), Karl Marx (1818–83), and John Maynard Keynes (1883–1946).

## Chapter III. The Leading Economic Theories: An Introduction

Here I discuss leading economic theories, including: 1) classical economics, also called the Smith-Ricardo-Mill-Malthus doctrines, or more popularly, capitalism, 2) socialism and communism, 3) the demand-side macroeconomic theory developed by Keynes, and 4) two morality-based theories advanced by Rawls and Sen as examples of egalitarian economics. I also describe how various nations adopted their economic models.

## Chapter IV. The Leading Economic Theories: A Critical Analysis

Here I provide a critical analysis of the leading economic theories, pinpointing their strengths and weaknesses. I argue how and why communism and socialism are flawed systems and are impotent in creating wealth. I also advance a scathing criticism of capitalism and show how it has degenerated into an immoral arrangement and how it recently has become something like a Ponzi scheme in the United States. I also show that egalitarian economics suffers from the same weaknesses as socialism with its lack of focus on wealth creation. This chapter is a primer for why we need a better framework, the subject of Chapter VII.

Although I briefly address wealth generation in this chapter, I devote Chapter VII to a more detailed discussion on the subject. In this chapter, I focus on fairness in income distribution. I show that capitalism in its rawest form is equivalent to economic Darwinism—a term I use similar to Social Darwinism (or eugenics), which I describe in Book 4 (see next chapter) as an immensely immoral theory. I argue that economic Darwinism is morally bankrupt and therefore unacceptable. I trace the immorality of capitalism to three sins: 1) overemphasizing the role of capital, 2) reducing the status of the working class to that of inanimate objects, and 3) Wall Street's hijacking of the term "technology". I show that the descent of capitalism into immorality, at least in the

United States, began in earnest after abandoning the gold standard in 1971.

I also discuss growth theories of economics and provide a critical analysis of the various terms used in equations for economic growth. Most economic theories relating to growth don't escape my critical review.

Next, I present a moral argument for restricting the wealth that large corporations and their owners may accumulate. My argument is based on the role of technology (in addition to capital and labour) in big businesses. Most tech companies, whose valuations run in hundreds of billions of dollars, relied on public funding of technology in government and academic labs. I cite references to show that a whopping 65 to 85 per cent of those multi-hundred-billion-dollar valuations come from publicly owned technology. I argue that those technologies, which MIT economist Robert Solow called the "common pool of technological progress", belong equally to all members of society. Therefore, their benefits should belong equally to everyone.

I then argue how an overemphasis on capital in capitalism has led to the rise of monopolies and, using multiple examples, show how such monopolies have driven capitalism towards immorality. Later in the chapter, I provide scientific proof of why monopolies are also an improper arrangement for wealth creation.

The chapter finishes with a discussion of mixed systems, in which capitalist countries have adopted certain socialist tools to remedy some of their shortcomings and communist countries have adopted a few capitalist tools to remedy some of their deficiencies. I analyse the economies of China, Russia, and France to show how each system has tried to borrow from the others, and I argue that the combinations have made the resulting arrangements even worse.

## Chapter V. The Laws of Thermodynamics

This chapter begins by answering the most consequential questions: Why do we need a new framework, and why do we need guidance from the hard sciences to build such a framework? I show how certain laws of sciences—the laws of thermodynamics, the Boltzmann law of distribution of energy, and Darwin's law of evolution—can provide templates for every possible economic issue.

This chapter has two parts. In the first, I introduce the relevant laws of science—including the first, second, and third laws of thermodynamics—in language accessible to the average reader. In the second part, I introduce the key terms of thermodynamics: temperature; entropy; closed, isolated, and open systems; and spontaneous and non-spontaneous processes. As I describe the terms, I briefly explore how I will later relate them to the economic terms already introduced.

## Chapter VI. Work and Energy: Where Thermodynamics and Economics Meet

In this pivotal chapter, I show how and why the concepts of thermodynamics are like those of economics. The concept of work connects the disciplines. To define work in terms of thermodynamics, I introduce 1) the ideal gas laws (Boyle's and Charles's laws), 2) the definition of work in thermodynamics and what is meant by pressure-volume work, 3) a commentary on work that relates it to conversions of energy, 4) the role of a machine and an agent in generating work, and 5) the heat engine and its defining principles, including the Carnot cycle. I also introduce several other thermodynamic terms: chemical energy, activation energy, internal energy, enthalpy, Gibb's free energy, and the Boltzmann law of distribution. Such laws rule the vast inorganic world. But the tiniest of the tiny organic world evolved through another law of nature, Darwin's theory of evolution, which I also describe, since it helps establish certain economic scenarios.

Chapters V and VI are quite technical, but I present them in everyday language. To keep the reader engaged, I describe how each concept will later connect to a corresponding concept in economics. Prep and collegiate readers will find these two easily digestible chapters particularly helpful in learning the basic principles of science.

## Chapter VII. The Framework of a New Economic Order

In this chapter, I develop our new economic framework and present its various components. This is the chapter where the proverbial rubber meets the road, where I translate the laws of science into the laws of economics. I establish the economic equivalents of temperature, energy, internal energy, enthalpy, Gibbs free energy, and the first and second laws of thermodynamics. I show why polarity in wealth distribution is essential for wealth creation, why natural laws do not provide an advantage to monopoly, and why forward and backward integrations, where called for, can provide better economic efficiencies. Next, I show that the size of a corporation does not provide any additional benefit, except in special cases.

While presenting the new economic framework, I show how nature demonstrates that socialism and communism are flawed systems and why they fail to create wealth. I also show why the new framework can be a force for wealth creation while providing a fair distribution of a nation's wealth to its citizens. Regarding distribution, I show that nations should distribute their GNP in two buckets: common and private. The common bucket should be based on the set of government-subsidized technologies that various companies have since privatized—what Solow called "the common pool of technological progress". All citizens of the nation should share equally of this bucket. The private bucket should belong to those who work hard to create wealth and/or use their proprietary technology to create value.

I discuss in detail a moral conundrum that can result from a competition between wages of labour and the efficiency of corporations in various countries, and I provide a solution in the aggressive use of technology to boost labour productivity in high-labour-cost countries. I also establish that the laws of nature encompass the concepts of private property and inheritance rights.

To be sure, the new framework is not a compromise between socialism (or communism) and capitalism. It is a new system built on nature's laws and subordinate only to moral laws. Yet a critical analysis of this system suggests that we could implement many of its tenets gradually as amendments to the capitalist model. These tenets include the following:

- Distributing a portion of national income as common property to every individual
- Providing free education
- Establishing a fair level of wealth inequality (a distribution of excess wealth) for optimum wealth creation

- Creating a method for the collection of federal revenue based on consumption tax only
- Drastically reducing the role and size of the federal government
- Reducing the role of capital in businesses through banking and financing reforms
- Eliminating monopolistic practices (lateral integration)
- Supporting vertical integration (both forward and backward) of business within maximum size limitations
- Establishing an independent reserve currency anchored to an appropriate basket of products and services
- Incentivizing creativity to spark a chain reaction of wealth creation

To implement the new framework, I propose a movement approach rather than a revolution or evolution. My purpose is therefore to convince concerned intellectuals and the average reader of the need for change and of the merits of the proposal. The result would be popular support for the new framework. Revolutionary change is destructive and short-lived, and evolutionary change takes too long to correct the current situation. A movement, a steady and well-thought-out process, has a parallel in nature: the activation energy needed for chemical reactions to occur.

I keep the new arrangement at the framework level so that details can be added to specific issues as needed within the scope of the established principles. We must therefore treat the new framework as a living document and not something carved in stone.

I argue that the new framework will remove the sins of capitalism and be superior to anything thus far. We can implement it with only modest efforts—amendments to capitalism, if you will. But before we can do so, the US dollar must be dethroned from its role as the international reserve currency and be replaced by an international reserve currency anchored to tangible assets—namely, to a basket of commodities.

Throughout this chapter and the book, I remind my readers that we are unique in the universe as a moral entity. Accordingly, as we seek guidance from nature to show us the path, we must also seek guidance from the laws of morality. Whenever conflict arises between the products of our inquiry and the laws of morality, the latter must prevail over the former.

## Chapter VIII. Healthcare and the New Economic Framework

No economic framework can be complete without a discussion of healthcare, which consumes, depending on the country, between 2 and 17.4 per cent of GDP. I open this chapter with a snapshot of various countries' per capita healthcare spending and the results of that spending. I divide the countries into three major groups based on life expectancies at birth, which we can take as a rough measure of the effectiveness of healthcare spending. The United States spends the most in absolute amounts ($11,000) *and* percentage of GDP (17.4 per cent) per capita on healthcare, yet it fails to make the first-tier group. It belongs to the second group and is tied with Poland, which spends $1,104 and 6.5 per cent of its GDP on health care, according to 2019 statistics.

After establishing the above facts, I analyse various healthcare issues, including quality of care and the effectiveness of government control of healthcare. I also discuss various issues surrounding a woman's right to abortion. Next, I present how we would deal with healthcare under the new framework. The new framework largely leaves management of healthcare to individuals, who can pay for it using their common share of the nation's income. The following, however, would be freely available to everyone: 1) emergency hospital care, 2) contraception for every female of childbearing age, and 3) free abortion until the fetus begins developing nerve cells. I provide both moral and scientific arguments in favour of each aspect of healthcare under the new framework.

## Chapter IX. Brave New World Dream

I begin this chapter by summarizing the twenty pillars of the new economic framework:

1. The laws of nature as our templates
2. Minimal federal government
3. Judicial oversight
4. National income to replace welfare programmes
5. Free education
6. Optimal inequality
7. No unions
8. No tenure for teachers
9. Same financing rules for all businesses, regardless of size
10. No business is too big to fail

11. No monopoly or horizontal integration
12. No federal income tax
13. Consumption tax
14. No inheritance taxes
15. Independent reserve currency
16. No Medicaid, Medicare, or other mandated healthcare programmes
17. Free emergency healthcare services
18. Free contraception
19. Time-limited free abortion
20. Implementation through a grassroots movement

I then use six hypothetical cases to explore how the new framework will affect the lives of people belonging to different socioeconomic strata in the real world. Not everybody will prosper, but most will do better under the new framework. Humanity wins when the great majority wins.

## Review

For me to gain confidence in the approach I adopted and the product it generated, I had my manuscript reviewed by someone who had intimate knowledge of the field of thermodynamics and adequate exposure to the field of economics. The following quote is from a renowned professor of chemical engineering, who also happened to be the spouse of a professor of economics.

> Dr. Chakrabarti's new economic framework guided by morality is particularly timely given the current

national emphasis on social justice and equality. Dr. Chakrabarti's approach—based on the fundamental scientific laws of thermodynamics—is unique and draws on his vast experience as both an entrepreneur and as a senior leader for over 25 years in Fortune 500 companies.

—Jennifer S. Curtis,
Professor Emeritus and former Dean of Engineering,
University of California, Davis

# 14

# About Book 4

## *The Highest Reality: A Treatise on Religion, Truth, Morality, and the Purpose of Life*

Life is a journey. It is also a learning experience. And it is more than a learning experience; it is about reflecting on what we learn. And it is more than reflecting on what we learn; it is about discovering new things that go beyond how the physical world works. It also concerns non-physical things—*spiritual* things. It is about discovering how the physical world interacts with our emotional world. It is about probing the nature of truth. It is about pondering religions—the good and the bad in them. It is about understanding the importance of helping others and philanthropic activities. It is also about pondering the purpose of life. Book 4, the last volume of my memoir series, is about all the above. It brings everything together by relating each idea to my inquiries and to the inquiries of those who have contemplated the same matters in the past.

As we journey through life, we accumulate varied experiences that contribute to our world views. Our experiences often take us from one pole of reality to another. Adam Smith, the father of the capitalist order of economics, taught us that if we take care of our self-interest, an "invisible hand" will take care of the collective interest. But in countries where citizens follow their self-interest with zest, they become corrupt and immoral. As children, we were taught to love our country, but when we love it with fervent passion, we pave the way for tyrants like Adolf Hitler. We were also taught not to accept injustice, but as the quote often attributed to Gandhi goes, "An eye for an eye leaves the whole world blind." We find that science has done great things for us, but if we use our science without moral constraints, we will destroy ourselves. Many a religion teaches that it is the only true religion and that all others are false or even evil. When we follow such advice, the result is jihads and crusades that kill millions.

No wonder we get confused. I have gone through such confusion and swung from one belief to another until I established my worldview, which balances science with morality, materialism with spirituality, and self-interest with the interests of others—always trying to distinguish a process from the product of a process. The process must follow the laws of science, but morality must rule the product.

When we were born, we had no religion, values, or biases. We acquired those from our families, cultures, and the environment in which we spent our early years. Children born into Muslim families grow up to be Muslims. When a Christian family raises an infant born to Muslim parents, the child grows up to be a Christian. The same is true for almost every other religion and sect. In a sense, we are born as a "clean slate" that eventually accumulates characteristics from our native culture and environment. As we grow older, we develop the ability to reason and examine our predilections through the prism of our judgement. Some of us apply this judgement and accept some predilections while rejecting others. But many among us remain confined in them—willingly and happily so—for life.

Born into a Hindu Brahmin family, I followed the practices of Hinduism with abiding faith. In our conservative family, these practices included a formal religious festivity almost every month. As the saying goes, a Hindu performs thirteen religious ceremonies in twelve months. My family's ceremonies involved worshipping various deities—God in human images, both male and female. We prayed to these deities, asking them to grant us every favour possible: to give us knowledge and make us successful as students, to keep our family healthy and safe, to give us good fortune and wealth, to protect us from snake bites, and so forth.

In addition, every morning we would pray before our family goddess, Lakshmi, the goddess of good fortune and wealth. If any misfortune struck the family or if one of us fell sick, I would prostrate myself before our family deity. If I were not home, I would kneel before an imaginary image of Vishnu (Hinduism's supreme preserver God) seated on a lotus flower. When the misfortunes disappeared, as they usually did, I thought my prayers had worked, and my religious faith deepened. I became a strong believer in the power of the deities we worshipped.

Hindus consider religious activities an act of sacrifice for the good of the family and society. My unfailing devotion to religion and my faith in the power of the divine became so intense that at one point in my life, I thought about abandoning everything material and becoming a sanyasi in the hope that I would do much good for society in that capacity by connecting directly with God, although I was unsure what that good would be. Since I did not know how to become a devoted sanyasi, I sought a guru—a successful sanyasi—who could help me achieve my aspiration, which endured until I completed my master's degree and began conducting research for my doctoral degree.

My blind faith in God and everything religious came to an abrupt halt when I met a sanyasi, who, as rumour had it, was a God-sent saviour. He turned out to be a fraud. After that experience, I began questioning my religious beliefs. I decided to test whether God existed as I believed He did. I thought if I could please God by worshipping him, I could also annoy Him by disrespecting Him. So, I stopped worshiping and dared God to stop me from pursuing my doctorate. When I earned my doctorate with flying colours, I thought my so-called experiment proved that my faith in God was a mistake. Of course, as a scientist, I should have known that a negative result does not prove the opposite. Yet this "experiment" shook my belief in God. I became agnostic—someone who neither admits nor denies the existence of God.

Although agnostic, I continued attending public religious ceremonies like Durga Puja but viewed them as cultural programmes rather than religious ones. Later, when our children and then our grandchildren were born, my wife and I performed their annaprasana (a Hindu rice-eating ceremony) at the age of one, hatey khari (marking the beginning of literacy), and for my grandson, the upanayana (a sacred thread ceremony)—all as cultural observances. My children and grandchildren remember these ceremonies fondly, but they do not practise religion, at least not in the way I did when I was their age.

Although I left the practice of certain Hindu religious rites, I remained a Hindu—a Hindu by birth. More than 80 per cent of the world's population belongs to some form of religion, and almost 98 per cent of that group belongs to one of the four major religions: Christianity, Islam, Hinduism, and Buddhism. This situation has persisted more or less unchanged for generations. My studies revealed that even some of the most renowned scientists had faith in God or some divine power. Richard A. Muller, PhD, the great physicist celebrated as a co-discoverer of dark energy, wrote in *The Physics of Time*, "I pray every day, though I do not know to whom."

Being agnostic, I felt helpless and frustrated on some occasions. When I became distressed, I wished I could pray to some supreme power but only became more distressed when I realized I did not believe in any supreme power. I turned to studying the major religions, hoping to find some form of truth in them. If such a truth existed, I reasoned, it should be common to all religions. These studies led me to devise my theory of Truth. I theorized that religious truths can be true only if 1) diverse groups of people accept them as true, 2) they survive almost unchanged over many generations, and 3) science cannot contradict them. I found that the core message of all religions was the same, although they differed in their respective rituals. I also concluded that most religions harbour both truths and falsehoods, with the falsehoods evident as the root of religious hatred and violence.

As a successful entrepreneur, I realized that fulfillment in life does not come from personal success alone. It comes from promoting both self-interest and the interests of others, with the first finding its expression of contentment in the second. I explore these concepts in Chapters VIII and IX of Book 4, "Beyond Self-Interest" and "The Paritosh and Srimati Chakrabarti Ashram."

I close Book 4 with a chapter on the purpose of life, using examples from science, art, and philosophy. Here I explore the concept that the grandest of all existences is nothingness and that nothingness is also the womb of all realities. All realities emerge as pairs of opposites from nothingness, and they end up again as nothingness upon their collapse. Our ability to create reality as pairs of opposites—our scientific, artistic, and philosophical advances and the fact that these realities can accumulate from generation to generation—gives humanity the power to one day fully understand the purpose that lies behind the existence of the universe. When humanity reaches that goal, we will have succeeded in fulfilling our purpose, which until then should be to do everything in our power to keep humanity alive and united at peace with itself.

Finally, as someone who has practised science for most of his life, I can attest that nothing in this book is based on my personal beliefs alone. The rigour of sound logic and/or the process of science supports everything, including the chapter on belief as a province unto itself.

Below I provide a chapter-by-chapter summary of the ten chapters Book 4.

## Chapter I. Religion and Me

Here I describe the evolution of my religious experiences—starting as a blind believer in deities, then becoming an agnostic, and then to an agnostic spiritualist. I describe five episodes—Bitten by a Snake, A Tantrik in Agartala, The Sanyasi at the Sealdah Railway Station, Concern for a Sick Friend, and Concern for a Sick Relative—that triggered the turning from one phase to another.

## Chapter II. An Inquiry into the Nature and Domain of Truth

I begin this chapter with a dissertation on the position of man in nature. I then reflect on truth and describe why I had to devise *My Own Theory of Truth* to fully explore the domain of truth. This theory is based on Darwin's principle of evolution. I describe with examples scientific truth, philosophical truth, moral truth, and religious truth. My theory can explain them all and bring them together in an expanded view of Truth. I describe these various forms of truth within the context of our free will, consciousness, the nature of the physical universe, and the contemplative power of our mind that can probe existence beyond the physical universe. Finally in this chapter, I provide a commentary about science and the scientist, where I show that a scientist is a person who is not married to the practice of science only—he is a person with his own spiritual, cultural, and religious beliefs as well.

## Chapter III. Deliberation on Religion

I start by providing a statistical distribution of the top ten religions. Then I examine the key components of the leading Abrahamic religions—Judaism, Christianity, and Islam—and two Eastern religions, Hinduism and Buddhism. I describe how these views coincide with or differ from one another in their description of ethics, morality, virtue, sin, peace, justice, love, compassion, charity, self-respect, and respect for others. I also describe their characteristic concepts about God, emissaries of God in the form of humans (messiah, prophet, and avatar), the soul, and the afterlife. I briefly describe the scriptures of these various religions in this chapter. In later chapters, I cross-reference the contents of this chapter as I explore what are the good and immutable facts of all religions and what is bad and false in them.

## Chapter IV. Establishing Religious Truth: Convergent Religious Discourses

This chapter is a discussion about universal truth—the core concepts that are common in all religions. I identify three areas where all major religions converge. These three areas are 1) the definition of morality, 2) the existence of a spiritual God, the supreme creator, and 3) possibly the existence of a soul. I test these concepts through the lens of my theory of truth and conclude that at least the first two aspects of religion are fundamental and spiritual truth, much the same as the laws of physics are scientific truth of the physical world.

## Chapter V. Observances and Experiences at the Interface of Truth and Falsehood

Here I examine the prescriptive or ritualistic practices of various religions. These practices—which differ significantly from one religion to another—must not be, I assert, confused with the fundamental truths of these religions. Rituals are processes or paths by which each religion teaches how to arrive at their ultimate destiny—the realization of God. They are temporal and as such change with time. These practices can be enlightening or narrow-minded. They are also the source of superstitions and religious violence. In this chapter, I also explore monotheism and polytheism—the concepts and misconceptions about them. I end this chapter with a discussion on belief—a field of inquiry unto itself that is different from religion and faith. I exemplify belief by an episode—My Father Was Reborn as My Elder Son Debtosh—admitting that beliefs can only be coincidences and might not mean anything more.

## Chapter VI. Falsehoods in Religion

Here I show the falsehoods in religion in much the same way that I showed the common truths among religions. The falsehoods, I conclude, lie in four main areas: 1) an exclusive claim to the true God, 2) justifying violence in the name of religion, 3) justifying caste and gender-based discriminations, and 4) theories about the creation of the universe: heaven and hell. These concepts and claims do not muster the test of commonality and temporal permanence, and/or they conflict with scientific facts. I end this chapter with a general commentary on religious falsehoods.

## Chapter VII. Challenges to the Concept of God and Spirituality: Communism and Nihilism

In this chapter, I explore the movements that denied any truth in religion—with particular emphasis on 1) Karl Marx and

Communism and 2) Friedrich Nietzsche, the man who called God the father of evil. I show how their dark views of religion are fundamentally wrong and conflict with the definition and nature of Truth that I explored before. I end this chapter with a few additional comments about both Nietzsche and Marx where I recognize their extraordinary talents as skilful writers.

## Chapter VIII. Beyond Self-Interest

Here I discuss the key concepts of morality. In Chapter II, I talked about the Darwinian principle as the basis for developing my theory of truth. That involved a process, not the product. The process, I argue in this chapter (and in many other parts of my memoir series), must always be based on scientific principles. In other words, it must be always true and reproducible. The product, in this case morality, must muster the human laws, which in the words of Socrates is a social compact about a set of rules developed by humans for humans about how one should live.

The concept of morality has been an integral part of all religions, and utilitarian considerations have also confirmed it. Though I discussed morality in various parts of this book and will continue to do so in the subsequent chapters, I summarize these views in this chapter with a single sentence—while the Darwinian principle is based on survival of the fittest, morality is about protection of the weakest. I develop this concept further to mean that morality is acting beyond one's self-interest—*non sibi*, Latin for "not-for-self". Once we believe and promote a concept to be true, we must also act accordingly.

In this chapter, I list most of my major philanthropic (not for self) activities. Because resources are limited, I chose my philanthropic activities—which span the areas of supporting education, promoting cultural harmony, creating new entrepreneurs, and several other projects—carefully to support those that could have scalable (multiplying) effects. I use two episodes—The Parents' Own Clinic for Deaf Children of Kolkata and The Plight of a Grandmother—to show the urgency and give human faces to the types of philanthropy I practise.

## Chapter IX. The Paritosh and Srimati Chakrabarti Ashram: An Initiative for Sustainable Global Peace

Although improving the economic health of people with fairness—a subject of Book 3 of this memoir series—is an important foundation for building a peaceful world, history has taught us that those aims are not nearly enough. To build lasting peace, we must build harmony among people with various orientations to religion, culture, regional origin, and race. This is a much tougher task than building substantive and fair economic arrangements. War, which is of course a form of violence, cannot be effective in curtailing religious violence, as history has taught us repeatedly.

In this chapter, I propose establishing a pilot think tank for creating a harmonious and peaceful world. The chapter starts with an outline of the objectives of the pilot. It then provides a discourse on the importance of protecting humanity—a unique phenomenon in this vast universe endowed with a unique purpose. A brief discussion then follows about the threats humanity faces from within and without and an outline of the conceptual framework of the ashram that purports to provide a solution to racial, religious, and cultural problems. To give my readers an understanding of the depth of the problems we face, and the ones that the ashram will address, I discuss the problems in each of the three areas of discord.

Under *racial discords*, I bring to the surface the anti-Semitism that engulfed Europe during the nineteenth and twentieth centuries, a brief biography of Adolf Hitler (who personified anti-Semitism), and caste-based discrimination in India. Under *falsehoods of religion*, I describe how, in spite of the grand unifying spiritual principles of all religions, religious violence—both inter-religious and intra-religious—has inflicted incalculable harm and loss of life in society. Under *cultural discords*, I describe several cultures and show how cultural diversity can enrich humanity and give it a sense of strength, even when we seek integration with historically ancient cultures.

Lastly, I describe how a group of backward-looking seniors used the legal process to delay and eventually derail the initial grand plan for the Ashram. Great ideas are not supposed to die. From this was born the concept of the virtual ashram, and I conclude this chapter with a detailed description of this ashram and its mode of operation and funding.

## Chapter X. The Purpose of Life

One aspect of human life is a quest to understand its purpose. I deal with it in the last chapter of the last book of my memoir—after I have presented my experiences as a student, a teacher, working in the industry, building a chemical company, and presenting my thoughts on economics, culture, religion, morality, and peace. This is because each of these experiences and thoughts was critical in coming to the final goal of the memoir—finding the purpose of life.

Some believe that there is no purpose in life other than living. To this group belongs the Nobel Prize-winning French writer-philosopher Albert Camus, who asked the question "We are born, we live, we die—to what end?" He answered, "To the end of living." But to many others, which include Albert Einstein and many other prominent scientists, ethicists, and social leaders like Gandhi and Martin Luther King, *life has a higher purpose* than just living. I belong to this latter class.

To address the question of the purpose of life it will be helpful to first understand the nature of reality and the place of humans, or more accurately of the human mind, in it. I discuss this in some detail in this chapter and conclude that reality is an expression of a neutral position into pairs of opposites. The neutral position, as I describe it, is *shunya* (nothingness), a concept developed in ancient India that means zero in mathematics, but literally, it means much more. I describe this conception of reality as an unfurling of shunya through seven examples, starting with the balance sheet of a company. On a balance sheet, assets always equal liabilities, meaning that a company is an unfurling of zero into assets and liabilities. My final example is the singularity from which the universe and space-time came into existence in the *big bang*. I show that the singularity is a point in the *absolute* shunya, something that is devoid even of space-time, meaning that it is beyond the universe. Science cannot probe this absolute nothingness because it is devoid of space-time. We can contemplate absolute shunya only with our minds. To be sure, in my way of thinking, shunya is not non-existence. On the contrary, it is the grandest of all existences and the womb of all realities. The various descriptions of God from the major religions look almost identical to the description of absolute shunya, as I show by quoting from various scriptures.

One way to think of a purpose is that it has a direction. Whenever we do something, we do it with a purpose. The fact that the universe is constantly gaining entropy, meaning that it has a forward-moving arrow of entropy, a concept I used as a template in Book 3 to develop a new economic framework, may on the surface seem to be at odds with the concept of the unfurling of the universe from nothingness. But it makes sense if we consider that one day, as physicists attest, the expansion of the universe will stop, and then it will start to contract. During this contraction, the arrow of entropy will reverse, and the universe will eventually disappear into a singularity in a *big crunch*.

Another concept that can help before we discuss a higher purpose of life is to understand the *potential and expectations* of others. As teachers or parents, *we want* to see high-potential students grow up to develop their full potential and make a positive contribution to society. The teachers' or the parents' expectations, though often remaining unspoken, are real. Our expectations, which are embedded in the words "we want", do not stop at the individual level—they extend to whole societies and even to all humanity. We expect every generation to make a positive contribution to the progress of humanity. To put it more clearly, to fulfil the higher purpose of life, we need to think beyond strengthening our individual potentials to include strengthening generational interests as well; we need to think *beyond self-interest* to the interests of all.

Yet another way to understand the purpose is to recognize the importance of *appreciation*. Just as with teachers and parents, we try our best to help good students reach their maximum potential. So we expect successful students to appreciate our sincere efforts and sacrifices to help them achieve their potential. We also do good to others for the sake of gaining their appreciation.

The above considerations and others led me to conclude that the higher purpose of life is not just living. It is to help humanity reach its apex, and this involves not only becoming the best we individually can be but also helping others become the best they can be. This is also part and parcel of understanding reality from both physical and spiritual perspectives. Finally, if a creator God existed, He must also expect that someone understands and appreciates his creation—maybe humanity came into existence to provide that appreciation.

The above definition of purpose prompted me to do the things I did in life, including those mentioned in this memoir, particularly in Books 3 and 4. It is the realization of a higher purpose in life that prompts us to do things that a nihilist philosophy never can.

# 15

# Valediction

*Death is the mother of beauty.*
—Wallace Stevens

*On the day when death will knock at thy door*
*what wilt thou offer to him?*
*Oh, I will set before my guest the full vessel of my life—*
*I will never let him go with empty hands.*
*All the sweet vintage of all my autumn days and summer nights,*
*All the earnings and gleanings of my busy life*
*will I place before him at the close of my days*
*when death will knock at my door.*
—Rabindranath Tagore, *Gitanjali*, Poem 90

When a wise storyteller writes a story, the first line is always fixed in truth. Then he gradually starts inventing as the story progresses until it becomes his creation. If he does a good job, something extraordinary happens, and the last line writes itself.

A journey is similar. The traveler begins his adventure from a known place. He explores along the way, and when the journey is near completion, the thrill of the adventure has already been known. The end is not something to worry about; it flows easily and spontaneously. A good story always ends well, as does a good journey.

Life is a journey. It begins with our birth and a genetic inheritance from our ancestors. What we do with it is of our own making and is the extent of our exploration and inventions. We should not worry about the end. The most important thing is the journey itself—the thrill and exhilaration that follows when we turn our journey into an adventure. If we do this well, the journey will end well. The end of a good adventure is always beautiful.

There is, however, a subtle difference between the enjoyment derived from a story and a journey. In the case of the former, not only does the writer enjoy the pleasure of his or her creative work, but the work also brings pleasure to the reader. In the case of a journey, the pleasure of the adventure remains confined to the traveller unless the traveller is also a good writer and can share his or her joy with the reader.

When a traveller's journey becomes an adventure, it leads to extreme pleasure. So it is with death when the journey of life becomes an adventure and death becomes the mother of beauty. But life, if we can describe its true experience as a piece of literature, can bring edification and enjoyment to the generations that follow. Tagore's welcoming message to death contains the same broader and higher meaning. Death is not just the mother of beauty; it is a tribute to itself. Most stories begin in the middle of an episode. For Tagore, death is the culmination of a life that spans a person's entire experience, beginning at birth. Death thus assumes a sublime significance beyond beauty, a special meaning that only Tagore could describe.

I have tried to live a life of courage, adventure, and invention. I have also fulfilled my desire to leave behind my life's experience in a four-volume memoir. In my farewell message, I will try to describe how and why I am ready and eager to welcome death.

## Fearing Death or Welcoming It as a Saviour?

Most people fear death. People in their eighties, nineties, and beyond cling to life, even as their bodies suffer. Why? Fear of the unknown. The unknown gives them anxiety and causes stress. They have not lived a life of adventure. They're afraid to veer away from the familiar. They live a life that the generations before them lived. They deliberately chose well-established paths because they fear the unknown. They seek food, clothing, shelter, warmth, sex, and entertainment just as their parents and grandparents did. When ambitious, they may want a better life, but better only means more of the same: richer food, more luxurious clothing, a bigger home and lawn, more comfortable surroundings, more toys, a sexier spouse, and so on.

When they travel, they visit places that others have already visited. They raise their children the same way their parents raised them. If they try something different, they make sure the different way has been well-tested and well-established. Their children study the same subjects their parents studied. They pursue known careers. A businessman's son becomes a businessman, a scientist's child becomes a scientist, a farmer's a farmer, and so on. They stay within their comfort zone.

Various ethnic groups come to America in search of wealth and opportunity, but in their minds, they live in their country of origin. They listen to their own music, view movies of their own people, and speak in their mother tongue. They socialize with their own kind, marry their own class, and form small groups of their own heritage at large gatherings. They don't want to cultivate a taste in American music, food, or movies. They avoid American culture and the use of English, although they speak their adopted country's language out of necessity. They don't make friends with people who aren't of the same ethnicity and class.

I remember a professor and his wife in Agartala. They lived in a heavenly hilltop bungalow. Free of congestion and suffused in fresh air, they could breathe deeply. But they hated it and wanted to go back to where they had come from, congested Calcutta and its polluted air. They missed the noise and the crowds.

The wise know that life offers infinite possibilities. They've ventured outside the known, invented things, and followed their attraction to the unknown. They know progress means exploring the unknown. They are trailblazers. They know the true thrill of adventure. They don't want to live a life without adventure. When the adventure ends, they no longer find life attractive. Thus, they see beauty in death.

Only adventure can make a person wise. A wise person knows that, as individuals, we are merely links in an infinite chain of humanity. Death is an essential part of that chain, and its role is to strengthen the link and make room for the next link to grow. The wise know that humanity has a purpose and that each individual's purpose is to help humanity fulfil that purpose. They know that the womb of existence is nothingness and that death means merging with that all-powerful nothingness. They welcome death when they have fulfilled their duty.[1]

## Why I Welcome Death as a Friend

I have lived a life of adventure. When I was a child, my family did not want uncertainty; yet, it was thrust upon us. When we moved from war-torn Burma to our ancestral home in Silaur, our parents dreamed of us living there for the rest of our lives as our ancestors had. That hope was dashed by a dacoity, the partition of India during independence, and our village becoming a part of Pakistan. As practising Hindus, Muslim Pakistan threatened us. Father built a house in the nearby princely state of Agartala, which had committed to join secular India. We felt we had finally moved somewhere we could call home. But our move to the chaos of Calcutta again dashed that hope of settling down.

Since then, most steps I took in my life—my audacity to sit for the School Final examination as a private student at the age of thirteen, my decision to pursue science in college in deviation from family tradition, changing my major from mathematics to the unfamiliar field of chemistry, giving up the certainty of a well-paying industrial job to undertake the unprecedented step to pursue research for DSc and skipping the conventional path of PhD, the decision to quit FMC Corporation upon an altercation with Sherman Reed, the uncertainties at every step of upward movement first at GAF and then at PPG Industries, my decision to resign from PPG

1. I explore nothingness and the purpose of life in detail in Book 4.

when my future looked better than ever before and instead start PMC Group with the inherent risk in such a venture, the audacity to challenge the centuries-old economic frameworks and propose new framework, and the many other steps that I took—were deviation from convention and the familiarity of paths trodden by other members of my family, my ancestors, and my friends. They were adventures onto the paths of the unknown from the familiarity of the tested ones. I certainly encountered pain along the way, but those pains were what made the adventures worthwhile and the journey of life worth taking.

My next big challenge was to understand spirituality. Scientists like Albert Einstein, Richard A. Muller, Charles H. Townes, Arno Penzias, Joe Taylor, and Isidor Isaac Rabi felt attracted to some kind of spiritual world beyond the physical world.[2] Their ideas were based on their feelings, not reasoned arguments. "I do pray every day, although I am not sure to whom," Richard A. Muller wrote on the final page of his book, *The Physics of Time*.[3] I couldn't pray without understanding whom I was praying to. Faith without logic seemed empty to me.

I gave up my aspiration of becoming a sanyasi when I was twenty-two years old after my search for a guru yielded a fraud posing as a sanyasi But the impulse that had led me to seek a guru never completely died. I turned to the life of Henry David Thoreau, the nineteenth-century Harvard man who became a self-proclaimed mystic, transcendentalist, natural philosopher, and "seeker of spiritual truth". I immediately noticed a significant difference between how he

2. Muller, 2016.
3. Muller, 2016, p. 338.

lived and how I lived. To Thoreau, the best way of living was to live "simply and wisely".[4] He built a cabin in the woods, which he said cost him only $28 and 12.5 cents in materials to construct—less than a Cambridge student's monthly rent for boarding.[5] He also grew vegetables for the sake of self-sufficiency.[6] On the contrary, I have lived with my family in seven houses since 1970. Of these, I custom-designed three, each of which displays a unique combination of modern amenities and features. The challenge of learning about construction and building our houses allowed me to test my acquired knowledge. More than anything else, they fed my spirit of adventure. They were far from the small cabin Thoreau built on the shore of Walden Pond.

Thoreau called for austerity in living. I do not agree with his philosophy. If everyone followed his advice, we would push our society back centuries. But I understand the need he felt to live close to nature to stimulate his thoughts.[7] That was his adventure. Thoreau and Emerson combined wordplay with their own real-life experiences to write timeless classics that readers have enjoyed for generations. As Thoreau put it, "For what are the classics but the noblest recorded thoughts of man?"[8] He endured hardships to do so, and the result of his efforts, combined with his literary magic, was marvelous—a discourse on civil disobedience that inspired future civil rights leaders like Gandhi to disobey unjust laws. But I did not find in them anything that could help me discover spiritual truth in the way I wanted to understand it.

4. Thoreau, 1986, reprint, p. 13.
5. Ibid., pp. 92, 93.
6. Ibid., p. 108.
7. Ibid., p. 62.
8. Ibid., p. 146.

I enjoy reading classics. I take leave from the hustle and bustle of life when I want to sit in my solarium to observe nature: snow falling in winter, birds chirping and leaves fluttering in the breeze in spring, a cool rain refreshing the lawn in summer. On those days, I cannot deny the value, beauty, and power of the classics. I enjoy them and they inspire me. But in the end, they do not answer my quest to understand the spiritual world. For such a journey, I followed my own path.

I do not feel guilty about building our mansions. Housing and automobiles are the two biggest drivers of our economy. Moreover, they were gifts to my wife, although she never craved luxury. I also learned from Suratha's mistake. Although named among the fifty richest people in New Jersey by *NJBiz* in 2016, I did not let the prestige go to my head. I did not crave the pompous lifestyle of the rich. Nor did I like the lifestyle of the poor. The former stoked my ego, and the latter stood in the way of productivity. Instead, I paid heed to Aristotle's advice: "Virtue lies in the middle." I do not think that Emerson and Thoreau would have minded my disagreement with them. "Each generation must discover the world through its own eyes," he wrote, "rather than through the eyes of the previous generation."[9]

My spirit of adventure led me to look at my religious experiences, study other religions, and examine various spiritual propositions, many of which contradicted one another or were based on blind faith. I could not be satisfied with such statements as, "My soul is blatantly obvious to me, even though I have a hard time expressing what I mean by it," even if it came from a celebrated physicist like Richard Muller himself.[10] To

9. Ibid., pp. 10–11.
10. Muller, 2016, p. 272.

determine the merits of a proposition, I had to discover my theory of the evolution of truth. That inquiry opened a whole new world to me and led to Book 4 of my memoir series.

My inquiry into the field of spirituality provided the profound realization that we could define morality in just a few words—tending to the interests of others, including society at large, even at the cost of one's interest. Thus, I turned my attention to philanthropy. I did so with zeal and a spirit of adventure, discovering ideas that common philanthropy neglects. The pain I encountered in making these sacrifices was among the most gratifying of all. I describe my philanthropic activities at length in Book 4.

My inquiry into the world of spirituality helped me discover nothingness as the womb of all reality. It showed that reality arose by splitting nothingness into pairs of opposites, and that realization convinced me that humanity would be able to solve every problem, provided we did not allow our inventions to destroy us beforehand. If moral laws guide us above all others, the future of humanity is bright. Individual death, I have concluded, is about merging our spiritual self with the vastness of nothingness. The body that stays behind has very little significance. It is like a vessel without passengers or an abandoned house exposed to the decaying forces of nature.

My inquiry into spirituality ultimately illuminated the purpose of life. It made it apparent, as I convincingly argue in Book 4, that humanity did not arise as just another phenomenon in the physical universe. It arose with a grand purpose: discovering the purpose and secrets of creation itself. No one can solve such a problem in his or her lifetime. Each person and generation must pass on their knowledge to the next until humanity reaches the status of super-humanity. Each of us is just a link in the chain of humanity. The purpose of each individual is to generate knowledge as best as he or she can and then give it to others to expand it further. Like a good quarterback who must throw the football to another player, we must pass our knowledge to our successors. When seen from this angle, death is the fulfilment of our duty and a satisfying event.

I have lived a life of adventure. Life without adventure is boring to me. I cannot think of living a life without it. When my ability to lead a life of adventure ends, death will be my most welcome guest.

Stevens and Tagore summarized my thoughts about death. As I near the end of life, death looks increasingly beautiful to me. It is an essential part of the life cycle, which is responsible for evolution and progression. Without death and the repeated propagation of life cycles by successive generations, the ultimate purpose of life cannot be realized.

My new-found appreciation of the spiritual world allows me to pray. I pray to the all-powerful nothingness, not for favours but to express my awe at the beauty and magnificence of creation, whose limitless abundance is absorbed within itself. But for what grand purpose? Our ability to pass on our wisdom. I have done my part in this journey. When I breathe my last breath, I do not want my loved ones to mourn my death. I want them to celebrate it.

As for the physical body that I leave behind, I do not want it consigned to nature's organic process of gradual decay. Rather, I want my family to accelerate that process and have it burned to ashes. Then my survivors can spread the ashes in the ocean so that they might become a part of the infinite vastness that the ocean symbolizes in our finite world.

# APPENDIX 1

## Some Historical Dates, Books 1 To 4

### Geological and Evolutional Events

| Event | Years ago |
|---|---|
| Big Bang—origin of the universe | 13,800,000,000 |
| Our galaxy | 10,000,000,000 |
| Our solar system | 5,000,000,000 |
| Early beginning of Earth—formation of continents | 4,500,000,000 |
| First life appeared on earth | 4,000,000,000 |
| Appearance of plants | 2,500,000,000 |
| Appearance of soft-bodied animals | 1,500,000,000 |
| Appearance of the first bird forms | 180,000,000 |
| Extinction of dinosaurs | 135,000,000 |
| Appearance of mammals and primates | 67,000,000 |
| Appearance of Hominids | 4,000,000 |

| Appearance of Homo sapiens | 200,000 |
|---|---|
| Appearance of modern human | 40,000 |
| Agriculture | 9,000 |
| Age of Hinduism | 3,700 |
| Age of Judaism | 3,300 |
| Age of Buddhism | 2,500 |
| Age of Christianity | 2,000 |
| Age of Islam | 1,400 |

## The Size of the Universe

The diameter of the universe is about 93 billion light years. The light year is a measure of distance, not time. One light year equals six trillion miles, the distance travelled by light in one year. Therefore, the diameter of the universe is 558,000,000,000,000,000,000,000 miles, or to put it simply, 558 × 1021 miles, or 898 × 1021 kilometres.

# APPENDIX 2

## Historical Da Tes of People and Events Mentioned in the Memoir

| Person or Event | Date(s) | Comment |
|---|---|---|
| Socrates | 470–399 BCE | Philosopher |
| Aristotle | 384–322 BCE | Philosopher |
| Thomas Hobbles | 1588–1679 | Philosopher |
| Robert Boyle | 1621–1691 | Physicist: Inventor of Boyle's Law |
| Baruch Spinoza | 1632–1677 | A Dutch philosopher of Portuguese-Jewish origin |
| John Locke | 1632–1704 | Philosopher and physician |
| David Hume | 1711–1777 | Philosopher and historian |
| Jean-Jacques Rousseau | 1712–1778 | Philosopher and writer |

| | | |
|---|---|---|
| Immanuel Kant | 1724–1804 | Philosopher |
| Declaration of US independence | 4 July 1776 | |
| First Amendment to the US Constitution | 15 December 1791 | The Bill of Rights |
| Most recent Amendment to the US Constitution | 7 May 1992 | The 27th, on Senators' and Representatives' salary |
| Adam Smith | 1723–1790 | Father of Capitalism. Famous writings: *The Theory of Moral Sentiment (1759); An Inquiry into the Nature and the Causes of the Wealth of Nations (1776–1778)* |
| Marquis de Condorcet | 1743–1794 | Philosopher and social reformer |
| Jacques Charles | 1746–1823 | Formulator of Charles's Law (1780) |
| Jeremy Bentham | 1748–1792 | Philosopher and jurist |
| Mary Wollstonecraft | 1759–1797 | Philosopher and writer |
| Thomas Robert Malthus | 1766–1834 | Economist; Famous writing: *In Principles of Political Economy* (1820) |

| | | |
|---|---|---|
| David Ricardo | 1772–1823 | Political economist; Famous writing: *On Principles of Political Economy and Taxation* |
| Jean-Baptiste Say | 1767–1832 | Economist; Famous writing: *Traite d'Economie Politique* |
| John Stuart Mills | 1806–1873 | Philosopher and political economist; Famous Writing: *Principles of Political Economy* (1848) |
| Abraham Lincoln | 1809–1865 | 16th President of the United States |
| Charles Darwin | 1809–1882 | Naturalist and geologist; Writing: *On Origin of Species* (1859) |
| Bruno Bauer | 1809–1882 | Philosopher |
| Karl Marx | 1818–1883 | Father of Communism. Famous writings: *The Communist Manifesto* (1848) and *Das Capital* (1867) |
| Rutherford B. Hayes | 1822–1893 | 19th President of the United States |

| | | |
|---|---|---|
| Laws of Thermodynamics | 1824–1860 | The empirical and fundamental laws of physics that govern conservation of mass and energy; direction of flow of energy; generation of work from flow of energy; and directions of chemical reactions. |
| Friedrich Nietzsche | 1844–1900 | Philosopher. Called God "The Father of Evil" |
| *The Communist Manifesto* (see also Karl Marx) | February 1848 | Authors: Karl Max and Friedrich Engels |
| John Dewey | 1859–1952 | Philosopher |
| Vladimir Lenin | 1870–1924 | Head of Soviet Union (1917), (1922–1924) |
| Albert Einstein | 1879– 1955 | Special Theory of Relativity 1905; General Theory of Relativity 1915 |
| Rabindranath Tagore | 1861–1941 | Poet, Nobel Prize in literature 1913 |
| Mohandas Karamchand Gandhi | 1869–1948 | Humanitarian. India's freedom fighter, called "Father of the Nation" |

| | | |
|---|---|---|
| John Maynard Keynes | 1883–1946 | Economist |
| Adolf Hitler | 1889–1945 | Führer of Germany 1933–1945 |
| Subhas Chandra Bose | 1897–1945 | India's freedom fighter. Famously known as *Netaji* |
| Roy F. Harrod | 1900–1978 | Co-inventor of the Harrod-Domar Economic Growth Theory |
| Albert Camus | 1913–1960 | Writer and philosopher; Nobel Prize in Literature 1957 |
| Milton Friedman | 1912–2006 | Economist; Nobel Prize in economics 1976 |
| Introduction of Federal Income Tax in the United States | 3 February 1913 | |
| Creation of the Federal Reserve Bank of the United States (FED) | 23 December 1913 | |
| Evsey David Domar | 1914–1997 | Co-inventor of the Harrod-Domar Economic Growth Theory |
| Edward Denison | 1915–1992 | A pioneer in the measurement of the US Gross National Product |

| | | |
|---|---|---|
| Paul Samuelson | 1915–2009 | Economist; Nobel Prize in economics 1970 |
| Overthrow of tsarist regime in Russia by Lenin-led revolution. | 7 November 1917; as per old calendar, 25 October | |
| Dissolution of Dollar's dependence on Gold Reserve in the U.S. | 1968 | |
| Elimination of the dollar's convertibility to gold | 1971 | |
| John Rawls | 1921–2002 | Philosopher; Famous work *A Theory of Justice* (1985) |
| Amartya Sen | 1933– | Welfare Economist; Nobel Prize in economics 1998 |
| Robert Solow | 1924– | MIT Economist; Nobel Prize in Economics 1987 |
| World Bank | Established July 1944 | HQ: Washington DC |
| International Monetary Fund (IMF) | Established 27 December 1945 | HQ: Washington DC |

# Bibliography

(Consolidated for Books 1 to 4)


Ali, Ahmed. 1993. *Al-Quran: A Contemporary Translation*. Princeton University Press, Princeton, New Jersey.

Armstrong, Karen. 1993. *A History of God*. Ballantine Books, New York.

Atkins, Peter, Julio de Paula, and James Keeler. 2018. *Atkin's Physical Chemistry:* 11th Ed. Oxford University Press, Oxford, UK.

Atkinson, Brooks, Ed. 2000. *The Essential Writings of Ralph Waldo Emerson*. The Modern Library, New York, NY.

Barnes, Jean-Paul, Transl. and Intro. 2001. *Being and Nothingness* by Jean-Paul Sartre. Citadel Press, New York, NY.

Bartlett, John. 1980. *Bartlett's Familiar Quotations*. Little Brown & Company, London, England.

Bose, Sugata. 2011. *His Majesty's Opponent: Subhas Chandra Bose and India's Struggle Against Empire*. The Belknap Press of Harvard University Press, Cambridge, Massachusetts.

Cannan, Edwin. 1994. *Adam Smith: The Wealth of Nations*. Random House, The Modern Library Edition, New York.

Chopra, Deepak and Rudolph E. Tanzi. 2012. *Super Brain.* Ebury Publishing, London.

Clark, Ronald, W. 1971. *Einstein: The Life and Times*. Avon Books, New York, NY.

Dewey, John. 1989. *Freedom and Culture*. Prometheus Books, Buffalo, New York.

Dickens, Charles. 1981. *Great Expectations*. Bantam Books, New York, NY.

Domar, Evsey. 1946. 'Capital Expansion, Rate of Growth, and Employment'. *Econometrica*, 14 (2): 137–47.

Edgerton, Franklin (Translation). 1993. *The Bhagavad Gita*. Harvard University Press, Cambridge, Massachusetts.

Einstein, Albert. Translation by Alan Harris. 1979. *The World as I See It*. Citadel Press, Secaucus, New Jersey.

Frost Jr, S.E. 1989. *The Teachings of the Great Philosophers*. Doubleday, New York, NY.

Galbraith, John K. 1987. *Economics in Perspective—A Critical History*. Houghton Mifflin Company, Boston, Massachusetts.

Galloway, Scott. 2020. *Post Corona—From Crisis to Opportunity*. Penguin Press, London.

Gangopadhyay, Sunil. Ed. 1999. *Smarak Grantha*. Saraswaty Press, Kolkata.

Gardner, Marin. 1997. *Great Essays in Science*. Oxford University Press, Oxford, England.

Garraty, John A. and Peter Gay. 1972. *The Columbia History of the World*. Harper & Row Publishers, New York, NY.

Greenspan, Alan and Adrian Wooldridge. 2018. *Capitalism in America: A History*. Penguin Press, New York, NY.

Halpern, Paul. 2020. *Synchronicity: The Epic Quest to Understanding the Quantum Nature of Cause and Effect*. Basic Books, New York, NY.

Hannah-Jones, Nicole. Ed. 2021. *The 1619 Project*. One World (Random House), New York, NY.

Harari, Yuval Noah. 2015. *Sapiens: A Brief History of Humankind*. Harper Collins Publishers, New York, NY.

———. 2017. *Homo Deus: A Brief History of Tomorrow*. Harper Perennial, New York, NY.

———. 2018. *21 Lessons for the 21st Century*. Spiegel & Grau, Random House, New York, NY.

Harrod, Roy F. 1939. 'An Essay in Dynamic Theory'. *The Economic Journal*, 49(193): 14–33.

Hesse, Hermann, 1951. *Siddhartha*. Bantam Books, New York, NY.

International Religious Foundation. 1995. *World Scripture: A Comparative Anthology of Sacred Texts*. Paragon House, St Paul, Minnesota.

James, Lawrence. 1994. *The Rise and Fall of the British Empire*. St Martin's Griffin, New York.

Johnson, Boris. 2014. *The Churchill Factor: How One Man Made History*. Riverhead Books, New York, NY.

Kaufmann, Walter. 1989. *The Genealogy of Morals: Friedrich Nietzsche*. Vintage Books, New York, NY.

Keay, John. 2000. *India: A History*. Grove Press, New York, NY.

Kelley, Kevin W. Ed. 1988. *The Home Planet*. Mir Publishers, Moscow.

Kevles, Daniel J. 1986. *In the Name of Eugenics: Genetics and the Uses of Human Heredity*. University of California Press, Berkley, CA.

Kershaw, Ian. 1998. *Hitler, 1889-1936*. W.W. Norton & Company, New York, NY.

Klamer, Arjo. 1983. *Conversations with Economists*. Rowman and Littlefield, Savage, Maryland.

Kukathas, Chandran and Philip Pettit. 1990. *Rawls: A Theory of Justice and Its Critics*. Stanford University Press, Stanford, California.

Kyokai, Bukkyo Bendo. 1986. *The Teaching of Buddha*. 445th Ed. Kosaido Printing, Tokyo, Japan.

Little, Arthur D. 1994. *An Exchange of Knowledge Among Leading Practitioners in Product and Technology Management: Best of the Best*. An Arthur D. Little Colloquium. Cambridge, MA.

Lock, Peter. 2006. *Routledge Companion to the Crusades*. eBook ISBN 0415-39312-4.

Max Muller, F (Translation). 1962. *The Upanishads: Part I*. Dover Publications, New York, NY.

McCloskey, Donald. 1985. *The Rhetoric of Economics*. The University of Wisconsin Press, Madison, Wisconsin.

———. 1989. *Formalism in Economics, Rhetorically Speaking*. Xerox.

Meacham, Jon. 2018. *The Soul of America: Battle for Our Better Angels*. Random House, New York, NY.

Morgan, Michael L. Ed. 1992. *Classics of Moral and Political Theory*. Hackett Publishing Company, Indianapolis, Indiana.

Muller, Richard. 2016. *The Physics of Time*. W.W. Norton & Company, New York, NY.

Newman, Melvin S. Ed. 1963. *Steric Effects in Organic Chemistry*. John Wiley & Sons, Inc., New York, NY.

Ritter, Lawrence S. and William L. Silber. 1984. *Money*, Fifth Edition. Basic Books of Harper Collins, New York, NY.

Roger, Charles Barclay. 5 October 2020. 'Amartya Sen and the Idea of Justice'. At https://www.opendemocracy.net/en/amartya-sen-and-idea-of-justice/

Ruhe, Peter. 2001. *Gandhi*. Phaidon Press Inc. New York, NY.

Samuelson, Paul. 1970. *Economics*, Eighth Edition, McGraw Hill, New York, NY.

Schacht, Richard. 1992. *Nietzsche*. Routledge, New York, NY.

Sen, Amartya. 1988. *On Ethics & Economics*. Blackwell Publishing, Malden, Massachusetts.

———. 1992. *Inequality Re-examined*. Harvard University Press, Cambridge, Massachusetts.

———. 2000. *Development as Freedom*. Anchor Books (Random House), New York, NY.

———. 2009. *The Idea of Justice*. The Belknap Press, Harvard University Press, Cambridge, Massachusetts.

Sinclair, Gavin. 1997. *All Things Work for Good: A Book of Encouragement for People with Cancer, Their Family and Friends*. The Positive Press, Gainesville, Florida.

Solow, Robert M. 1987. 'Growth Theory and After'. The Nobel Prize Lecture, 8 December 1987.

———. 1994. 'Perspective on Growth Theory'. *Journal of Economic Perspectives*, 8 (1): 45–54.

Sowell, Thomas. 1977. *Classical Economics Reconsidered*. Princeton University Press, Princeton, New Jersey.

Swami Vidyatmananda, Ed. 1972. *What Religion Is: In the Words of Swami Vivekananda*. Advaita Ashrama Publications, Kolkata.

Thoreau, Henry David. *The Wisdom of Thoreau*. Kensington Publishing, New York, Citadel Publication 1967.

Updegrove, Mark, K. 2017. *The Last Republicans*. HarperCollins Publishers, New York, NY.

Wilkerson, Isabelle. 2010. *The Warmth of Other Suns*. Random House, New York, NY.

———. 2020. *Caste: The Origins of Our Discontents*. Random House, New York, NY.

Witherspoon, W. Roger. 1985. *Martin Luther King Jr: To the Mountain Top*. Doubleday & Company Inc., New York, NY.

Yunus, Muhammad. 1999. *Banker to the Poor: Micro-Lending and the Battle Against World Poverty*. Public Affairs, New York, NY.

# Index